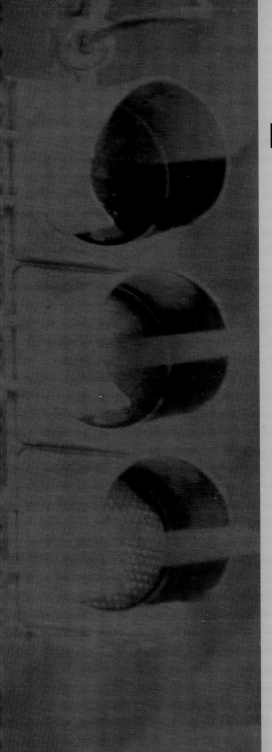

LIGHTWAVE [6.5]
MAGIC

By Dan Ablan

With contributions from Julian Kain, Graham McKenna,
Stuart Penn, Phil South, and Gary Whitley

New Riders

201 West 103rd Street, Indianapolis, Indiana 46290

LightWave [6.5] Magic

International Standard Book Number: 0-7357-0996-3

Library of Congress Catalog Card Number: 00-100498

Printed in the United States of America

First Printing: December 2000

05 04 03 02 01   7 6 5 4 3 2 1

Interpretation of the printing code: The rightmost double-digit number is the year of the book's printing; the rightmost single-digit number is the number of the book's printing. For example, the printing code 01-1 shows that the first printing of the book occurred in 2001.

Trademarks

Warning and Disclaimer

Publisher
David Dwyer

Associate Publisher
Al Valvano

Executive Editor
Steve Weiss

Product Marketing Manager
Kathy Malmloff

Managing Editor
Sarah Kearns

Acquisitions Editor
Theresa Gheen

Development Editors
Jennifer Eberhardt
Katie Pendergast

Project Editor
Michael Thurston

Copy Editor
Audra McFarland

Technical Editors
Julian Kane
Doug Nakakihara

Interior Designers
Steve Gifford
Kim Scott, www.bumpy.com

Compositor/Project Opener Images
Wil Cruz

Proofreader
Teresa Hendey

Indexer
Cheryl Lenser

Software Development Specialist
Jay Payne

CONTENTS AT A GLANCE

ABOUT THE AUTHORS

Dan Ablan (**www.danablan.com**, **www.agadigital.com**) is a native of Chicago and holds a BA in Broadcast Journalism and a minor in Photojournalism from Valparaiso University. He is known for his three best-selling New Riders' books, *LightWave Power Guide, Inside LightWave 3D, and Inside LightWave [6]*. He's also president of AGA Digital Studios, Inc., which creates 3D animations for broadcast and corporate productions. AGA Digital is also a NewTek-authorized LightWave 3D training facility.

Julian Kain (jkain@mail.com) is currently a computer engineering student, studying at the University of Central Florida in Orlando. Although he is pursuing a major in the technical field of computers, his interests lie in the merger of art and technology, something he is adamantly working toward. He has written several LightWave-related articles and edited the popular *Inside LightWave [6]*. Julian has worked with LightWave for three years on both a technical and artistic basis, and is now developing several plug-ins for the software.

Graham McKenna, author of Project 2, "Photorealistic Fur and Hair Without Plug-Ins," holds five years experience in the field of digital combat and a degree in "that looks right," carrying a wide variety of skills from point manipulation to camera and light trickery. Somewhere within this broad spectrum, he has accumulated a wealth of knowledge for character subtleties, breathing life into the most dormant of objects.

Graham currently holds a senior artist position at Scottish-based studio, Axis Animation (**www.axisanimation.com**), and his personal achievements can be viewed at **www.charontheboatman.com/graham**.

Stuart Penn started his working life as a scientist, gaining his physics doctorate in 1991. In 1997, he introduced himself to LightWave and soon realized it was far more fun than working. After winning the September, 1998 LightWave Mailing List contest, he realized that maybe this bit of fun that took up most of his evenings could be turned into a career. After many late nights working on his showreel and the odd freelance job, he made the break to a full-time job in 3D in the summer of 2000 when he joined Framestore in London. The results of Stuart's labors can be seen at **www.sapenn.demon.co.uk/lw3d**.

Phil South (phil@ideasincluded.co.uk) is a new media designer who lives and works in the UK. He runs Ideas Included (**www.ideasincluded. co.uk**) from a small studio in the South West, specializing in Web design, animation, and multimedia for corporate clients. As well as being a LightWave user since version 1 on the Amiga, Phil uses Flash, Photoshop, and Commotion in his daily work.

Recent projects include four 5-minute animations based on stories by children for Disney Channel UK, 3D character design for a multi-player digital TV game for nGame Ltd., and illustrations and animation for **www.seethru.co.uk**, the Web site for the BBC TV drama series, "Attachments". In what spare time he has, he is a low-budget filmmaker (**www.zombiesatemybrain.co.uk**).

Gary Whitley first started doing computer graphics in 1980, using an HP9872 plotter and HP9825 computer, while working as a mudlogger on oil exploration rigs in the Far East.

He used his redundancy pay to buy an Amiga 1000 in 1987 and began making animations for film and TV, working as a video editor and sound recordist in a video co-operative in England. Since then he has had a number of film- and television-related jobs, as well as working as a freelance journalist and video technician.

Gary began to work in 3D with the arrival of Videoscape3D (Allen Hasting's precursor of today's LightWave) and then with LightWave when the Video Toaster was launched for the Amiga. He wrote many tutorials and reviews for British Amiga magazines and was commissioned to write a book on Amiga desktop video.

He is now working mostly with PCs; however, his old Amiga 2000 still gets regular use for those jobs PCs still cannot do as well or efficiently as an Amiga can.

Gary has produced in-shot graphics and animations for a number of TV and feature film productions, and continues to collaborate with friends on film, video, Internet, and multimedia projects, as well as designing Web sites, making music, growing vegetables, making his own bread, beer, jams, and wines, generally trying to keep the wolf from the door while living a low-impact lifestyle.

DEDICATION

This book is dedicated to the tireless efforts of the LightWave 3D development team at NewTek. It is also dedicated to the thousands of loyal LightWave users around the globe.

ACKNOWLEDGMENTS

It isn't often someone gets an opportunity to work with a rare team of people who dedicate themselves to creating the best training materials on the market. I've had the pleasure of working with the New Riders team for nearly five years, and have enjoyed every minute of it—well, almost! A huge thanks to Steve Weiss at New Riders for yet another cool and fun project to be a part of. Right there next to Steve is Jennifer Eberhardt, the driving force behind this book. Thanks Jennifer for whipping this thing into shape! Special thanks goes to Brad Peebler and his team at NewTek for keeping me up to date (literally) with LightWave 3D. As always, Doug Nakikihara saves the day as the best tech editor. This book wouldn't be possible without the additional material from Julian Kain, Stuart Penn, Gary Whitley, Phil South, and Graham McKenna. Thanks Guys! Thanks to the one and only "LightWave Dave" (Dave Adams) for the humor, and Jeff Fowler for the cool ideas and original design work.

Also, Thanks to Foad Afshari and Steva Giles of Logicalinsanity, Inc. (**www.logicalinsanity.com**), and Chip Thompson at Remlight Design Studio (**www.remlight.com**) for all of their hard Web site work. And I better not forget to thank my darling, wonderful, fantastic, kind, talented, and beautiful wife for understanding the extra workload. How's that for sucking up?

A MESSAGE FROM NEW RIDERS

As the reader of this book, you are our most important critic and commentator. We value your opinion and want to know what we're doing right, what we could do better, in what areas you'd like to see us publish, and any other words of wisdom you're willing to pass our way.

As the Executive Editor for the Graphics team at New Riders, I welcome your comments. You can fax, email, or write me directly to let me know what you did or didn't like about this book—as well as what we can do to make our books better. When you write, please be sure to include this book's title, ISBN, and author, as well as your name and phone or fax number. I will carefully review your comments and share them with the authors and editors who worked on the book.

Please note that I cannot help you with technical problems related to the topic of this book, and that due to the high volume of mail I receive, I might not be able to reply to every message. If you run into a technical problem, it's best to contact our Customer Support department, as listed later in this section. Thanks.

Email: steve.weiss@newriders.com

Mail: Steve Weiss
           Executive Editor
           Professional Graphics & Design Publishing
           New Riders Publishing
           201 West 103rd Street
           Indianapolis, IN 46290 USA

Visit Our Web Site: www.newriders.com

On our Web site, you'll find information about our other books, the authors we partner with, book updates and file downloads, promotions, discussion boards for online interaction with other users and with technology experts, and a calendar of trade shows and other professional events with which we'll be involved. We hope to see you around.

Email Us from Our Web Site

Go to www.newriders.com and click on the Contact link if you

- Have comments or questions about this book.

- Want to report errors that you have found in this book.

- Have a book proposal or are interested in writing for New Riders.

- Would like us to send you one of our author kits.

- Are an expert in a computer topic or technology and are interested in being a reviewer or technical editor.

- Want to find a distributor for our titles in your area.

- Are an educator/instructor who wants to preview New Riders books for classroom use. In the body/comments area, include your name, school, department, address, phone number, office days/hours, text currently in use, and enrollment in your department, along with your request for either desk/examination copies or additional information.

Call Us or Fax Us

You can reach us toll-free at (800) 571-5840 + 9+ 3567 (ask for New Riders). If outside the U.S., please call 1-317-581-3500 and ask for New Riders. If you prefer, you can fax us at 1-317-581-4663, Attention: New Riders.

Technical Support and Customer Support for This Book   Although we encourage entry-level users to get as much as they can out of our books, keep in mind that our books are written assuming a non-beginner level of user-knowledge of the technology. This assumption is reflected in the brevity and shorthand nature of some of the tutorials.

New Riders will continually work to create clearly written, thoroughly tested and reviewed technology books of the highest educational caliber and creative design. We value our customers more than anything—that's why we're in this business—but we cannot guarantee to each of the thousands of you who buy and use our books that we will be able to work individually with you through tutorials or content with which you may have questions. We urge readers who need help in working through exercises or other material in our books—and who need this assistance immediately—to use as many of the resources that our technology and technical communities can provide, especially the many online user groups and list servers available.

- If you have a physical problem with one of our books or accompanying CD-ROMs, please contact our Customer Support department.

- If you have questions about the content of the book—needing clarification about something as it is written or note of a possible error— please contact our Customer Support department.

- If you have comments of a general nature about this or other books by New Riders, please contact the Executive Editor.

To contact our Customer Support department, call 1-317-581-3833, from 10:00 a.m. to 3:00 p.m. U.S. EST (CST from April through October of each year— unlike the majority of the United States, Indiana doesn't change to Daylight Savings Time each April). You can also access our tech support Web site at http://www.mcp.com/support.

INTRODUCTION

LightWave has become one of the industry's best-known 3D applications. More than half of the effects you see on television today are created in LightWave 3D from NewTek, Inc. Known for its powerful modeling engine, easy to navigate interface, and the highest quality rendering engine, LightWave 3D gets you the best performance for the best price.

This book uses version LightWave[6.5] for it's projects. However, in order for all of our readers to follow along with the projects, we are using the "6.0 Style" menu configuration. Be sure to set Layout and Modeler menu configurations to the "6.0 Style" option. When you open the Configure Menus panel in both Modeler and Layout, you'll find this option available.

WHO WE ARE

This book is brought to you by a team of LightWave users and experts from around the globe. Led by LightWave veteran Dan Ablan (*LightWave Power Guide, Inside LightWave 3D, Inside LightWave [6]*), the authors have pooled their talents to bring you insight on creating top-notch effects with LightWave.

WHO YOU ARE

As seasoned LightWave users, you often need a resource for quick solutions to your animation needs. If you are familiar with LightWave, and have read through the manuals, and perhaps *Inside LightWave [6]*, but need that extra "effect" for your animations, this book is for you.

WHAT'S IN THIS BOOK

This book covers some of the most commonly requested effects topics such as how to create fire, water, and smoke, just to name a few. You can quickly find and learn an effect without any fluff or fanfare. We bring you the information straight.

The CD

The CD that accompanies this book includes all of the project files needed to complete the exercises. You'll also find rendered examples for many of the effects as well, so you know exactly what you're creating. Please refer to the "What's on the CD" appendix at the back of the book for a complete listing of its contents.

Our Assumptions as We Wrote This Book

When creating this book, the authors assumed you understand the LightWave 3D workflow and it's interfaces. It is also assumed that you know your way around the program and are familiar with the particular common areas such as the Graph Editor, Keyframing, and so on. This book does not go into lengthy descriptions of buttons and techniques. It is a cookbook filled with recipes of cool effects for you to quickly set up and render. It is aimed at the intermediate to advanced LightWave user.

Conventions Used in This Book

This book has a unique style, unlike any other LightWave book. As you flip through the book, you'll notice we have an interesting layout. Because we know most of you are really into graphics and 3D, the project openers contain cool eye candy. But the real meat of the projects start on the next page. Take a look:

In the left column, you'll find step-by-step instructions for completing the project, as well as succinct but extremely valuable explanations. The text next to the number contains the action you must perform. In many cases, the action text is followed by a paragraph that contains contextual information when appropriate. If you want to perform the steps quickly and without any background info, you need read only the text next to the step numbers. This is the magic of *LightWave [6.5] Magic*. Get in, get out, get it done, get paid!

In the corresponding columns to the right, you'll find screen captions illustrating the steps. You'll also find Notes and Tips, which provide you with additional contextual information or customization techniques.

At the end of each project, you'll find unique customization information. Each *Magic* project is designed to be highly customizable; therefore, we provide as many tips and examples of what you can do with the techniques you've learned so you can apply them to your own work quickly and easily. You'll also notice that many of the effects throughout the chapters can be combined to create fantastic scenes.

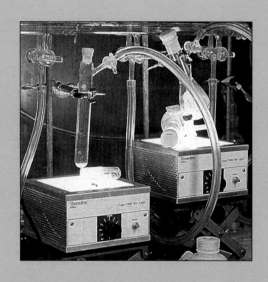

GEAR
EXPRESSIONS

"Someone told me that

each equation

I included in the book

would halve the sales."

—PROFESSOR STEPHEN HAWKING,
A BRIEF HISTORY OF TIME (1988)

Controlling Animation with Expressions

Expressions provide a powerful way of controlling animations. They allow the properties of one item to be controlled by the properties of other items and by mathematical formulas. Properties that can be controlled include an object's position and rotation, a surface's color, and a light's intensity. Because LightWave [6.5] uses a unified Graph Editor for all envelopes, anything that has an envelope can be controlled by an expression. In this project, you will use expressions to automate a piston engine so that keyframing one object will control the entire engine's motion.

Project 1

Gear Expressions

by Stuart Penn

GETTING STARTED

In this section, you will set up a basic expression to make one gear rotate in time with another. This may seem like a basic example, but it demonstrates the method for adding expressions to an object.

1 Start Layout and load **ExpressionStart.lws** from the Projects/Scenes/Chapter 1 folder on the accompanying CD.

   This scene contains two objects, both of which include gear wheels. One of them, Cam.lwo, is attached to a crankshaft and will be used to control the animation. The other object, GeneratorGear.lwo, is a simple gear object that you will make rotate in synchronization with Cam.lwo.

Note: A few keyframes have been added to this object's pitch to give us a trial animation.

4

2 Open the Display Options panel (**d**). Set the Viewport layout to **1 Left**, **2 Right**. Use the drop-down menu on the top-right viewport to change its view to Front.

Having multiple viewports will make it easier to see the various movements of the gears from different angles.

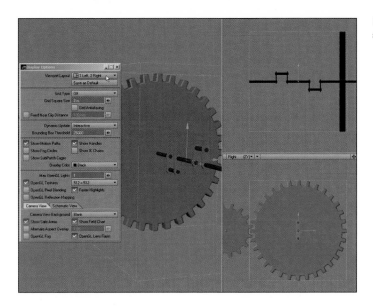

Load ExpressionStart.lws and set up the viewports.

3 Open the Graph Editor and activate the GeneratorGear object by double-clicking it in the Scene List. This list is located on the bottom left and is marked "Channels."

When you activate the GeneratorGear object, a list of channels associated with that object is displayed in the Curve Bin (the list at the top left of the Graph Editor marked "Channel").

4 Select the GeneratorGear.Rotation.P channel by clicking it.

Because GeneratorGear is aligned so that it rotates about its pitch axis, this is the channel you want to add an expression to. Click on the Expressions tab.

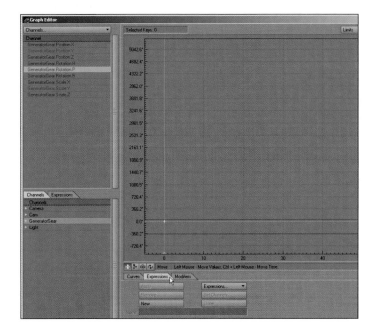

Open the Graph Editor and click over to the Expressions tab for the GeneratorGear.Rotation.P channel.

5   Click the New button under the Expressions tab. Set
the Name to Generator Gear Rotation Pitch, or
something similar.

6   Enter the following into the Value input field, and
then close the Expressions panel:

   –2*Cam.rot(Time).p

This expression sets the pitch of GeneratorGear to
twice that of Cam and in the opposite direction. You
need to use the factor of 2 because the driving gear
(Cam) has twice as many teeth as the driven gear
(GeneratorGear). The value in parentheses specifies
at what time the pitch should be evaluated. In this
case, the word "Time" means to evaluate the pitch at
the current frame. If the value were a number, such
as 1.0, it would have used the pitch of the Cam at 1
second into the animation. In this scene, which has
30 frames per second, that would be at frame 30.
Click Apply.

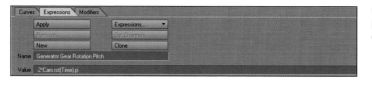

Open the Expressions
panel and enter the
expression value.

Note: Expressions are case sensitive. The case of the object names must
match the case in which they appear in the Graph Editor. Object names
cannot contain spaces. The reserved word "Time" must start with a capital T.
However, it is also worth noting that channel descriptions start with capital
letters in the Curve Bin (for example, Position, Rotation, Dissolve), but when
used in expressions, they must use lowercase letters (for example, position,
rotation, dissolve). Some of the more commonly used channels have abbrevia-
tions; position can be written as pos and rotation as rot.

Note: After you enter an expression, the modifier list
shows the expression rather than LW_Expression.

Note: When making gears, it is best to keep the size
of the teeth on each gear the same. This ensures that
the gears run smoothly together. When the size of the
teeth is kept the same, the number of teeth on a gear
is proportional to the diameter of the gear. So if you
double the diameter of a gear, it should have twice as
many teeth.

7 Because Cam already has some keyframes applied, if you move the frame slider, you will see the two gears move in harmony. You might have to move the Graph Editor out of the way to see your Layout, or simply minimize the panel.

8 Click on the Limits drop-down menu in the Graph Editor and select Numeric Limits. Enter a Min Value of **−150** and a Max Value of **50**.

Two lines will now be visible in the Graph window. The solid line shows any keyframed motion that has been applied to the channel, and the dashed line shows the effect of any modifiers, such as expressions.

You can expand the Graph window by clicking on the down arrow below the window.

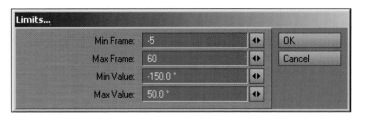

Set the numeric limits in the Graph Editor.

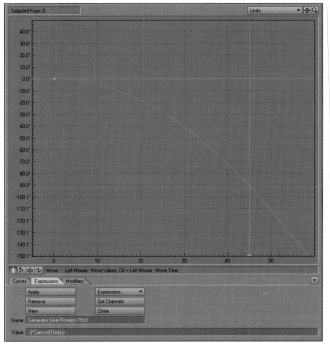

The Graph Editor now shows the motion in the Graph window.

This simple motion could have been created just as easily with the LW_ChannelFollower modifier instead of the LW_Expression modifier. If you want to try it out, open the Graph Editor and make the GeneratorGear.Rotation.P channel active as you did in Steps 3 and 4. Click the Expressions tab, click the Remove button, and then add the LW_ChannelFollower modifier from the drop-down list. In the Channels list, click on the small arrow next to Cam to expand the list of available channels. Double-click on Rotation.P to select it. You have now selected the channel you want to use to drive the rotation of GeneratorGear.

Set Scale to **–200%**. The rest of the settings can be left as default. It looks odd that the End Frame is set to **–1**, but this just tells ChannelFollower to be active for all frames.

The animation will now behave just as it did with the expression.

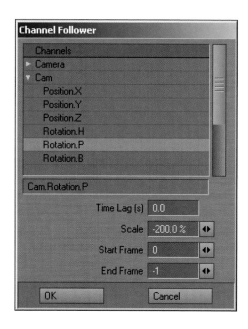

Replace the expression with LW_ChannelFollower.

SETTING UP THE RIGHT-HAND PISTON

This section will show how expressions can be used to control pistons that are connected to the cam/crankshaft. This type of piston is commonly found in engines. The expressions needed to do this include some trigonometry. Don't panic if you are not mathematically inclined; the necessary expressions will be supplied, and you will be shown how to modify them for your own projects.

1 Load the objects **RodR.lwo**, **PistonR.lwo**, **RodL.lwo**, and **PistonL.lwo** from the book's CD-ROM.

Note: Remember that in LightWave [6.5], you can hold the Shift key to select multiple items to load at once.

The pivots of the objects have been left in their default positions at the origin. You could have set up the objects' positioning and pivot positions in Modeler so that when they are loaded into Layout, everything is in position. However, for this example, it is useful to see how the objects are moved relative to each other. The objects' relative positions define some of the numbers that are used in the expressions.

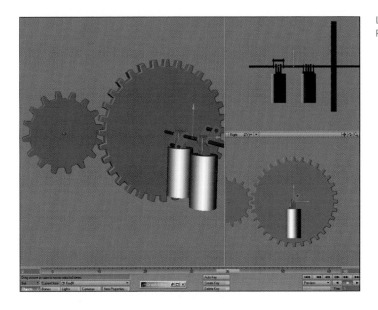

Load RodR.lwo, PistonR.lwo, RodL.lwo, and PistonL.lwo.

2   Open the Scene Editor and use drag and drop to parent the objects as outlined here:

>   RodR to Cam
>
>   PistonR to RodR
>
>   RodL to Cam
>
>   PistonL to RodL

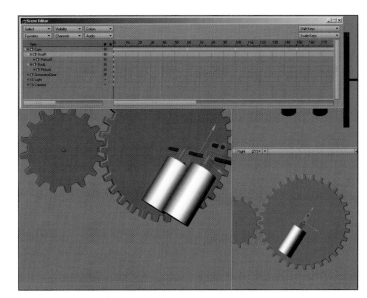

Parent the piston and rod objects in the Scene Editor.

3 In Layout, move RodR and PistonR to the following positions, remembering to create a keyframe at zero to lock them in place:

 RodR XYZ: **0**, **700mm**, **0**

 PistonR XYZ: **0**, **−2m**, **0**

The objects are now in place and ready for animation. Notice the distances that RodR and PistonR have moved in the Y direction because they will appear in the expressions you will create later.

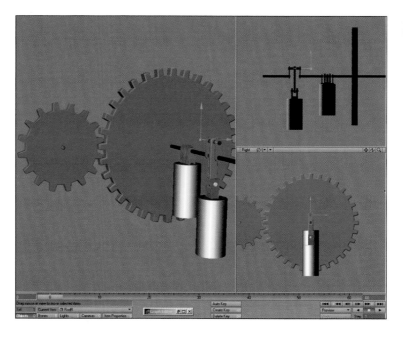

Move RodR and PistonR into place.

4 Select RodR and open the Graph Editor. Add an LW_Expression modifier to the RodR.Rotation.P channel. Click over to the Modifiers tab, and from the drop-down list, select LW_Expression.

5 Open the LW_Expression modifier and enter the following into the input fields:

 Expression: **B+C**

 A: **0.7/2.0**

 B: **deg(asin(A★sin(rad(Cam.rot(Time).p))))**

 C: **−Cam.rot(Time).p**

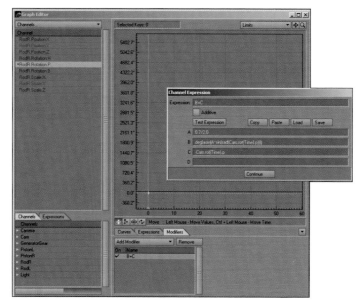

The LW_Expression modifier with scratch variables.

The A, B, and C input fields are known as "scratch variables" and are useful for breaking down complex expressions. The scratch variables in A, B, and C are calculated in order before the contents of the Expression field. In this case, A calculates the ratio of the two lengths we moved RodR and PistonR in Step 3 (700 mm = 0.7 m).

B and C use the rotation of the Cam and some trigonometry (specifically a relationship known as the Sine Rule) to calculate the angle of RodR. In B, you will see an "A." In the calculation, this is replaced by the value calculated in the A field. Four functions are used in B:

rad() Converts angles in degrees to radians.

sin() The sine function.

asin() The arcsine or inverse sine function.

deg() Converts angles in radians to degrees.

The rad() and deg() functions are needed because LW_Expressions trigonometric functions use radians, and references to objects rotations are in degrees.

6 Close the Expression panel, and then move the frame slider to observe the motion.

The expression you entered keeps the far end of the rod—where the pivot point of the piston meets the rod—directly below the axis of the Cam.

Note: If you want to modify this example to use piston rods and cams of different dimensions, you need to adjust the numbers in the A field.

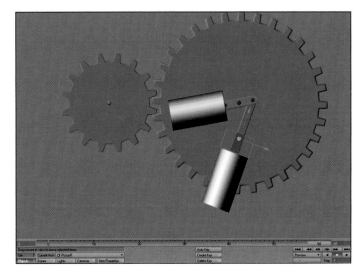

Move the frame slider to see that the far end of the rod stays directly below the Cam's axis.

7 In the Graph Editor, open the expression modifier for RodR.Rotation.P and click the Copy button. Click Continue to close the Expression panel.

8 Make PistonR the active object by double-clicking it in the Scene list. Add an LW_Expression modifier to the PistonR.Rotation.P channel.

9 Open the LW_Expression modifier and click the Paste button. Modify the expression so that it reads as follows:

Expression: **B**

A: **0.7/2.0**

B: **–deg(asin(A*sin (rad(Cam.rot(Time).p))))**

Click Continue to close the panel.

10 Rotate the pitch of the Cam, or move the frame slider and observe the motion.

The expression you entered adjusts the angle of PistonR so that it remains vertical.

The automation of this piston is now complete. Now you need to set up the left-hand piston.

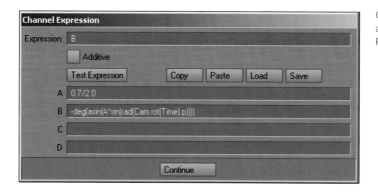

Open the LW_Expression modifier and enter the expression for PistonR.Rotation.P.

Note: If you are using scratch variables, it is a good idea to enter any expressions into them before entering anything into the main expression input. If you do not do this and you reference the scratch variables when they are still empty, you may receive an error report.

SETTING UP THE LEFT-HAND PISTON

With the automation of the right-hand piston complete, it's time to set up the left-hand piston.

1   In Layout, move RodL and PistonL to the following positions to prepare them for animation, making sure to create a keyframe at zero to lock them in place:

> RodL: XYZ   **0, −700mm, 0**
>
> PistonL: XYZ   **0, −2m, 0**

The objects are now in place and ready for animation.

Move RodL and PistonL into place.

2   In the Graph Editor, make RodR the active object by double-clicking it in the Scene list (if necessary). Select RodR.Rotation.P from the Curve Bin. Right-click on it and select Copy. Select RodL.Rotation.P, right-click on it, and select Paste.

This copies the channel settings from RodR.Rotation.P to RodL.Rotation.P.

3   In the same manner as the preceding step, copy the channel settings from PistonR.Rotation.P to PistonL.Rotation.P.

The expressions from the right-hand piston have now been copied to the left-hand piston. Rotate the Cam, and you will see that the motion of the left-hand piston is not yet correct because the sign of some parts of the expressions is wrong.

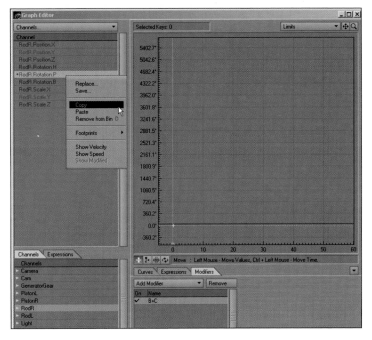

Copy the channel settings from RodR.Rotation.P and paste into RodL.Rotation.P; copy the settings from PistonR.Rotation.P and paste them into PistonR.Rotation.L.

4 Select RodL.Rotation.P, and then double-click on the expression in the Modifiers tab to open it. Change Expression from **B+C** to **−B+C**.

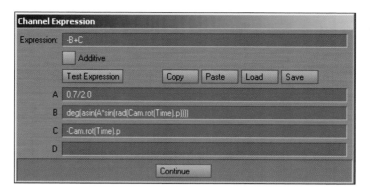

Modify the expression for RodL.Rotation.P.

5 Select PistonL.Rotation.P, and then double-click on the expression in the Modifiers tab to open it. Change Expression from **B** to **−B**.

The expression set up for the pistons is now complete. You can now either make a preview or render the animation from frames 1–300 to see the pistons in action.

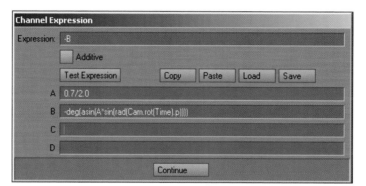

Modify the expression for PistonL.Rotation.P.

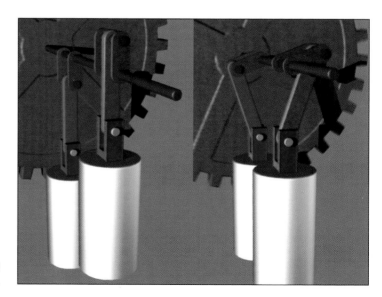

Move the frame slider and observe the motion of the pistons.

IT'S NOT ONLY MOTION

In this section, you will add a few additional objects to fill out the scene and give your pistons a setting. You will then use expressions to control envelopes rather than motion channels.

1   Load the objects **Engine.lwo**, **Beams.lwo**, **Generator.lwo**, and **Floor.lwo** from the book's CD-ROM.

2   Move the Generator object to XYZ **0m**, **0m**, **–6.5m**.

    This scene represents a fictitious steam engine that is driving an electric generator.

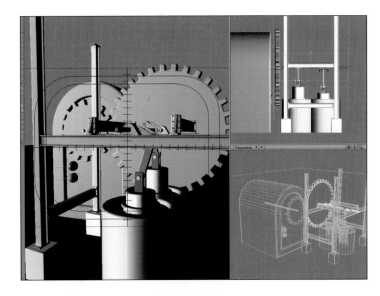

Load Engine.lwo, Beams.lwo, Generator.lwo, and Floor.lwo and move them into position.

3   Add a Point Light by choosing these commands: Action/Add/Add Light/Add Point Light. Name it **RedLight**, and parent the light to the Generator object.

4   Move RedLight to XYZ **–5m**, **–3m**, **–2m** to place the point light inside the red dome on the generator.

5   Select RedLight, open the Light Properties panel (**p**), and set the following light properties:

    Color: RGB **255, 0, 0**

    Intensity Falloff: **Inverse Distance**

    Range/Nominal Distance: **2m**

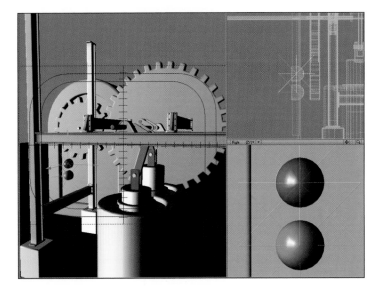

Add a Point Light, name it RedLight, and move it into position inside the red dome on the Generator.

15

6 Click on the Envelope button (**e**) next to Light Intensity to open the Graph Editor.

> **Note:** Clicking on any Envelope button (E) opens the same Graph Editor that is used above to modify the motion of the objects.

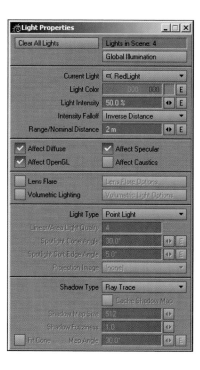

Open the Light Properties panel and set the Color and Falloff of RedLight.

7 Go to the Modifiers tab and add an LW_Expression modifier to the RedLight.Intensity channel.

8 Enter the following into the Expressions panel:

> A: **(Cam.rot(Time).p − Cam.rot(Time − 1/Scene.fps).p)**
>
> Expression: **2★A**

The expression in A calculates the difference between the pitches of the Cam in the current frame and the previous frame. Scene.fps gives you the frames per second for the scene, so 1/Scene.fps is the duration of one frame. The expression gives us a measure of the speed of rotation of the Cam. This makes the light intensity proportional to the speed

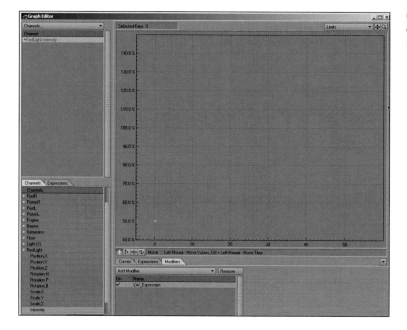

Click on the RedLightIntensity envelope button and add an LW_Expression modifier.

of the pistons. The scaling factor of 2 was chosen because it gives light intensities in a suitable range for the animation.

9   Add another Point Light, as in Step 3, and name it GreenLight.

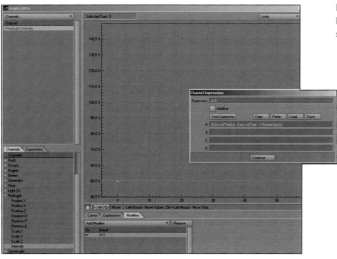

Enter the expression to make the light intensity proportional to the speed of the pistons.

10 Move GreenLight to XYZ **–5m**, **–4m**, **–2m** to move the light to a position inside the green dome on the generator.

11 With GreenLight selected, open the Light Properties panel (**p**). Set the Light Color to RGB **0**, **255**, **0**.

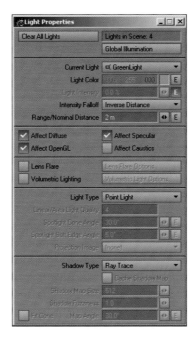

Add a Point Light and name it GreenLight. Move it into position inside the green dome and change its color to green.

12 Click on the envelope button for GreenLight's Intensity. Add an LW_Expression modifier to the Intensity channel.

13 Open the LW_Expression panel and enter the following expression:

A: **(Cam.rot(Time).p − Cam.rot(Time − 1/Scene.fps).p)**

B: **A*Scene.fps**

Expression: **B > 120.0 ? 1.0 : 0.0**

This introduces a conditional expression. As in Step 8, A represents the difference in pitch between the current and previous frames. Multiplying this by the Scene.fps gives you the angle of change per second. This is then used in the conditional part of the expression B > 120.0 ? 1.0 : 0.0, which means that if B is greater than 120, the expression is equal to 1.0; otherwise, it is equal to 0.0. This effectively creates a light that turns on only when Cam is turning faster than 120 degrees per second.

Render the animation from frames 1–300 to see the expressions in action. An example of the animation, Expressions.avi, is available on the book's CD-ROM.

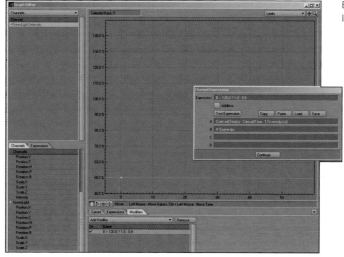

Enter the expression for the Intensity of GreenLight.

Note: When the expression gives a value of 1, this is equivalent to an intensity of 100%. The same applies to other parameters that are expressed as percentages.

MODIFYING THE PROJECT

This tutorial has given you an idea of the power of expressions. It is important to remember that expressions can be applied to any property or parameter that can have an envelope or be keyframed. This provides an almost unlimited number of possibilities of things that you could do with expressions. This list outlines just a few of those possibilities:

■ Create hydraulic pistons of the type that you might find on the arms of robots.

Note: If the object that is controlling the expression is being controlled with IK, you will need to add the LW_IKCapture modifier to its Motion Options panel (**m**). Otherwise, the effect of the expression will be ignored.

■ Prevent an object from passing through the floor by applying the following expression to the object's Y channel:

Value < 0 ? 0 : Value

> **Note:** The keyword Value returns the value of the current channel before the expression is applied. It does take into account any other modifiers that are in the list before LW_Expression. Sometimes it can be useful to add Value to part of an expression so you can keyframe in additional movement. Adding Value to the whole expression is equivalent to turning on the Additive option in the Expression panel.

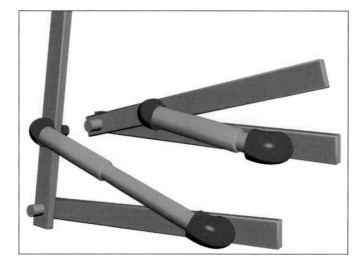

Hydraulic pistons.

■ Use dynamic parenting for things such as firing missiles from an aircraft or allowing a character to put down an object or pass it to another character. The basic method for doing this is to use a conditional statement. The parenting can be applied to one or more channels. Possible conditions that control the parenting could include the position of an object, the intensity of a light, or the passing of a specific time or frame. For example, consider the following conditional statement:

Time < 5.0 ? ObjectA.wpos(Time).x : ObjectB.wpos(Time).x

This expression makes a channel follow the X coordinate of the world position of ObjectA if the time is less than five seconds; otherwise, it will follow ObjectB.

■ Display inertia or extrapolated motion. For example, if you create a spaceship flying though space and you detach a life pod, the life pod will continue in the direction the ship was travelling at the time the pod was released.

In the Inertia.lws example, PodDocked is a null that marks the position of the docked pod. The expression on the x channel of the pod reads like this:

Expression: Time < A ? PodDocked.wpos(Time).x : C

A: LaunchNull.pos(0).x

B: (PodDocked.wpos(A).x − PodDocked.wpos(A − 1/Scene.fps).x)★Scene.fps

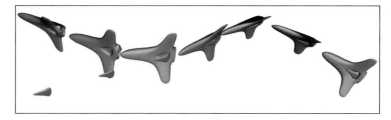

Inertia. An escape pod is attached to a spaceship, but when launched, it heads off in the direction the ship was heading when the pod was launched.

C: PodDocked.wpos(A).x + (Time − A) ⋆ B

A defines the time of the launch. B is the speed that the carrying ship is travelling at launch time. C extrapolates the motion of the pod given the position from which it was launched. Similar expressions would have to be applied to the Y and Z channels.

The h rotation channel reads as follows:

Time < LaunchNull.pos(0).x ? Ship_Carrier.rot(Time).h : Ship_Carrier.rot(LaunchNull.pos(0)).h

This keeps the rotation of the pod with that of the ship before launch and then fixes it with the rotation it had at the launch. Similar expressions are applied to the other rotation channels.

- Add the effect of motion blending. You can add the motion of two or more objects together using nulls or other objects to control the proportion of the motions added. The following expression uses a null to blend the x channel motions of ObjA and ObjB:

    Expression: A ⋆ ObjA.pos(Time).x +
    (1 A) ⋆ObjB.pos(Time).x

    A: Null.pos(Time).x

If Null.pos.x = 1, the expression gives the position of ObjA; if Null.pos.x = 0, it gives the position
of ObjB. Therefore, this can be used as a form of dynamic parenting. If the value was 0.5, the
expression would give a course halfway between the two objects.

Motion blending can also be used to add small secondary motion to existing keyframed motion. For example, you could add some noise or random motion.

- Make the wheels of a vehicle rotate at the correct rate for the vehicle's speed.

- Give thrown objects physically correct projectile motion.

Note: If you want one object to follow another but the pivots of the two objects do not line up, it is a good idea to parent a null to the control object and position it at the rest position of the pivot of the controlled object. In the expressions for the controlled object, refer to the world position (wpos rather than pos) the null, but still use the rotations of the control object. See Inertia.lws for an example.

Note: To access multilayer objects, you must use a special syntax. If a layer is named Object_Layer, you would access it in an expression with Object_Layer.

Note: It is useful to control some values, such as the time or position where something happens, with a null. This can save you from having to edit expressions if you want to adjust the value later on. This can be a great time saver, especially if the same value is used in many places, for example, on every channel of an object's motion.

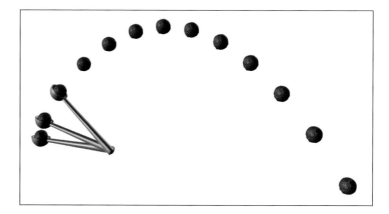

Catapult. The rock is linked to the motion of the catapult and then follows a projectile motion.

- Create muscle bones that move or stretch to cause a bulge when a joint is bent.

- Create morph targets, and then link the morph channels created by morphmixer to the motion on bones and nulls. This can create many effects that add to the realism of characters, for example:

    Add wrinkling at joints.

    Create folds of flesh that wobble as a character moves.

    Create bulging muscles (see ArmMuscle.lws).

    Control the stretching/flapping of wing membranes on dragons and bats.

- Use a single null to control bones to make a claw or hand flex.

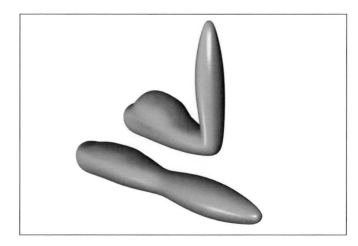

This muscle bulge was created using a morph target linked via an expression to the angle of the arm joint.

MODIFYING WITH PLUG-INS

Although the built-in expressions in LightWave [6.5] have a lot of power, there are still many situations in which third-party plug-ins can make life easier.

- Prem Subrahmanyam's Relativity is a very powerful expressions plug-in with a user friendly interface. You can find it at **http://www.premdesign.com/ppp.html**.

- project:messiah is an impressive character animation plug-in that also has an easy-to-use expressions system. For more information about messiah, produced by Lyle Milton, Fori Owurowa, and Dan Milling, visit **http://www.projectmessiah.com**.

PHOTOREALISTIC FUR AND HAIR WITHOUT PLUG-INS

"Laugh it up, Fuzzball."

—HAN SOLO IN *STAR WARS*

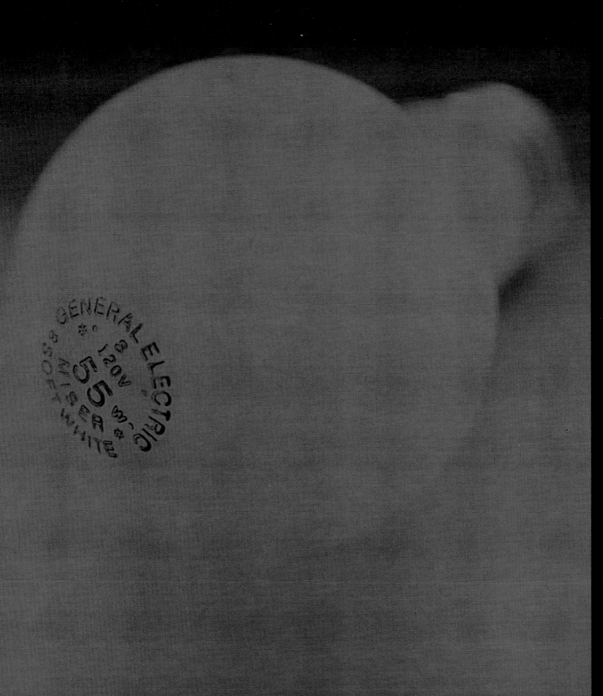

CREATING EXTRAORDINARY HAIR AND FUR SURFACES

Too many times you see exceptional modeling

of human characters and fantastic creatures,

only to find your eyes telling your brain that

something is not quite right with what you are

viewing. A lot of this stems from a lack of

photorealism in certain surfaces that, in the

past, have proven to be most elusive, namely

fur and hair.

Project 2

Photorealistic Fur and Hair Without Plug-Ins

by Graham McKenna

GETTING STARTED

The objective of the first steps toward achieving this effect is to create your geometry and apply a surface within Modeler. With these pieces in place, you can migrate to layout for the rest of the effect, whereby you will transform this primitive shape into your very own furball.

Birth of Furball: Creating Geometry

In these first steps, you will create two unique spheres, one 50% smaller than
the other.

1   Start Modeler, choose the Ball tool, and create a
    tessellated sphere at subdivision level 4, with 8
    segments and a 1.75 radius on all axes.

    Note: Press n to open the numeric panel to enter the
    appropriate values.

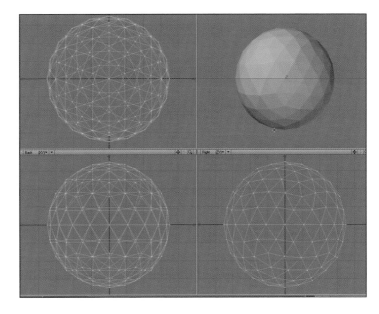

Create a tessellated sphere
and morph target.

2   Open the Change Surface dialog box (**q**) and name
    the entire ball surface **Fur**. Save the sphere as
    ball.lwo.

3   Choose the Size tool (Shift+h) and reduce the
    size of the sphere by a factor of 75%, centered on 0
    (zero). To do this, open the numeric requester for
    Size (**n**), enter the values, and then click Apply.
    Save the geometry as ballmorf.lwo.

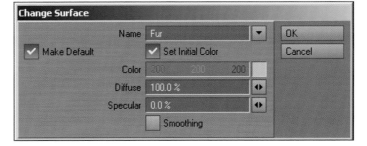

Name the ball surface Fur.

APPLYING GEOMETRY SURFACE ATTRIBUTES

Now that you've created the basic geometry, you need to set the ballmorf.lwo object surface parameters, including specular and glossiness values, and you need to apply bump and color textures. Follow these steps:

1   Start LightWave Layout and load the **objects ball.lwo** and **ballmorf.lwo**, which you created in the preceding steps.

Alternatively, you can load the objects from the book's companion CD.

2   Select the ballmorf object, and press **p** to enter Object Properties. In the Object Properties panel, click the Rendering tab, turn off all shadow attributes, and then check Unseen by Rays, Unseen by Camera, and Unaffect by Fog. Press **p** to close the Object Properties panel.

3   Open the Surface Editor and set Edit by to Object. Set the Specularity to **100%** and the Glossiness to **20%**. Click the Smoothing option. Then click the Advanced tab and set Color Highlights to **100%**.

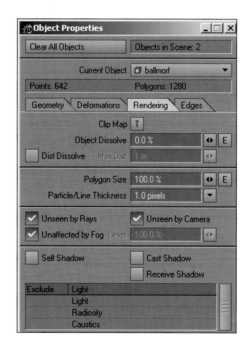

Ballmorf.lwo is ultimately never being rendered.

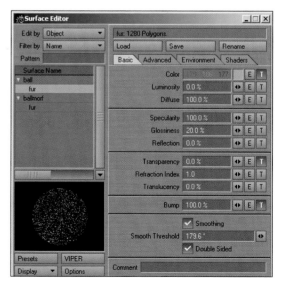

Set the sphere's surface attributes.

4 Go back to the Basic tab of the Surface Editor and open the Bump Texture Map options by pressing the T button next to Bump. Then enter the following settings:

> Layer Type: **Procedural Texture**
>
> Blending Mode: **Additive**
>
> Layer Opacity: **100%**
>
> Procedural Type: **Fractal Noise**
>
> Texture Value: **70%**
>
> Frequencies: **3**
>
> Scale: XYZ   **100mm, 100mm, 100mm**

The first layer of Bump Mapping adds general unevenness to the surface.

5 While still in the Bump Texture panel, apply a second bump texture by selecting Procedural from the Add Layer drop-down list. Enter the following settings:

> Procedural Type: **Crumple**
>
> Texture Value: **50%**
>
> Frequencies: **12**
>
> Small Power: **1**
>
> Scale: XYZ   **400mm, 400mm, 400mm**

The second layer of Bump Mapping creates a fine grain wash that, when motion blurred, helps create the illusion of tiny strands.

6 Apply a third procedural bump texture, with the following settings:

   Procedural Type: **Crumple**

   Texture Value: **50%**

   Frequencies: **3**

   Small Power: **2**

   Scale: XYZ **700mm**, **700mm**, **700mm**

The third layer of Bump Mapping adds deep pocket craters that form larger clumps of strands when motion blurred.

7 Apply a fourth procedural bump texture with the following settings:

   Texture: **Ripples**

   Texture Value: **60%**

   Wave Sources: **10**

   Wavelength: **0.2**

   Wave Speed: **0**

   Scale: XYZ **100mm**, **100mm**, **100mm**

8 Click Use Texture to close and accept the bump map textures. At this point, it's a good idea to save the object. In Layout, choose the Actions tab and select Save/Save All Objects.

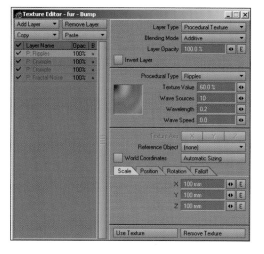

The fourth layer of Bump Mapping.

Note: Many bump maps are needed to give the render the best look. You can reduce the number of maps at your discretion when you reach this level. Bump maps give irregular swirls and a natural look to the fibers in the effects. You could get a similar effect by removing layers 2 and 4 and reducing the value of 1 (200%) and the value of 3 (10%). But to be honest, the effect works best with all four layers and is true to the renders.

The ripples map evens out the previous maps in appearance. But they still hold their own effects when motion blur is applied. The ripples also give a larger swirl to the fibers when used with motion blur.

9 Set a texture map for surface color by clicking the T button next to Color in the Surface Editor, under the Basic tab. Enter the following settings:

Layer Type: **Procedural Texture**

Blending Mode: **Additive**

Procedural Type: **Fractal Noise**

Texture Color: RGB **155, 108, 66**

Frequencies: **3**

Contrast: **1**

Small Power: **0.5**

Scale: XYZ   **1m, 1m, 1m**

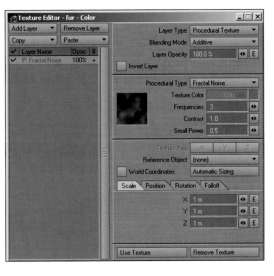

A color texture procedural for added texture.

10 Add an additional procedural color texture map with the following settings:

Layer Type: **Procedural Texture**

Blending Mode: **Additive**

Procedural Type: **Fractal Noise**

Texture Color: RGB **109, 64, 50**

Frequencies: **3**

Contrast: **1**

Small Power: **0.5**

Scale: XYZ **1m, 1m, 1m**

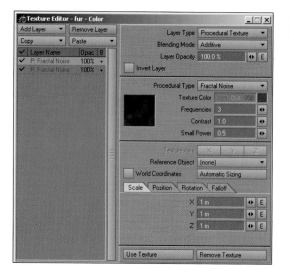

A second layer of color texture procedural is added.

11 Click Use Texture to close the texture panel and accept the color texture map settings. Save the object. Press **F9** to see what the surface looks like after you've made your changes.

Here is the surface with a motion blur applied.

Morph Target Setup

To make the sphere appear soft around the edges and to create the illusion of
fibers, you'll apply repeating morph and motion envelopes for the ball object.
You'll also set up the render and motion blur parameters.

1   Open the Object Properties panel (**p**) for ball.lwo.
    Under the deformations tab, set the morph option
    for morph ball.lwo in ball.morf.

Setting the initial morph target.

2   Click the Envelope tab (**e**) for Morph Amount.
    Create a keyframe at frame 1 in the Graph Editor. Set
    Post Behavior to Repeat, set the Value to **100%**, and
    exit the Graph Editor.

    Using the repeating envelope is the key to making
    the edges of the sphere appear soft. It now contracts
    in size over one frame repeatedly, constantly creating
    the look of a soft edge.

3   Choose ball.lwo and create a keyframe at 1. At frame
    0, reduce the size by 50%. You can do this by first
    selecting Size from the Actions tab in Layout, and
    then pressing **n** to highlight the numeric values.
    Enter a value of **0.500** for X, Y, and Z for a 50%
    scale of the default 1.0 setting. Create a keyframe
    at 0 to keep the size change.

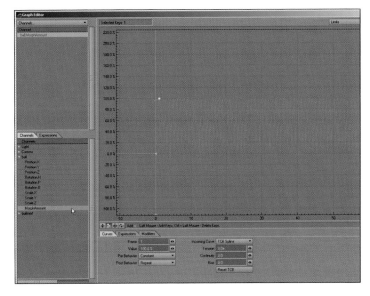

Soften the edges of the
sphere by setting a repeating morph envelope.

4   In the Graph Editor for ball.lwo, set Post Behavior
    to Repeat for Ball.Scale.X, Ball.Scale.Y, and
    Ball.Scale.Z. Close the Graph Editor.

Note: Be sure to press the a key in the Graph Editor
to fit the curves to view.

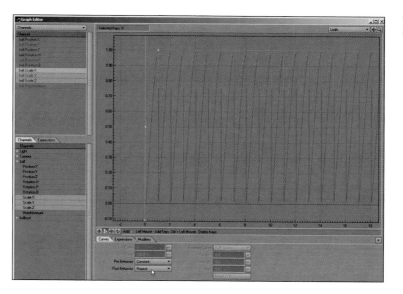

The scale is repeated in
the Graph Editor.

5   Open Camera Properties (**p**) and set the
    following options:

    Resolution: **VGA (640 × 480)**

    Pixel Aspect Ratio: **1.0**

    Antialiasing: **Enhanced Medium**

    Motion Blur: **Dithered**

    Blur Length: **50%**

The Dithered Motion Blur option makes for a
smoother effect on the motion blur, resulting in
smoother strands. Normal motion blur has a more
banded look but will render more quickly.

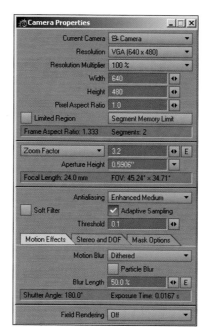

Set the camera motion blur settings.

6 Go to frame 1 and press **F9** to render.

> **Note:** Because of the bump maps you applied earlier, you can start to see the illusion of fiber strands. This is caused by the motion blur streaking the texture again over one frame.
>
> To lengthen the fibers, you use the same repeating envelope technique in the motion channel for the ball object. That technique gives far better results than if you were to increase the motion blur length or exceed the morph target percentage.

Repeating morph envelope and motion blur work together to soften the edges of the sphere.

DISPLACEMENT MAP SETUP

Although things are shaping up nicely, the strands look as if they are being emitted from the center of the sphere in a linear fashion. To correct this, you can introduce some kink into the fibers to give a more natural appearance. A displacement map works well for this purpose.

1 In the Object Properties panel, enter the Displacement Map Texture panel (**t**) for the ball.lwo object. Enter the following values:

> Layer Type: **Procedural**
>
> Blending Mode: **Additive**
>
> Layer Opacity: **100%**
>
> Procedural Type: **Fractal Noise**
>
> Texture Value: **0.3**
>
> Frequencies: **12**
>
> Contrast: **0.5**
>
> Small Power: **0.5**
>
> Scale: XYZ **5mm, 5mm, 5mm**

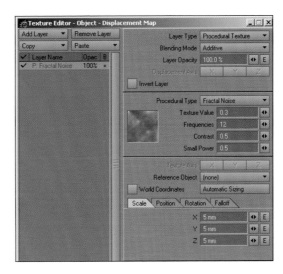

Displacement map settings.

2 Click Use Texture to keep the displacement map settings.

3 Exit the Object Properties panel and save the object. Then press **F9** to render.

Repeating the displacement envelope gives a more natural look to the strands.

TRANSPARENCY MAP SETUP

Now the strands look more natural, but you can still apply one more enhancement to embellish the final look. You can add shadow detail by applying a transparency texture.

1 Open the Surface Editor and choose the fur surface. Check the Double-Sided option.

2 Apply a Transparency texture map by clicking the T button next to Transparency. Then enter the following values:

    Layer Type: **Procedural Texture**

    Blending Mode: **Additive**

    Layer Opacity: **100%**

    Procedural Type: **Fractal Noise**

    Texture Value: **75%**

    Frequencies: **3**

    Contrast: **10**

    Small Power: **2**

    Scale: XYZ **8mm, 8mm, 8mm**

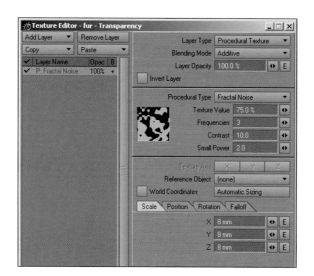

Additional surface attributes.

3   Click Use Texture to accept the Transparency
    texture map values.

4   Save the object and press **F9** to render.

With the transparency texture applied, you have a finished
effect. By adding the transparency texture, you introduced
grainy detail within the shadow, which adds to the realism
of the render.

The final effect.

How It Works

The fur technique uses a variety of procedures to create desired effect, but
the repeating envelope procedure is the main ingredient. By applying various
surface parameters to an object's surface in conjunction with motion blur, you
can create an endless number of effects.

Modifications

Don't be afraid to change any of the outlined settings to achieve the look you
need. It doesn't end here. Try deforming the geometry with a skeleton, or
parent your sphere to a null and keyframe from side to side to show the effect's
potential where dynamics are concerned. All in all, this is a simple but effective
effect to keep you warm over the winter.

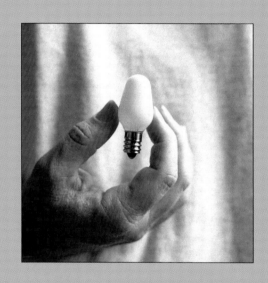

WELDING

SPARKS

"Don't ever take a fence down until

you know why it was put up."

—ROBERT FROST

WORKING WITH PARTICLE SPRAYS TO CREATE SPARK EFFECTS

Using LightWave [6.5]'s integrated particle

system along with HyperVoxels 3.0, you can

create quick and easy spark effects that can

be useful in many animation situations. In

addition, the variations are never-ending. This

technique can be used for welding sparks, of

course, but also for any sort of particle spray

you might be inclined to create, such as dust,

dirt sprays, or even water droplets.

Project 3
Welding Sparks

by Dan Ablan

GETTING STARTED

The goal of this tutorial is to help you create a laser beam that moves along a metal plate and generates sparks. This is a great technique for logo reveals, logo signatures, or even true sparks for when animated metal hits metal—like the braking wheels of a train.

> **Note:** So you don't have to waste a lot of time setting up a scene, a simple laser beam and metal plate scene was put on the book's CD for you. Look for the 03WeldingStart.lws scene.

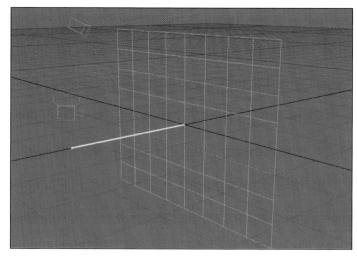

Load the wireframe scene in Layout to begin creating a cool effect.

CREATING THE LASER BEAMS

The first task is to create crossing laser beams. Follow these steps:

1. Load the **03WeldingStart.lws**, go to the Camera View (press **6** on the numeric keypad), and change the view style from Front Face Wireframes to Texture Shaded Solid.

2. Select the 03LaserBeam.lwo object. Press **y** on the keyboard to activate Rotate.

   Note: Be sure the AutoKey feature is off.

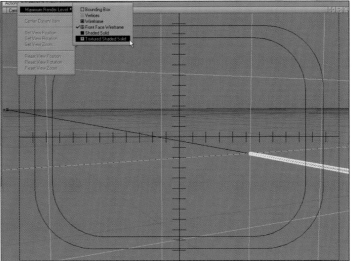

Change the view mode to Texture Shaded Solid.

3. Rotate the laser beam so that it's pointing to the upper-left corner of the Layout window.

   The laser beam's pivot point is at its base, so when it's rotated, you can have more control.

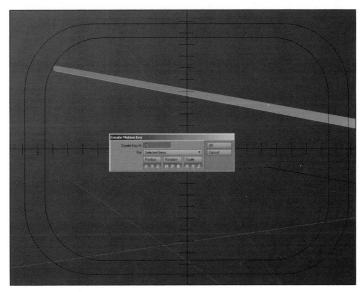

Rotate the laser beam's first keyframe to the top left of the Layout.

4 Create a keyframe at 0 for the laser beam. Then rotate the beam to the upper-right of Layout and create a keyframe at frame 45.

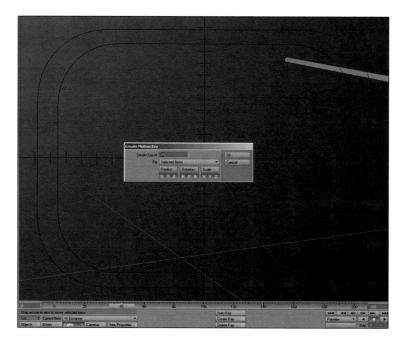

Rotate the laser beam's keyframe to the top right-hand corner of the screen at frame 45.

5 Rotate the laser beam a third time, down and over to the left-middle of Layout. Create a keyframe at 80.

With these steps, you're simply creating a fast zigzag motion for the laser beam. This will accentuate the welding sparks.

6 Rotate the laser beam over to the right middle side of the layout.

A quick laser swoosh across the screen will yield nice-looking results when the sparks are added to the end of the laser beam.

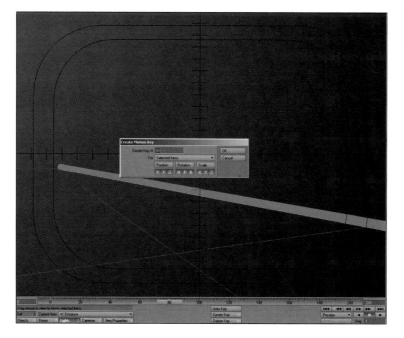

Rotate the laser beam to the left-middle of Layout and create a keyframe at 80.

7 Create a keyframe at 90.

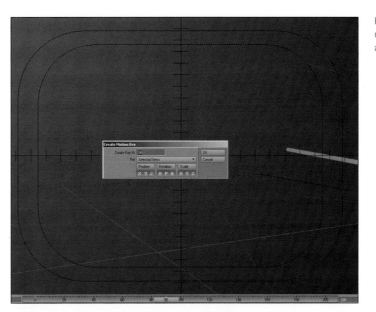

Rotate the laser beam to the right middle side of the layout at frame 90.

8 Rotate the laser beam to the bottom-left corner of the layout and create a keyframe at 105.

9 Rotate the laser to the right and out of view, and then create a keyframe at frame 125.

Note: This demonstrates how to create sparks with particles. The crossing laser beam motions you just created simply make it easier to see the particles move. More specific examples could be a laser beam drawing out and revealing text, while generating sparks.

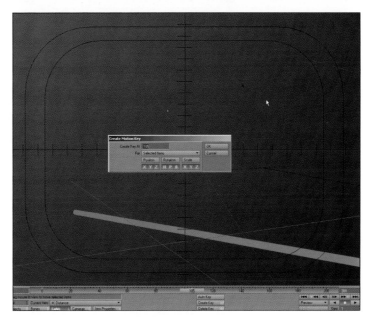

Rotate back to the other side of Layout for a keyframe at frame 105.

GENERATING SPARKS

Now the fun starts. The keyframed motions are set for the laser beam object, so you can begin adding sparks to the tip of laser beam. LightWave [6.5]'s integrated particles make it extremely easy to set up particles and get results instantly.

In the following steps, you'll use LightWave's particle engine to create an emitter object, and the emitter object will be parented to the tip of the laser.

1   Select the Extras tab, and then click the Plug-in Options button.

The Plug-In Options panel.

2   Select the FX_Browser plug-in.

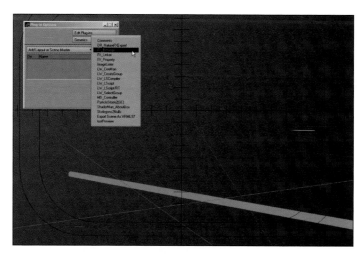

Using the Particle FX Browser, you can quickly add particle effects directly in Layout.

3   From the Add drop-down list, select Emitter.

The Particle FX Browser interface.

Selecting Emitter from the Add category instantly adds a particle emitter into Layout.

4 Click Continue in the FX Browser, and then return to Layout.

A large bounding box has been added to your scene. This is the particle emitter.

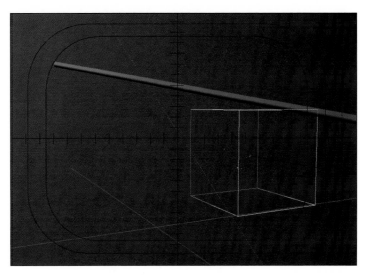

In Layout, the particle emitter is displayed as a default 1m bounding box.

5 Open the Plug-in Options panel and select the FX_Property plug-in.

Note: Instead of bringing up the FX Properties panel, you can leave the FX Browser open and then select the controller from the Select pop-up menu. From there, you can click the Property button to open the FX Property panel. This saves you the extra steps of using the generic plug-in panel.

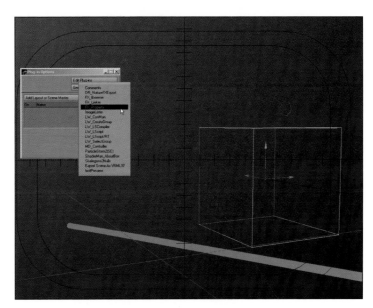

Select the FX_Property plug-in from the Plug-in Options panel.

6 Select the emitter in Layout.

7 Press the **m** key to call up the Motion Options panel. Parent the emitter to the 03LaserBeam object.

The emitter will jump and join itself to the end of the laser beam. Close the Motion Options panel.

8 In the bottom-right corner of the layout interface, change the last frame of the animation to **200**.

9 In the FX Property panel, change the Generator Size setting for the emitter to XYZ **0.1**, **0.1**, **0.1**.

This scales the size of the emitter in Layout.

Note: Don't forget that in LightWave [6.5], you can drag and drop one or many items directly in the Scene Editor for instant parenting. This method is great for parenting many items at once.

Note: Remember that with LightWave's non-modal panels, you can keep the FX Property panel open as you work. You can see here that the particle emitter is scaled down and parented to fit the tip of the laser beam. Also, you can quickly add Wind, Gravity, and more through access to the Properties panel for each.

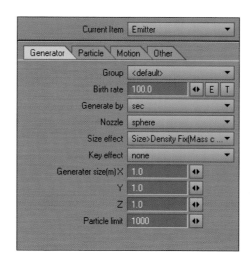

Open the FX Property panel, where particle data is controlled.

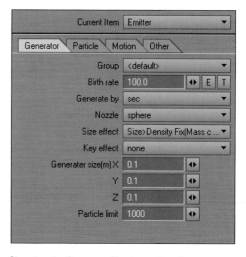

Changing the Generator Size from 1.0 to 0.1 scales down the emitter in Layout to better fit the tip of the laser beam.

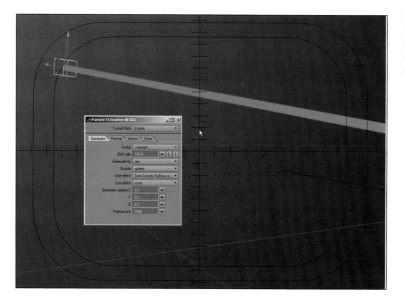

Notice that the full Layout interface with the FX Property panel is still open. The smaller emitter is now parented to the laser beam.

10 Click the Play button.

Because the emitter is parented to the laser beam
and you've set up keyframes for the laser beam, the
particle emitter moves with it, spraying particles
along the way.

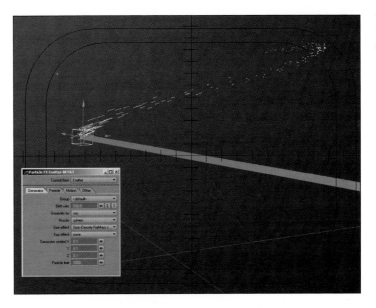

The animation at this point.
Next, make the particles move
and react with the scene.

11 Click the Motion tab from within the FX Property
interface. Change the Explosion rate to **0.5**.

By default, the particles look pretty good. But by
changing the explosion rate, you can make them
react better to what's happening in the scene.

Note: Remember that you can keep the FX Property
panel open and keep the animation playing at the same
time. Clicking the Play button sets the scene into
motion and loops it until you click the Pause button.
When you change particle information, it updates the
data in real time!

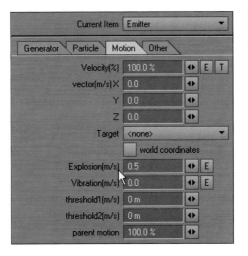

Setting the Explosion rate to 0.5
gives the particles a burst of
energy as they are emitted.

12 Click the Other tab within the FX Property panel. Set the Gravity Y to **–2.0**.

From here, you can tweak and adjust the particles in real time to create various effects. You can add effects such as wind, turbulence, or more texture effects. Project 14 will use more of LightWave [6.5]'s integrated particles to create a killer tornado!

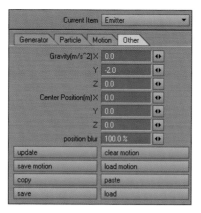

Set the Gravity Y position to –2.0 to add gravity to the particles, making them fall after they are emitted.

PARTICLE VISIBILITY

All right, so you've got the laser beam moving, and you threw some particles into the mix—but what will they look like when rendered? Right now, they won't look like anything. But you can make them look pretty cool with HyperVoxels. Adding HyperVoxels to your particles will make the sparks visible. The steps up to this point helped you generate the particles. From here, HyperVoxels will bring them to life with color and gradients.

Note: Particles can be seen only if you use HyperVoxels. They are not treated as normal LightWave particles, like single-point polygons used for stars. Single-point polygons will render on their own. The particles you've generated cannot render on their own.

1 Go to frame 70 of your animation. In the Effects panel, click the Volumetrics tab and select the HyperVoxelsFilter plug-in.

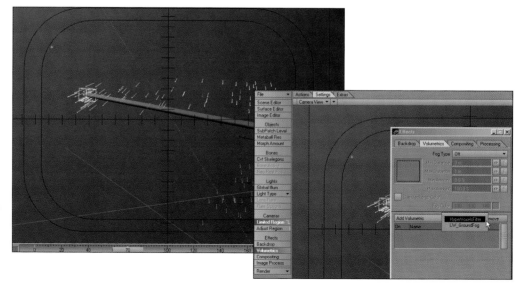

Review frame 70 of the animation before you apply HyperVoxels. Then add the HyperVoxelsFilter through the Effects panel's Volumetrics tab.

2   Double-click the HyperVoxels 3.0 plug-in listing to open its control panel.

3   In the Object Name list, double-click the ghosted name Emitter.

The name becomes bold as the particle emitter is activated in HyperVoxels.

4   Click the VIPER button at the bottom of the HyperVoxels interface. This opens LightWave [6.5]'s interactive preview renderer.

Note: You may want to click the Draft Mode button on the VIPER window for faster renders. This is for display only and has no effect on the final render.

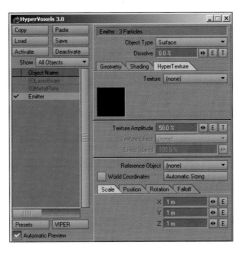

Double-click the object named Emitter in the Object Name list to make the particle object active in HyperVoxels 3.0.

5   Change the Object Type to Sprite.

Note: In your VIPER window, you can see that with HyperVoxels applied, the particles could be used to create great-looking smoke trails.

6   Change Particle Size to **30mm**.

This will make the Sprite HyperVoxels tiny and more independent of one another.

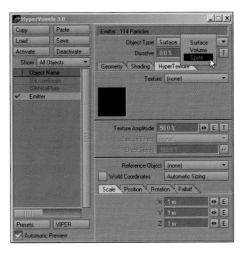

Change the Object Type to Sprite to change the particles to softer-looking objects.

Note: A Sprite is a 2D slice of a HyperVoxel that creates a softer-looking effect and helps speed up render times.

A Voxel is a pixel element with 3D attributes.

7 Set Stretch Direction to Velocity and click on Align to Path.

8 Click the Shading tab in the HyperVoxels panel, and then change the Color to a fire orange-red color using the setting RGB **236**, **151**, **074**.

Note: You can click on the Show Particles button in the HyperVoxels interface to show visible outlines of the voxels while in Layout.

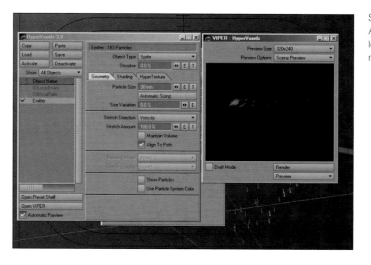

Set Particle Size, Stretch, and Align To Path, and the particles look closer to the intended final result.

9 Click the T button for Luminosity to open the Texture Editor.

10 Set the Layer Type to Gradient, and then click in the middle of the white gradient display to create a key. After you add the key, make sure it is selected. To do this, click on the small triangle on the left side. (Clicking the X on the right side deletes the key.)

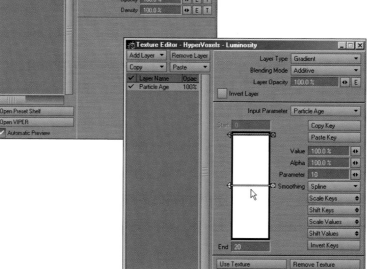

Clicking the T button next to Luminosity opens the Texture Editor.

Create a key for the Gradient Luminosity map by clicking in the white gradient area.

11 Set the following parameters:

> Blending Mode: **Additive**
>
> Layer Opacity: **100%**
>
> Input Parameter: **Particle Age**
>
> Value: **100%**
>
> Alpha: **0%**
>
> Parameter: **20**

VIPER updates the display, showing brighter particles that now look like they're glowing. This helps fade the particles out as they die. Note that you won't see this effect in the VIPER window, but only when you render.

12 Click Use Texture.

Note: You can employ almost the exact same settings from the Luminosity Gradient texture to the Color Gradient texture. Using the Particle Age Input Parameter, you can vary the color of the particles over their life. This technique can also be used for things like fireworks. Try it out!

Add a gradient with the Particle Age parameter to make the particles fade as they die.

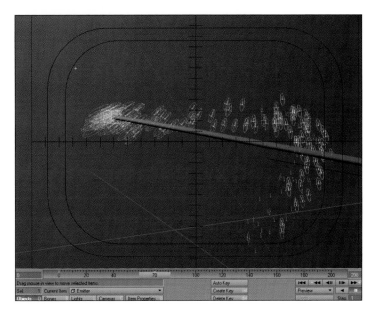

Apply the HyperVoxel settings to the emitting particles in Layout; they're represented by small wire outlines.

FINAL TOUCHES

The laser beam is glowing hot, and the particles are bright and full of color, but there's one thing missing: a hot spot. The laser beam and the particles are clearly two separate objects in this render. Adding a small lens flare to the end of the laser will help blend the laser beam tip with the particles.

> **Tip:** As a final enhancement to the scene, add Glow to the particles and the laser beam object. This will add a nice extra touch, creating a hot, soft look.

A rendered image of the animated particles with HyperVoxels applied at frame 70.

1   Under the Actions tab in Layout, select Add, Add Light, Add PointLight. Enter the name Flare when prompted.

2   Select the light and press **m** to call up the Motion Options panel. Parent the new point light to the 03LaserBeam object.

This point light will serve two purposes: to illuminate the tip of the laser and metal plate backdrop, and to create a soft transition between the laser and the particles.

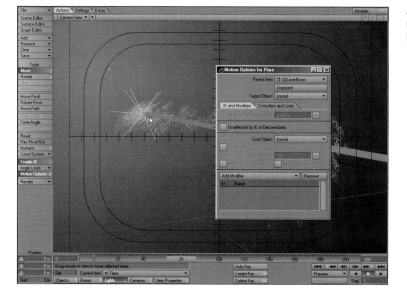

Add a point light to the scene and parent it to the laser for an added glow.

3 Open the Display Options panel (**d**) and turn on the OpenGL Lens Flares option.

4 Select the flare light, and then press **p** to call up the Light Properties panel. Bring the light color to a soft orange, using the settings RGB **255**, **156**, **108**. Leave the Light Intensity at the default setting of 50%.

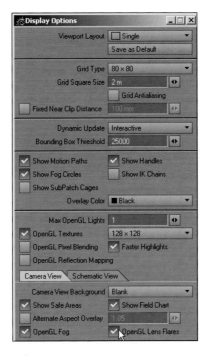

Activate OpenGL Lens Flares through the Display Options panel to set a lens flare without rendering.

5 Click the Lens Flare option.

You'll see the lens flare kick on in Layout. You might need to move the Light Properties panel over to the right to make the flare fully visible.

6 Click the Lens Flare Options button to adjust the flare properties. Set the following parameters:

> Flare Intensity: **80%**
>
> Fade Off Screen: **On**
>
> Fade Behind Objects: **Off**
>
> Fade in Fog: **Off**
>
> Fade with Distance: **Off**

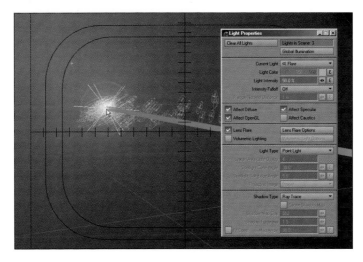

Once you turn on Lens Flare for a light and activate OpenGL Lens Flares from the Display Options panel, you can see your efforts directly in Layout.

Central Glow: **On**

Central Ring: **Off**

Glow Behind Objects: **Off**

Red Outer Glow: **Off**

Anamorphic Distortion: **Off**

Streaks: **None**

Reflections: **None**

Close the Lens Flare Options and return to Layout.

7 Make a test render by pressing the **F9** key.

A render of the sparks with all the elements in place.

HOW IT WORKS

The techniques here are simple to set up and adjust, thanks to the particle integration in LightWave [6.5] and VIPER. The OpenGL Lens Flares option also helps you design your scene by enabling you to see where your lens flare is and how it affects the rest of the scene. Although this is easy, the final results are the often much-needed finishing touches that make an animation come to life. This effect works because the particle system generates particles that often seem to have a mind of their own. Particles that react to movements of parented objects and LightWave [6.5] surfacing attributes help any animation take on a new dimension.

MODIFICATIONS

It should be evident how many variations you can make with this technique—from sparks on machinery or water droplets, to magic wands, smoke, and more. The particle effect demonstrated here could go even a step further within itself. If you've ever seen real sparks, you can sometimes see a small plume of smoke as well as the sparks. To re-create that event with the effect in this project, all you need to do is repeat the preceding steps from the beginning, adding another emitter to the scene. However, when it's time to add HyperVoxels, don't change the size and color as much. Play with the settings to make the sprite style HyperVoxel look soft and misty, like smoke.

Another possible effect for this particular particle animation is to delay the particles by adding an envelope that will start and stop the particles at specific times. Do this in conjunction with the laser beam entering the frame and slamming into the metal plate, creating the spark effect. Finally, you can use the Acid plug-in from Steve Worley's Polk plug-in collection (**www.worley.com**) or Surface Effectors from Prem Design (**www.premdesign.com**) to leave a "burned" result or a trail from the welding sparks.

How you can vary this effect and the others in this book really depends on your own creativity and ingenuity. Although it's great to have a handy "cookbook" of effects, it's even cooler to take all the "recipes" and make your own feast.

MAGNIFYING GLASS

"A day without sunshine is like,

you know, night."

—STEVE MARTIN

USING CAUSTIC PROPERTIES TO PRODUCE A FOCUSED LIGHT SOURCE

The idea for this tutorial came from John Mark Roquemore. John was curious how to create an animated magnifying glass with a focused light source—a *caustic*. Taking the effect a step further, this chapter will show you how to burn a small area of paper.

Project 4

Magnifying Glass

by Dan Ablan

GETTING STARTED

The effect you'll create can be used in many situations, from logo enhancements to scientific animations, spectacles, or even 3D detective work. You'll create the effect in three stages: focusing the lens, applying caustics, and setting up the burn. So, enough banter, on with the effect!

1 Starting in Layout, load the **04MagGlass.lws** scene from the book's CD. Press **F9** to render a test frame, of frame zero.

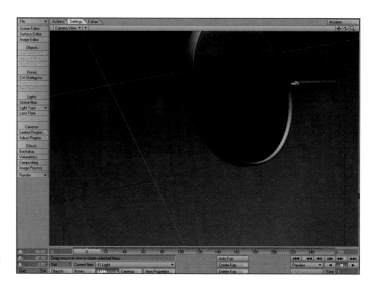

Load the 04MagGlass.lws
scene in Layout.

2   Press the **f** key and go to frame 250. Press **F9** again to render.

You can see that the magnifying glass now catches the light, but nothing develops from it underneath.

Although the magnifying glass now catches the light, the light does not refract through like it would in the real world.

3   From the Settings tab, click the Global Illumination button to open that panel. Click the Enable Caustics button.

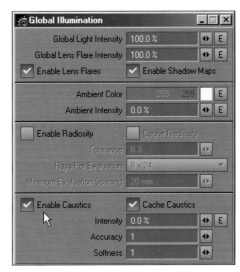

The Global Illumination panel.

4 Enter the following settings:

Cache Caustics: **On**

Intensity: **650%**

Accuracy: **60**

Softness: **100**

These values were derived from a simple "test it and see" method of calculation.

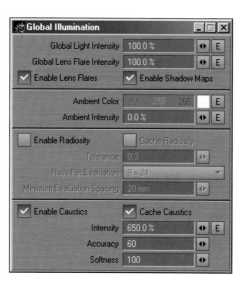

Apply caustics through the Global Illumination panel.

5 Press **F9** again to render.

Now you'll see the light source focused through the magnifying glass. This is a caustic.

> **Note:** Apply caustics to a scene with ray traced reflections and refraction will certainly add render time. But you can use LightWave [6.5]'s "Extra Ray Trace Optimization" feature in the Render Options panel. Turn this on to add a speedy increase to a raytraced scene.

6 Render the animation. The focus of light is centered under the magnifying glass.

Now you need to create a spot where the hot light is burning the paper.

Applying Caustics to the scene causes LightWave to calculate and imitate the reflection of light through a transparent surface.

Clip Map Burns

Clip Mapping is a very useful LightWave technique that you can use for many animations. It is a great way to cut holes in objects without actually modeling.

1 Go to the Settings tab and click the Image Editor. Load the image 04burnme.tga from the book's CD. Close the Image Editor and select the **04ParchPaper.lwo** object. Press the **p** key to open the Object Properties panel.

Note: You can also select Load Image from the Texture Editor. Using the Image Editor helps you load multiple images and manage them. The choice is yours.

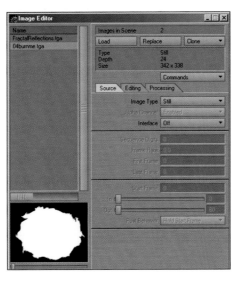

Load the 04burnme.tga image into LightWave's Image Editor.

2 Go to the Rendering tab and click the T button for Clip Map.

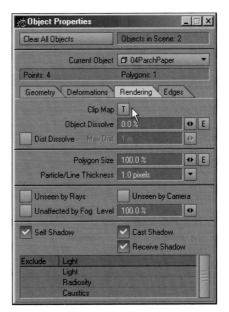

You can access the Clip Map Texture Editor via the Object Properties panel's Render tab.

3 Set the following parameters:

> Layer Type: **Image Map**
>
> Blending Mode: **Additive**
>
> Layer Opacity: **100%**
>
> Projection: **Planar**
>
> Image: **04burnme.tga**
>
> Width Tile: **Reset**
>
> Height Tile: **Reset**
>
> Pixel Blending: **On**
>
> Texture Antialiasing: **On**
>
> Strength: **1.0**
>
> Texture Axis: **Y**
>
> Scale: XYZ **1m, 1m, 1m**

The Texture Editor for Clip Map looks like the Texture Editor everywhere else in LightWave, so it should be easy to navigate. When you finish, click Use Texture.

4 Press **F9** for a test render.

Note: Now you have the hole, but it's off to the right and not underneath the magnifying glass. You can try to position the clip map numerically, but an easier way is to use a reference object.

5 Add a null object from the Actions tab in Layout. When prompted, name it ClipREF.

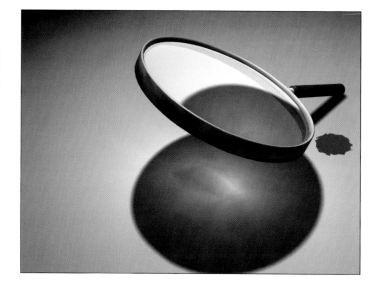

Adding a clip map to the parchment paper object cuts a hole based on the black and white luminance of an image.

6 Select the null object ClipREF from the Reference Object drop-down list in the Clip Map Texture Editor.

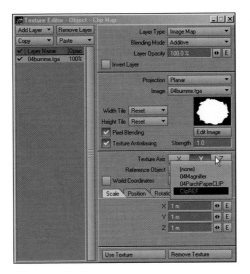

Adding a reference object such as a null gives you control over the clip map in Layout.

7 Back in Layout, move the ClipREF null object down the Z-axis to 3.0815m. Then move it on the X-axis to −366mm. Press **F9** to render a frame. Create a keyframe at frame zero to lock the position in place.

Note: The beauty of using a reference object with a clip map (or any image map) is that you have physical control of its placement in Layout. This reference object can also help you size the clip map in situations like this.

Using a reference object enables you to move the clip map, which now appears under the magnifying glass.

Burn Progression

The magnifying glass is focusing a hot spot of light on a piece of paper, and the clip map has created a hole, simulating a burn through the paper. But in reality, the hole would start small and burn its way outward. Although you can easily go into the Clip Map Texture Editor and keyframe the scale, an easier way is to use the added reference object.

1   Go to frame 0 in Layout. Select the ClipREF object and size it to **0.01** for the X, Y, and Z coordinates. Create a keyframe at 0.

2   Size the ClipREF object to **0.01** for the X, Y, and Z coordinates again. Press Enter and create a keyframe at 120 to keep the change

Because the magnifying glass turns over at frame 90, you want a second in there for the burn to start.

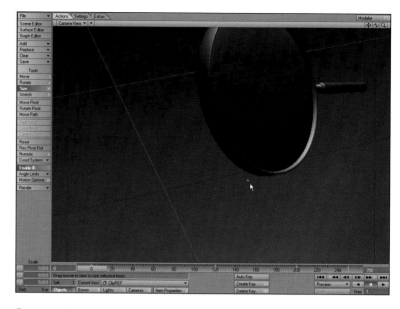

Decreasing the size of the null at frame zero makes the clip map start small and burn outward.

3   At frame 200, size the ClipREF back to **1.0** for the X, Y, and Z coordinates, and then create a keyframe to lock it in place.

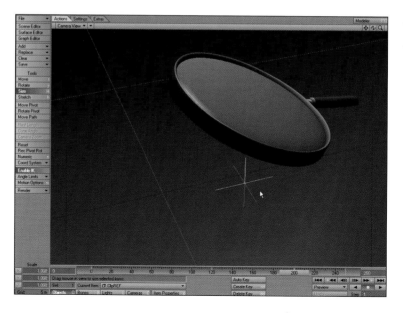

At frame 200, the clip map is sized to its normal position; it will now be animated over time.

4 Open the Graph Editor for the ClipREF object and ease in the keyframes. In the Graph Editor, select all channels for the ClipREF object.

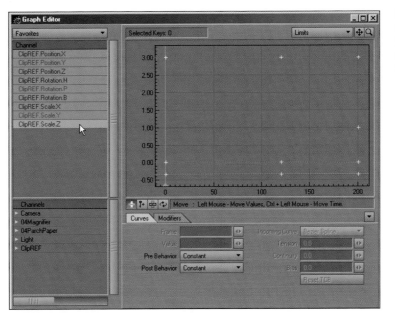

Select all channels from the channel bin in the Graph Editor to work with all their keyframes at once.

5 Hold the Shift key and double-click to select all keyframes in the Curve Window. Right-click on one of the keyframes and select Ease In/Out. This sets a TCB Spline with Tension of **1.0** for all selected keyframes. This will keep the ClipREF from drifting between keyframes.

Back in Layout, you can see your null object sizing over time. A quick AVI or Quicktime render of the animation will show the animated clip map.

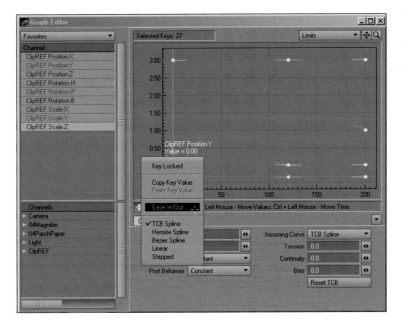

With all keyframes selected, right-click and choose Ease In/Out to keep frames from drifting.

HOW IT WORKS

By using LightWave's tools together, you can create many great and different effects. In this project, you use Caustics along with clip mapping to produce a light that's focused through a magnifying glass to create a burn. The caustic is a reflected light through a transparent surface (like the magnifying glass). The clip map is nothing more than a black and white image made in Adobe Photoshop. The white area of the image cuts a hole when applied as a clip, whereas the black area does not. This is a clever and quick way to cut holes in objects without adding extra modeling time.

VARIATIONS

You can take this technique one step further by using LightWave's integrated particle system to create a bit of smoke that rises from the burn as it happens. By using third-party plug-ins like the James K. Polk collection from Worley Labs (**www.worley.com**) or Surface Effectors from Prem Design (**www.premdesign.com**), you can color the edges of the burn on the clip map for added realism. Add smoke, and you're all set! For more details on creating smoke, refer to Project 19, "Smoke Plumes."

To take the clip map idea further, you can use this technique to create complex shapes like leaves or plants. A color, bump, and specular map along with a clip map can create a very realistic leaf out of just one polygon. This is extremely helpful when you're creating trees with large amounts of leaves. Other uses for clip maps could be for humans in architectural settings. A color map along with a black and white clip map can make a great filler for crowd scenes, and so on. The possibilities are truly endless with LightWave [6.5].

AGED FILM EFFECT

"Practice is the best of all instructors."

—PUBLILIUS SYRUS

USING IMAGE FILTERS AND PLUG-INS TO IMITATE AGED FILM

If you think about it, it's funny that the exact

things videographers and filmmakers have tried

to avoid and work away from over the years

are things animators are trying to achieve.

Things like lens flares, camera jitter, and aged

film are often avoided in the real world. But in

the 3D world, they are special effects. This

project shows you how to take any animation

and make it look like aged film using three

LightWave plug-ins: Bloom, Vectorblur, and

Virtual Darkroom.

Project 5

Aged Film Effect

by Dan Ablan

GETTING STARTED

This effect can be applied to any of your animations, from logos, to industrial plants, to automobile composites, and more. For this particular project, you'll use an animation of old cargo aircrafts flying to create the look of old war footage. The scene has been put together for you and is on the book's CD. Feel free to study the scene itself for lighting, camera motion, and backdrops.

Note: The lighting for the scene is simply a generic distant light. Because the final render will be color processed and grainy, you want the light to be general and even. Camera motions are easily created with LightWave's texture channel, which is explained in detail in Project 9, "Procedural Texture Motions." The plane motions are handled this way as well.

Note: Be sure the ShadFilt.p plug-in is loaded from the Layout Legacy plug-ins folder. This will load the Sepia plug-in used in this project.

Follow these steps to create the scene for the flying planes:

1　Load the scene **05PlaneStart.lws** from the book's CD. Select the 05PlaneBodyWings(3) object. This is the foremost plane in view at the base of the scene you'll use to age and blur.

Load the scene 05PlaneStart.lws into Layout.

Frame 120 rendered from the 05PlaneStart.lws scene. It looks cool, but not old and aged.

2　Press **4** on the numeric keypad to switch to Perspective view.

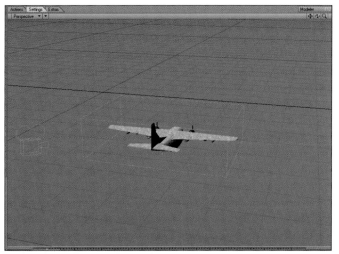

Select the 05PlaneBodyWings(3) object and switch to Perspective view.

3 Select 05PlaneBodyWings(3) and open the Graph Editor from the Actions tab. From the channel bin, select the channel 05Plane:PlaneBodyWings(3) Position Y.

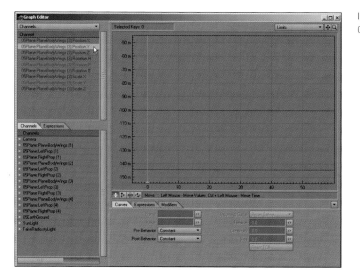

In the Graph Editor, select the channel 05Plane:PlaneBodyWings(3) Position.Y.

4 Select the NoisyChannel modifier from the Add Modifier drop-down list. Then double-click the NoisyChannel listing to open the controls.

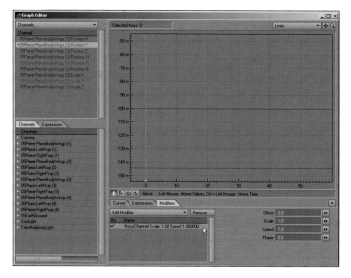

Add the NoisyChannel modifier. Double-clicking the NoisyChannel modifier opens its controls in the Graph Editor.

5 Resize and move the Graph Editor window so that the 05Plane:PlaneBodyWings(3) object is visible in Layout.

Note: Because Layout is in the Perspective view, you can move the view out of the way as you did the Graph Editor. All you need to see at this point is the NoisyChannel controls.

Note: If you have a dual monitor setup, just drag the Graph Editor window aside.

6 Click the Play button in the lower-right corner of Layout.

You'll see the plane object bounce around. It seems as if there is a little too much turbulence. Instead, you want a smooth flying motion.

7 Change the NoisyChannel Scale to **1.33** and the Speed to **0.06**.

8 Switch back to Camera View by pressing the **6** key.

The plane now floats softly on the Y-axis.

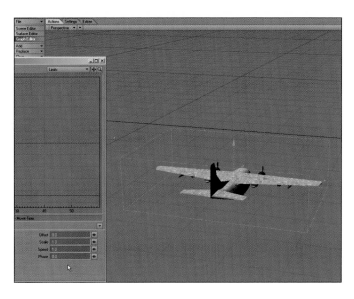

Reposition the Graph Editor and Perspective views so you can see the plane object as well as the Graph Editor.

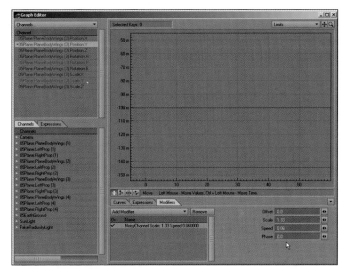

Changing the scale and speed of the NoisyChannel adjusts the plane's Y motion channel.

9   Add a NoisyChannel modifier to the
    05Plane:PlaneBodyWings(3)Rotation.B channel. Set
    the Scale to **0.15** and Speed to **0.08**.

    This will give the plane a nice rocking motion,
    making it appear as if it's floating.

10 Click Play to see the changes in Layout.

> **Note:** NoisyChannel is great for quick, random motion
> setup. You can also set NoisyChannel to a displacement-
> mapped sub-patched polygon for watery surfaces, and
> then add it to a boat to create rocking motions.

> **Note:** You can also add NoisyChannel modifiers to the
> other planes in the scene, as well as to the camera.
> The final scene on the CD, 05Planes.lws, has these
> already set for you.

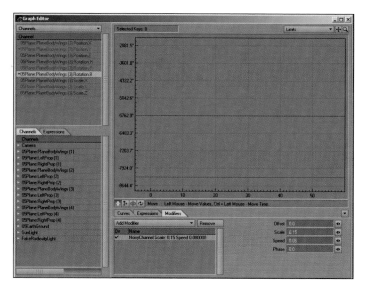

Changing the NoisyChannel values for
05Plane:PlaneBodyWings(3).Rotation.B
creates a slight rocking motion.

AGED BLUR

Computer animation is crisp and clean. While that's great for architectural
and industrial animations, old film has a blur to it. You can add image filters
to make the animation look blurry and old. The scene already has LW_Bloom
applied as an image filter. Bloom creates bright specular highlight glows.
LW_SoftReflections is also applied; it softens the reflective properties of the
scene. Finally, LW_VectorBlur has been applied to blur the propeller blades.
These filters help set up the animation for a nice bright daytime shot. The goal
from here is to add the aged film look.

1   Go to the Settings tab and click the Image Process
    button.

2   From the Add Image Filter drop-down list, select
    LW_DepthBlur. Double-click LW_DepthBlur in the
    listing to open the controls.

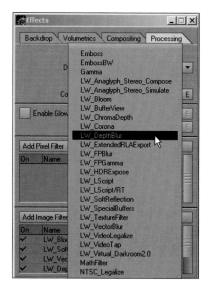

The LW_DepthBlur image
filter will help soften the
animation.

This will allow you to add a soft blur to the image, taking away that computer-generated-image feel.

3   Set the following parameters:

    Blur Strength: **50%**

    Blur Alpha Channel: **Off**

    Blur Background: **Off**

    Use Layout Lens: **Off**

    Focal Distance: **450m**

    Lens F-Stop: **8.0**

4   Close the LW_DepthBlur panel, keep the Effects panel open, and get ready for the next stage of the project.

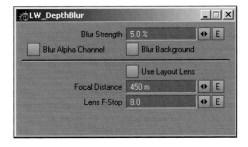

Add a soft blur to take away the computer-generated-image feel.

FILM GRAIN

The next phase of the animation effect is to create the film grain, like aged emulsion. You'll use LightWave's Virtual Darkroom plug-in as another image filter to further enhance your animation.

1   Add the LW_VirtualDarkroom image filter from the Effects panel.

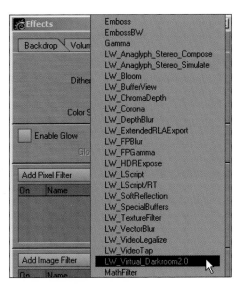

The LW_VirtualDarkroom image filter will help create the old film grain look.

2 Double-click the LW_Virtual_Darkroom listing to open the controls. Set the following parameters:

Output Type: **Black & White**

Negative LUX: **4**

Positive LUX: **3**

Negative Time: **0.15**

Positive Time: **1.0**

Enable Scattering: **On**

Negative Width: **15.0**

Negative Height: **15.0**

Enable Grain: **On**

Selwyn Granularity: **0.0012**

Apply the LW_Virtual_Darkroom interface settings for aged film.

The render up to this point at frame 120.

AGED COLOR

The color of old film is often black and white or sepia toned. Even old color processed film sometimes has a sepia tone from aging. This next and last section will guide you through re-coloring the animation.

1 Go to the Effects panel and load the Sepia filter. Double-click the Sepia filter in the list.

You'll see that it has no interface.

2 Press **F9** to render a frame.

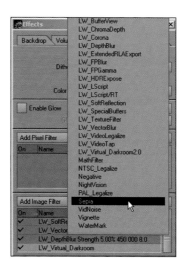

The Sepia image filter has no interface controls. Add the Sepia image filter for aged colorization.

How It Works

Because LightWave [6.5] allows you to layer as many filters and plug-ins as you want, you can do just about anything. In this project, you used six image filters to blur, grain, and color the rendered image. This will of course make the animation look more lifelike and realistic. It's important to note that the placement of these filters is crucial to the overall look of the project. If you put the LW_VirtualDarkroom filter last, for example, you would end up with sharper and brighter grain because the Sepia filter, which is currently last, would be applied before it. You can rearrange the order of the image filters by simply clicking and dragging them in the filter list.

Modifications

If you looked through the Image Filter plug-in list when you were adding the filters for this project, you might have seen the LW_TextureFilter. If you add that as an image filter, you can add textures to the render. Something like Turbulence or Fractal Noise on top of the blurring and sepia effects can help create the look of dust and scratches. Remember also that if you add the Texture Editor as an image filter, you can open the Graph Editor and animate those properties.

It's been said before, and it'll be said again: The possibilities are endless!

Note: You don't have to make a 3D animation to use the LW_VirtualDarkroom plug-in. It can also be used on video clips! Bring your image sequence—or pre-rendered animation—into LightWave, throw it into the background, and process the images. No need for another image processing program!

STORM CLOUDS

"Don't knock the weather,

nine-tenths of the people couldn't start

a conversation if it didn't change

once in a while."

—KIM HUBBARD

CREATING STORMY SKIES WITH HYPERVOXELS 3.0 AND LIGHTWAVE'S VOLUMETRIC OPTION

It seems that in most 3D animations, you see

pleasant peaceful skies. Pretty blues and some

orange, maybe even a deep purple makes it in

there as well. Animators often add nice bright

lens flares to finish it all off. But what about

those stormy days? Is it always sunny where

you live? It's got to be overcast sometime, so

why not animate it? This project instructs you

on the techniques needed to create realistic

billowing storm clouds with HyperVoxels 3.0.

Project 6

Storm Clouds

by Dan Ablan

GETTING STARTED

This effect will help you create storm clouds as well as an overcast sky. And although the goal is to teach you how to set up this type of sky, the technique can be used for any type of sky—sunny or not. You'll start in Layout.

1   Open Layout and start with a clear scene. You can create these clouds from the perspective of the ground or from the air. For this project, you'll start in the air and begin by changing the backdrop colors.

2 Click the Backdrop tab in the Effects panel.

3 Click the Gradient Backdrop option.

This creates a range of colors in Layout's backdrop.

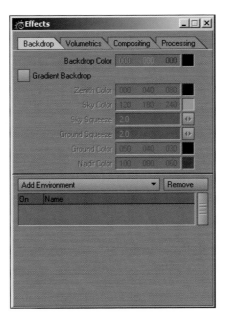

From the Backdrop tab in the Effects panel, you can start creating an atmosphere of storm clouds.

4 Set the following colors:

Zenith Color: RGB **100**, **111**, **125**

Sky Color: RGB **217**, **217**, **221**

Ground Color: RGB **217**, **217**, **221**

Nadir Color: RGB **176**, **176**, **176**

Leave the Sky Squeeze and Ground Squeeze settings at 2.0.

Use a gradient backdrop of colors to create a base for the storm.

Render the gradient backdrop.

MAKING 3D CLOUDS

You have a few choices of how to go about creating storm clouds, and which you use depends on the type of animation you are doing. You can go simple, rendering fractal noise on a flat plane. This is useful for filler sky shots in which the clouds are not key players. You can also use a pre-rendered picture or image map and use LightWave's Image World modifier to apply a cloud image to a scene.

But what if you want to really see some clouds and fly through them? You're going to do this the hard way. Well, it's not really hard at all, but it is the most efficient if you want to create a cloud fly-through or animate the clouds. You'll use HyperVoxels 3.0 to generate real storm clouds.

1   Click over to the Volumetrics tab in the Effects panel.

2   Slide the panel over to the right of the Layout window, and then add an object. From the Actions tab, select Add / Add Object. Add **06CloudPoints.lwo** from the book's CD.

Note: Often, you might find that using an image of clouds works best for animations that do not focus directly on the sky. When the clouds are the direct focus and you want to create a great realistic fly-through, HyperVoxel clouds are great.

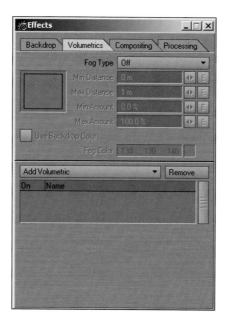

You will create clouds in the Volumetrics panel.

3   Go to the Camera View and select the
09CloudPoints object.

4   Move the 09CloudPoints object up on the Y-axis to
92m. Then move it on the Z-axis to 294m.

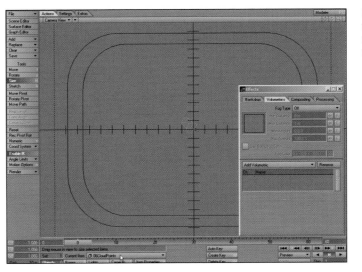

Load the 09CloudPoints object
with the Camera View and
move the Effects panel off to
the side.

5   Select Size, and set the scale to **10.0** for all axes.
Create a keyframe at zero to lock it in place.

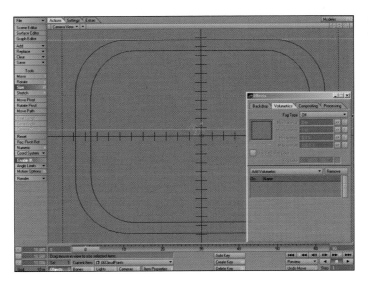

Size and position the
09CloudPoints object in Layout.

6 On the Layout screen's title bar, click the Maximum Render Level drop-down arrow and select Vertices. This allows you to see the cloud points.

Note: The 09CloudPoints object is nothing more than a clump of 25 points. This will be used to calculate HyperVoxels clouds.

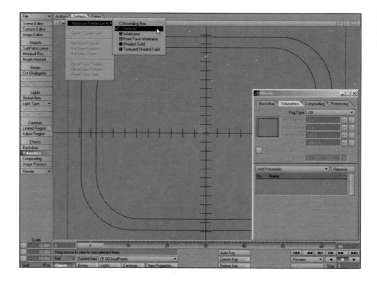

Changing the Maximum Render Level to Vertices will enable you to see the cloud points.

7 Select the HyperVoxelsFilter from the Add Volumetric list.

8 Double-click the HyperVoxels listing to open the controls.

Add one instance of HyperVoxels.

9   In the Object Name list, double-click the 09CloudPoints object to make it active. Click the VIPER window.

You can see that the sky is full of big, white balls at this point.

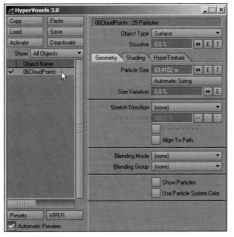

Double-click the 09CloudPoints object in the Object Name list to activate it for HyperVoxels.

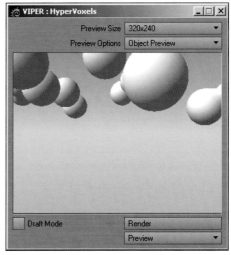

Open the VIPER window for HyperVoxels.

10   Change the Object Type to Volume. Click the Draft Mode check box.

VIPER will begin to draw a volume around the points, but it will be very slow. Clicking Draft Mode will help speed up the redraws in VIPER. After the volume change, the clouds look like black smoke. Using Draft Mode does not affect your final render, only the preview in the VIPER window.

Note: You might want to change the Preview options in the VIPER window to Scene Preview to see your sky backdrop.

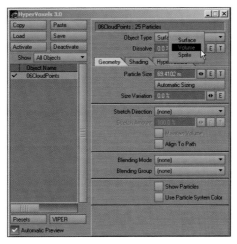

Change the object type with the Volume setting.

Switching the HyperVoxels Object Type to Volume changes the render in the VIPER window.

83

11 Open the Geometry tab and set the following parameters:

Particle Size: **100m**

Size Variation: **50%**

Show Particles: **On**

The Show Particles setting will show a volume representation in Layout.

12 Click the Basic tab / Shading tab and enter the following settings:

Color: RGB **200, 200, 200**

Luminosity: **100%**

Opacity: **100%**

Density: **100%**

Thickness: **20%**

Smoothness: **50%**

13 Click the Advanced Shading tab and set the following options:

    Render Quality: **Medium**

    Near Clip: **1m**

    Volumetric Shadows: **On**

    Texture Shadows: **Off**

    Shadow Quality: **Medium**

    Shadow Strength: **5%**

    Illumination: **Beer**

    Use All Lights: **Off**

    Light 1: **Light**

    Light 2: **None**

    Ambient Color: RGB **190, 206, 206**

    Ambient Intensity: **15%**

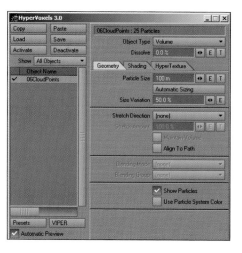

Set the Geometry of the HyperVoxels.

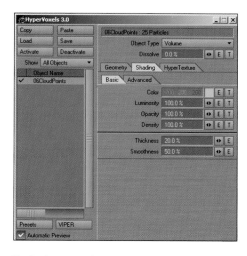

The basic settings for the HyperVoxels shading.

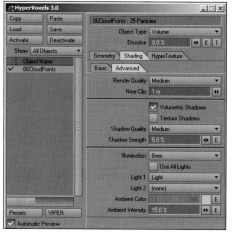

Set the Advanced Shading options for the clouds.

84

CLOUD TEXTURE AND MOVEMENT

Now that the basic shading is in place for the HyperVoxels clouds, you need to give them some texture and get them moving. These storm clouds are nasty and might even produce a tornado!

1 Click the HyperTexture tab in the HyperVoxels panel.

2 Set the following parameters:

Texture: **Turbulence**

Frequencies: **3**

Contrast: **0%**

Small Power: **0.5**

Texture Amplitude: **100%**

Texture Effect: **Turbulence**

Effect Speed: **20%**

Reference Object: **None**

World Coordinates: **Off**

Scale: XYZ **1m, 1m, 1m**

If you take a look at the VIPER window after your changes are redrawn, you see some nasty but cool-looking storm clouds looming above.

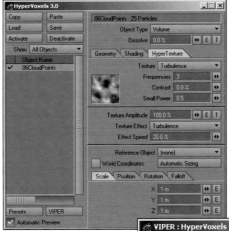

Add the HyperTexture settings for the storm clouds.

VIPER displays the clouds with the new settings applied.

Note: You've probably noticed at this point that the renders in the VIPER window are pretty slow. LightWave must do some major calculating to draw those volumes of clouds, but the wait is worth it. Remember that you can make a preview of the animated clouds in VIPER.

3 Close the HyperVoxels panel. You can add a few last things to finish off the scene, such as fog. Fog is great for adding atmosphere.

4 Turn on the OpenGL Fog setting in the Display Options panel.

This shows the fog in the Camera View only. However, the full effects will be shown in the final render.

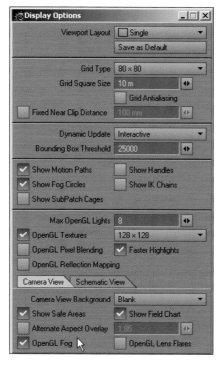

Turn on OpenGL Fog in the Display Options panel.

5 Go to the Volumetrics tab within the Effects panel and select Nonlinear 2 for Fog Type.

Your Layout display will fill with fog. The benefit of the OpenGL Fog display is that you can set your values in real time.

Add Fog from the Volumetrics tab of the Effects panel.

6 Drag the Max Distance slider to 1.5km (or type in the value). Click on Use Backdrop Color so the fog is the same color as the gradient backdrop. (You can, of course, experiment and adjust these settings to your liking.)

You've now set up some soft, nasty, rolling storm clouds. All that is left is to add a ground layer, or perhaps you can use the ground object from Project 5, "Aged Film Effect." Conversely, you can add a bottom layer of storm clouds. The choice is yours. You can even change the backdrop color to make the sky darker and more ominous. Try a few different options to see what you can come up with.

Implement fog settings for added atmosphere.

How It Works

LightWave's Volumetric options are quite powerful. HyperVoxels 3.0 adds yet another dimension to your scenes by drawing a physical volume around specific points. This volume can be colored, shaded, and animated to create effects like storm clouds.

Modifications

You can use HyperVoxels to create smoke, fire, dust, soft clouds, cotton balls, and more. Experimentation is key with this feature: You can sit for hours trying different settings. The bonus is that you can use VIPER to get interactive feedback of your changes. Try adding some clouds to Project 5's scene to complete the flying airplane scene.

RACK FOCUS
CAMERA

"You can't depend on your eyes when

your imagination is out of focus."

—MARK TWAIN

REPRODUCING CAMERA-LIKE FOCUS WITH DEPTH OF FIELD AND FOCAL DISTANCE

Part of the art of 3D animation includes the digital camera. No, not the one you take pictures of your kids or dog with, but the one inside your 3D animation program. The camera is the "eye" of the animations you create. Animators often forget that they can employ real-world properties such as depth of field and focus tricks during an animation. Effects such as these sell your animations—they're the proverbial icing on the cake.

In this exercise, you'll work with a non-aged version of the animation and add a rack focus camera effect using depth-of-field techniques. During the animation, the focus will change from the foreground plane to the plane in the distance.

Project 7
Rack Focus Camera

by Dan Ablan

GETTING STARTED

Too little emphasis is placed on the camera in LightWave. Think of it as your friend—your buddy. Get to know it. Okay, maybe that's a little over the top. But the idea is to think about the camera in every animation, not just the objects and lights. This project gets you started using depth of field. Then you'll change the depth of field over time during the course of the animation.

1   Open Layout and load the **07DOF_Start.lws** scene from the book's CD.

Right now the camera is set back behind one of the planes. A render shows that the animation renders completely in focus. If you were using a real-world camera to shoot the scene, the planes away from the camera would either be in focus or out of focus.

Load the 07DOF_Start.lws scene in Layout.

Note: The depth of field effects are not seen in LightWave Layout, only in the render.

Rendering without depth of field keeps everything in focus.

2 Press the **2** key on the numeric keypad to switch to a top view.

You can see that the planes are positioned across the Layout grid.

Note: The camera's focal point begins in the center of the camera, not at the visible lens. This camera object in Layout is only a visual representation.

The top view shows the planes across the Layout grid.

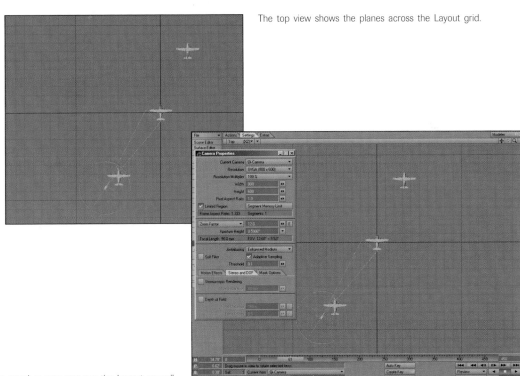

Position the Camera Properties panel so you can see the Layout as well.

3 In Layout, count the number of grid squares from the center of the camera to the center cargo plane object (07Plane:PlaneBodyWings(1)). There should be about 8 squares. At 20m per square, that's 160m. This is your focal length.

4 Click the Stereo and DOF tab in the Camera Properties panel. Click the Depth of Field check box to turn the feature on.

Note: You must have at least Medium Antialiasing set to activate depth of field.

Note: You can also use LightWave's Layout Ruler to measure your distance. To do so, follow these steps:

1. Add a null object.

2. Open the Object Properties panel for the null.

3. Add Custom Object, LW_Ruler.

4. In Layout, size the null up to XYZ **20**, **1**, **1000**.

5. Each line in the ruler is equal to 10m. Rotate the null in Layout so that it passes through the target plane, and then count the number of lines in the ruler to determine the distance between the null and the target.

6. Delete the null and continue.

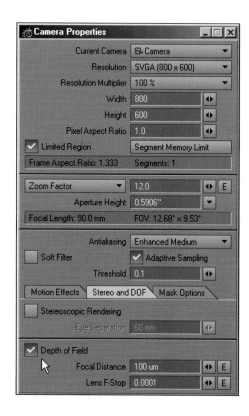

Enable Depth of Field on the Stereo and DOF tab of the Camera Properties panel.

5 Set the Focal Distance to **160m** (the amount you calculated in Step 3). To calculate the Focal Distance, use the grid size or the LW_Ruler custom object.

Note: With the Focal Distance setting, you tell the camera where to focus. Items before and after that focal point will be out of focus, depending on your f-stop.

6 Apply an f-stop to the lens and set it to **0.4**.

In a real-world camera, the f-stop regulates the amount of light entering the camera lens. In LightWave, f-stop controls the amount the lens opens (the aperture), which essentially determines a distance range for things that will be in focus. The real-world f-stop does not exactly translate to LightWave. An f-stop of 0.4 in the real world would be a huge aperture, but in LightWave, it works well for this particular tutorial.

Note: In the real world, small lens openings are large f-stops and need more exposure time. The longer the exposure time, the more things will be focused. In LightWave, a low f-stop setting yields a small in-focus range, making things more out of focus.

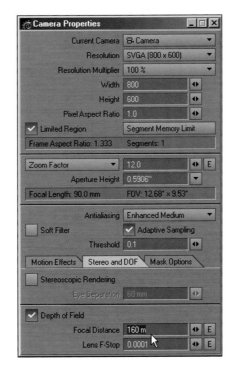

Entering a Focal Distance setting tells the camera to focus at a fixed focal point.

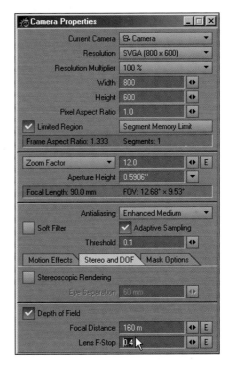

Assigning a low f-stop setting makes things more out of focus from the camera to the focal distance.

7 Press **F9** for a render.

You'll see that the foreground plane object is out of focus, while the cargo plane in the center of the shot is in focus. The plane in the distance is slightly out of focus.

Using the right Focal Distance setting, the right Lens F-Stop setting, and depth of field creates depth in the rendered image.

ANIMATED DEPTH OF FIELD

Now that your Focal Distance and Lens F-Stop settings have been applied, you can change those values over time. Doing this will help the viewer focus his or her attention during an animation. You can "force" the viewer to look at what you want by changing the focus.

1 Press **6** on the keyboard to switch to Camera View. Select the Camera, and move it down on the Y-axis to XYZ −140m, 23m, −184m.

2 Rotate the Camera to H 38.30, P 4.63, B 0.30.

3 Create a keyframe at 200.

This will lock the camera in place. It will also give the animation an added dimension of movement.

4 Press the **2** key on the numeric keyboard to jump to a top view again.

Adding a small movement of the camera over 200 frames gives a nice element to the rack focus effect.

94

5 Count the grid squares from the center of the camera to the cargo plane closest to the camera object. You should count 2.5 grid squares, which represents about 50m.

6 Click the E button in the Camera Properties panel.

7 Create a keyframe at 230. The camera moves over and rests on the closest plane at frame 200. One second later, you want it to come into focus (frame 230).

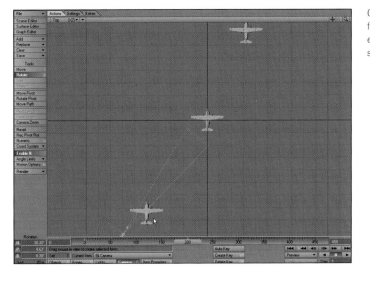

Calculating the focal distance for the first cargo plane is easy if you count the grid squares in Layout.

8 Set the Value at **40m** for frame 230. Press the **a** key to fit the graph in view. Hold the Shift key and double-click in the Curve window to select both keyframes at once. Set the Incoming Curve to TCB Spline with a Tension of 1.0.

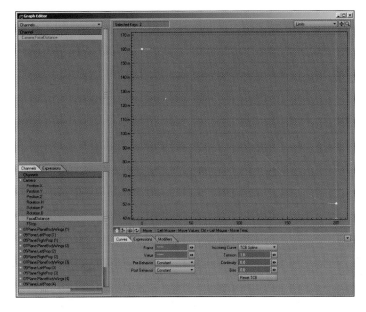

The Graph Editor with two keyframes for focal distance. One keyframe is at frame zero, the other is at frame 230.

9 Press **F9** to take a look at the render. The focus is now on the closer plane, and the planes in the distance are out of focus. However, the difference in distance between the two planes is still not clear enough. Also the blur on the distant planes is harsh.

10 Click the E button in the Camera Properties panel to open the Graph Editor.

With the focal distance changing over 200 frames, the planes in the distance are now out of focus.

11 Create a keyframe at frame 200 and set the Value to **1.0**.

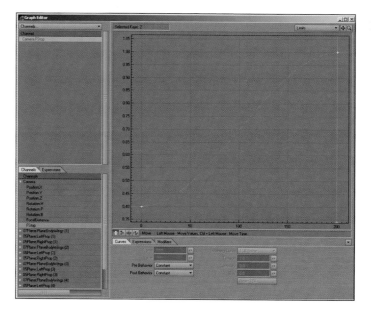

Animating the f-stop over time varies the range of what is in focus.

How It Works

Animating a rack focus is as simple as setting an envelope for the focal length of the camera lens, as you did here. Added to that is an envelope for the f-stop, which also changes the look of the focus over time. Although the technique is not complex to set up, the result looks complex. This is an ideal effect. It's easy to do, looks cool, and requires no extra render time.

LightWave requires that you have Antialiasing set to at least Medium quality in order to use depth of field. Your final animations should render with Medium Antialiasing (or higher) regardless, for quality. This is required because, in LightWave, depth of field is a blurring effect. LightWave moves the polygons each frame to create a soft blur, simulating depth of field.

This real-world principle has enormous potential and creates a very cool look.

Modifications

One of the final touches you can put on this effect is a smoothing of the camera motions, including the focal length and f-stop envelopes. You can add a Tension setting of 1.0 to ease in and out of the keyframes for smooth transitions.

Some other ideas for this technique could be a quick and jumpy focusing effect, sort of like you would get with a hand-held camera. If you take the effect of Project 9, "Procedural Texture Motions," and add a quick rack focus periodically, you'll only enhance the animation further. You can use this technique to simulate the effect of someone waking up out of a stupor. Or perhaps the focus change over time would imitate what someone would see when taking their glasses on or off.

Rack focus effects are also good for people shots. If you ever watch a news magazine show on television with a one-on-one interview, that "over the shoulder" shot often has some serious depth of field. You can rack focus between whichever digital person is speaking, controlling the viewer's eye. You can also give the new DepthBlur Image Filter a try. It is a fast but less accurate blur that doesn't require a medium antialiasing level.

Adding small but effective techniques like this in your animations will make not only your work stand out, but you as well.

FALLING RAIN
AND SNOW

"*For many years I was a self-appointed*

inspector of snowstorms and rainstorms and

did my duty faithfully, though I never

received payment for it."

—HENRY DAVID THOREAU (1817-1862)

USING INTEGRATED PARTICLES TO ADD SNOW AND RAIN

People often wonder what is the best way to make rain and snow. Some people use single point polygons with a motion blur for rain. Some people use a third-party program like Final Effects to generate snow over a rendered animation. But using LightWave 6.5's integrated particles, you can add rain and snow directly in your scene.

Project 8

Falling Rain and Snow

by Dan Ablan

GETTING STARTED

You don't need much to get this effect off the ground. Although short and simple, it's quite effective. You'll begin with a blank scene in Layout. The final scene is on the book's CD for your reference.

1   Open Layout and load the **08Setup.lws** scene.

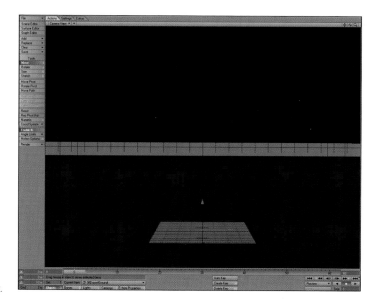

     Load the 08Setup.lws scene into Layout.

2 Press **F9** to render a frame. You'll see where the rain will be falling.

Rendering the scene shows a cloudy sky and a simple ground texture of LightWave gradients.

3 Click the Extras tab, and then select the Plug-In Options button to open the panel.

Open the Plug-In Options panel.

4 Select the FX_Browser from the Generics plug-in list to open the Particle FX_Browser window.

5 Select Emitter from the list. Close the Plug-In Options panel. This adds a particle emitter in Layout.

Select the FX_Browser from the Generics plug-in list. Add a particle emitter from the Particle FX_Browser panel.

6 Click the Property button to open the Particle FX_Emitter properties panel.

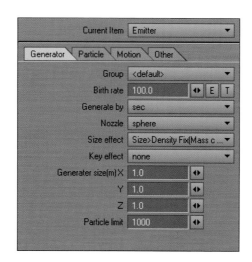

Open the Particle FX_Emitter properties panel.

7 Close the Particle FX_Browser panel and move the properties panel off to the side.

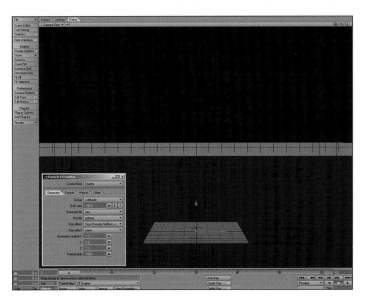

Position the Emitter properties panel so most of the Layout is visible.

8 Change the Generator Size to XYZ **400**, **1**, **400**.

The emitter object grows visibly in the Layout window.

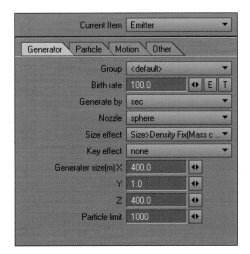

Increase the Emitter size to match the size of the scene.

9   Move the emitter object up 285m on the Y-axis, and then create a keyframe at 0 to lock the position in place.

> **Note:** After you add an emitter to Layout, you can move and rotate it like a regular object.

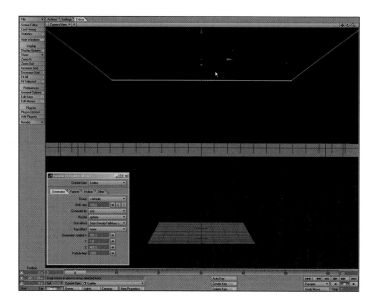

Move the emitter object up on the Y-axis to the top of the frame.

10   Click the Other tab and set the Y Gravity to **–400** in the FX_Emitter properties panel.

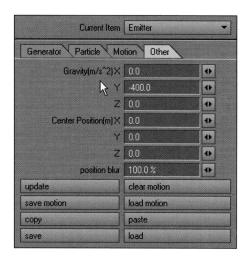

Add some gravity to the particle emitter to make the particles fall like rain.

11 Go back to Layout, set the last frame of the animation to **300**, and click the Play button in the lower-right corner of Layout.

Your particle rain should begin dripping down out of the sky.

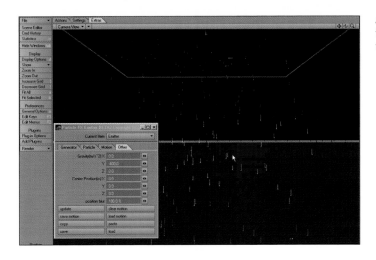

Apply gravity to the particles in frame 200 of the animation, and they fall like rain.

ADDITIONAL RAIN MOTIONS

At this point, the rain particles simply fall straight down the Y-axis. That's fine, but you can enhance the look slightly and make it look more natural by adding some variations in the motion.

1 In the FX_Emitter properties panel, click the Motion tab and set Explosion to **200**.

Adding variation to the motion results in a more natural look.

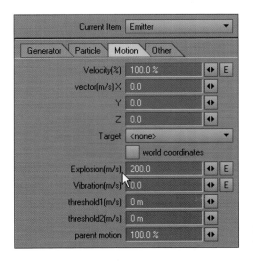

Note: The Explosion setting expands the trajectory of the rainfall. Conversely, a negative Explosion value will contract the rainfall—great for a waterfall look.

Use the Explosion setting in the Motion tab of the Emitter properties panel.

RAIN SURFACING

All you need to do now is set up the surfacing of the rain. To do this, you'll use HyperVoxels 3.0. Follow these steps:

1   On the Settings tab, click the Volumetrics button to open the Effects panel. From the Add Volumetric drop-down list, add the HyperVoxelsFilter.

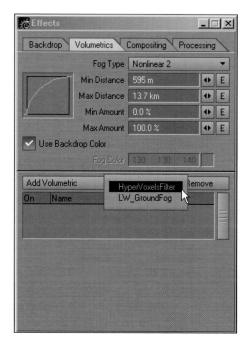

Add an instance of HyperVoxels from the Volumetrics tab of the Effects panel.

2   Double-click the HyperVoxels 3.0 listing to open its control panel. Then double-click the Emitter listing under Object Name. This will make the particles active for HyperVoxels.

3   Set the Object Type to Surface.

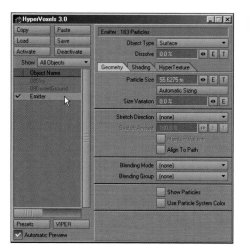

Activate the particle emitter object for use with HyperVoxels by double-clicking on it.

4 Click the Geometry tab and set the following parameters:

> Particle Size: **1m**
>
> Size Variation: **10%**
>
> Stretch Direction: **Y**
>
> Stretch Amount: **500%**
>
> Maintain Volume: **Off**
>
> Align to Path: **Off**
>
> Blending Mode: **Additive**
>
> Blending Group: **None**
>
> Show Particles: **Off**
>
> Use Particle System Color: **Off**

5 Click the Shading tab. On the Shading tab, click the Basic tab and enter the following settings:

> Color: RGB **200, 200, 200**
>
> Luminosity: **0**
>
> Diffuse: **60%**
>
> Specularity: **90%**
>
> Glossiness: **30%**
>
> Reflection: **80%**
>
> Transparency: **0%**
>
> Translucency: **0%**
>
> Bump: **100%**
>
> Self Shadows: **On**
>
> Full Refraction: **Off**

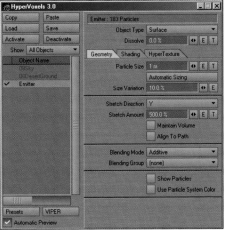

Set the Geometry settings for the rain.

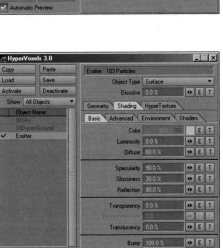

Set the basic color parameters for the rain.

Note: As an alternative to HyperVoxels, you can use LightWave [6.5]'s particle replacement feature by selecting the FX Linker plug-in. You can replace particles with objects, such as single point polygons, actual teardrop-shaped raindrops, or small animals!

6 Add a diffuse texture by clicking the T button next to Diffuse.

7 In the HyperVoxels Diffuse panel, set the following parameters:

>Layer Type: **Gradient**
>
>Blending Mode: **Additive**
>
>Layer Opacity: **100%**
>
>Invert Layer: **Off**
>
>Input Parameter: **Incidence Angle**

8 Create a key for the gradient and set its Value to **80%**. Set the Alpha for the key to **100%** and set the Parameter to **90**.

Note: Remember to use VIPER in the HyperVoxels 3.0 window to see quick and instant updates to your particles!

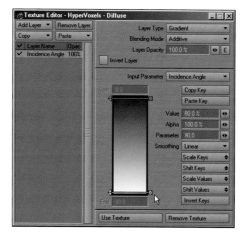

The added key for the gradient diffuse texture.

9 Set the Value to **20%** for the first key (at the top of the gradient). Set its Alpha to **100%** and set the Parameter to **0**.

10 Click Use Texture.

11 Click the T button next to Reflection to open its Texture Editor.

>Enter the following settings:
>
>>Layer Type: **Gradient**
>>
>>Blending Mode: **Additive**

The first key's Value settings for gradient diffuse texture.

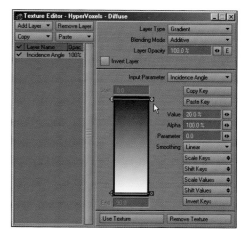

Layer Opacity: **100%**

Invert Layer: **Off**

Input Parameter: **Incidence Angle**

From here you can add a texture for the reflection.

12 Create a key for the Gradient and set its Value to **60%**. Set the Alpha for the key to **100%** and set the Parameter to **90**.

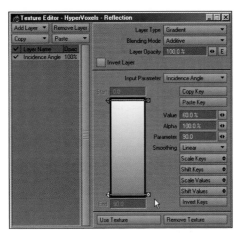

The added key for the gradient reflection texture.

13 Make sure the Value for the first key (at the top of the gradient) is set to **100%**. Set its Alpha to **100%** and set the Parameter to **0**.

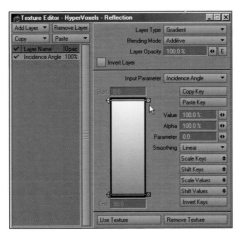

Adjust the first key's Value settings for gradient reflection texture.

14 Click Use Texture. Then press **F9** and test render a frame to see how the rain looks.

Using Incidence Angle (from the camera) is one of the coolest tricks for making your animations look real. You are basically changing the diffusion and reflectivity based on the angle of the surface to the camera. This is very much like a Fresnel effect.

Note: For diffusion, looking straight on is 90 degrees and thus very opaque. For reflection, you've got essentially the reverse gradient; therefore, straight-on is less reflective than surfaces pointing away.

The rendered particle rain with HyperVoxels 3.0.

ADDING MORE RAIN

As you can see, the rain blends nicely with the backdrop sky and ground because of the HyperVoxel textures you applied. The rain is sparse, so depending on what kind of look you want, you can increase the number of particles in the Particle FX_Emitter properties panel to create more rain.

1 Select the Emitter object in Layout. Select the FX_Property plugin from the Generic plug-in list.

2 Open the Generator tab and change the Birth Rate to **500**. Then change the Particle Limit to **6000** and the Particles to **522**.

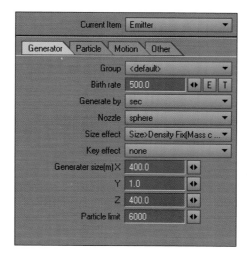

More particles are instantly added to create more rain.

3   Click the Play button in Layout, and you see that you instantly have more particles. A quick render shows that the HyperVoxels settings are still applied to the particles.

A few clicks of the mouse added more particles, making the rain more dense.

FROM RAIN TO SNOW

So you don't like rain? You would rather see snow? One thing to know is that snow is lighter than rain, so it will fall from the sky differently. This is not a problem, though, because you can change the motion values instantly in the Particle FX Browser properties.

1   Select the Emitter object in Layout. (Alternatively, you can select the Emitter directly from the FX Broswer.)

2   Open the Particle FX Browser by selecting the FX_Browser plug-in from the Generic plug-in list.

Note: You can leave the FX Browser panel open (as you can most LightWave [6.5] panels) so that you can make changes on-the-fly!

3 Access the Particle tab and set Particle Weight to **0.4**. Set Particle Resistance to **0.5** and change Life Time to **300**.

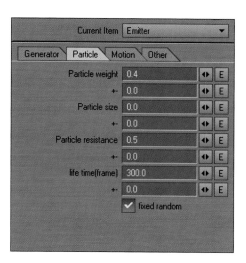

Make a few changes to the particles to affect the speed at which they fall.

4 Click the Motion tab and change the Vibration setting to **160**.

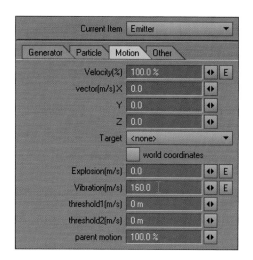

Changes to the motion make the snow fall more sporadically.

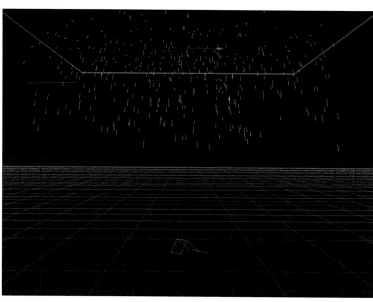

A screen grab shows a nice spead of particles

Note: If you play the quick preview in Layout, you'll see that the particles now fall more like snow, drifting from side to side slightly.

5 Click the Other tab and change the Y Gravity setting to **−300**.

6 Close the Particle FX Browser properties and reopen HyperVoxels.

7 Change the Object Type to Volume for the Emitter.

8 Click the Geometry tab and set Particle Size to **4m** and Size Variation to **20%**. Turn off Stretch Direction.

9 Click the Shading tab and set the following parameters:

> Color: RGB **225, 245, 255**
>
> Luminosity: **0**
>
> Opacity: **0**
>
> Density: **200**
>
> Thickness: **40%**
>
> Smoothness: **10%**

10 Add a texture for Luminosity with the following settings:

> Layer Type: **Procedural Texture**
>
> Blending Mode: **Additive**
>
> Layer Opacity: **100%**
>
> Invert Layer: **Off**
>
> Procedural Type: **Crust**
>
> Texture Value: **385%**
>
> Coverage: **0.2**
>
> Ledge Level: **0.6**
>
> Ledge Width: **0.3**
>
> Scale: XYZ **1mm, 1mm, 1mm**

11 Click Use Texture.

12 Select the Shading/Advanced tab and set the Render Quality to Low.

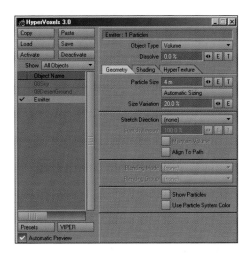

Apply a volume-type HyperVoxel to the emitting particles.

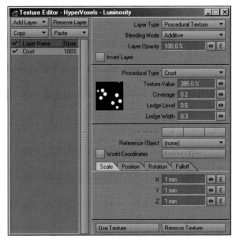

Adding the right procedural texture to the particles creates a nice, soft snow look.

13 Set the Near Clip value to **1m** and the Shadow Quality to Very Low. Set the Shadow Strength to **50%** and the Illumination to Beer.

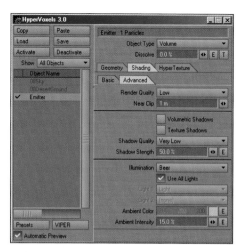

Set the Advanced Shading options for snow.

14 Click the HyperTexture tab and enter the following settings:

Texture: **FBM**

Frequencies: **1**

Contrast: **0**

Small Power: **0.2**

Texture Amplitude: **100%**

Texture Effect: **Displace**

Effect Speed: **75%**

Scale: XYZ **320mm, 320mm, 320mm**

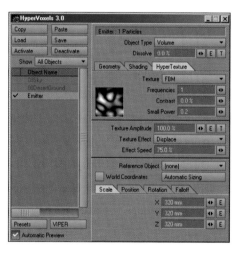

Add the HyperTexture settings to give the snow a noisy, transparent look.

15 Close the HyperVoxels panel and render the scene.

The full rendered image with HyperVoxels snow.

HOW IT WORKS

The integrated particle system in LightWave [6.5] is quite extraordinary. Without much effort and in real time, you can add animated particles. This project guided you through the simple exercise of changing particles into rain and snow. But don't let the ideas stop there.

MODIFICATIONS

There is so much more to the integrated particle engine than this project shows. It's great that you can easily add particles to your scene, but you can also add wind and collision. These particles can be transformed into blazing fires, waterfalls, or billowing smoke, all with different Motion settings and different HyperVoxel properties.

You can take this even further by adding some particle blur and wind. You could create another instance of particles, and using a wind generator (part of the particle engine), you can create a tornado using a HyperVoxel Volume setting. From there, you can set up another emitter that can be blown about from the tornado, and you can replace those particles with actual object files using the FX_Motion and FX_Link Motion plug-in modifiers.

Finally, if you'd like to vary the look and increase rendering speed, definitely try applying the Sprite mode in HyperVoxels to the falling rain and snow. It's very cool.

PROCEDURAL TEXTURE MOTIONS

"I always feel the movement is a sort

of mosaic. Each of us puts in one

little stone, and then you get

a great mosaic at the end."

—ALICE PAUL (1885-1977)

Using Textural Motions to Imitate a Hand-Held Camera

The most powerful of Lightwave [6.5]'s new features are the procedural texturing capabilities. They are used not only for surfacing, but for displacement, volumetric lights, backgrounds, and even motions. That's right, you can use a procedural texture to create motion! And that is what you'll do in this project.

Procedural Texture Motions

by Dan Ablan

GETTING STARTED

The effect described here will help you create a hand-held camera look. The reason this project is called "Procedural Texture Motions" and not "Hand-Held Camera Effects" is that the power of procedural texture motions expands well beyond the scope of just camera motions. With the information in the next few pages, you'll be able to apply this technique to any other variable in your animation. Be sure to read the "Modifications" section at the end of this chapter for more ideas.

A scene to work with has been provided for you on the book's CD. Project 12, "Creature Walk with Cyclist," shows you how to make a six-legged spider walk in real time with the movement of one null object. To enhance your learning, this chapter takes that scene a step further, adding real-world camera properties to it. The idea behind this effect is to create an animation that looks like a hand-held camera, without having to create a lot of messy keyframes.

CAMERA POSITIONING

Note: Make sure that the AutoKey feature is turned off.

Depth of field has been set up for added realism, and you can see from the view that LightWave [6.5]'s schematic view is in place in one of the viewports. This helps you select and organize a complex scene.

1   Load the **09spider_setup.lws** scene from the book's CD.

   This is the finished scene from Project 12, without camera motion. (For reference, the 09spider_final.lws scene on the book's CD is the finished scene for this chapter.)

2   Select the camera and move it to XYZ −1.49, 3.139, −14.665.

3   Rotate the camera to H 4.60, P 11.90, B 0.00.

4   Create a keyframe at frame 300 to keep the camera position.

   Now you have a panning shot of the spider scene. How about adding some real-world motion to it?

5   Open the Graph Editor, and expand it to full screen.

   Because the camera was already selected, LightWave automatically puts all the channels for the camera in the Channel Bin.

6   Click the Modifiers tab next to the Expressions tab.

   By default, the Camera.Position.X channel is already selected and is, therefore, active in the Curve Window.

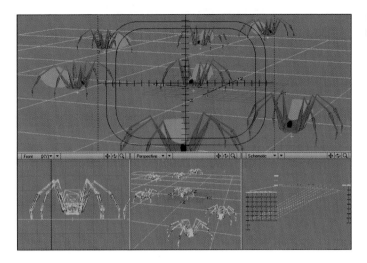

Load the 09SpiderStart.lws scene in Layout.

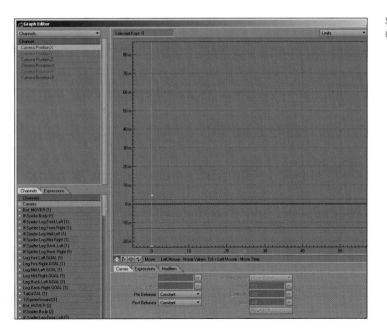

Select the camera in the Graph Editor.

7 Open the Add Modifier drop-down list and select the LW_TextureChannel modifier.

It will be added to the list of modifiers.

8 Double-click on the listing, and the LW_TextureChannel controls appear to the right of the Modifiers list.

Select the LW_TextureChannel modifier.

9 From the LW_TextureChannel controls in the lower-right corner of the Graph Editor, click the Texture button.

The familiar LightWave Texture Editor appears. Whatever you do in the Texture Editor window will affect the Camera.Position.X motion channel.

Note: Remember that what you are doing here for the camera can be applied to any other items in your scene, such as lights, additional cameras, or other objects.

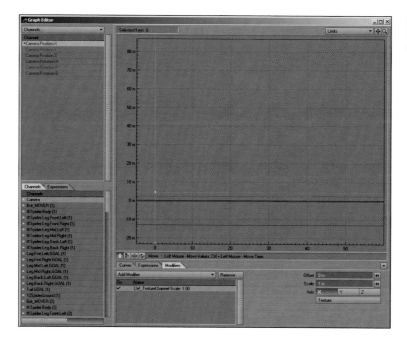

Double-click LW_TextureChannel from the list, and its controls appear to the right.

10 In the Texture Editor, set the following parameters:

    Layer Type: **Procedural Texture**

    Blending Mode: **Additive**

    Layer Opacity: **100%**

    Procedural Type: **Turbulence**

    Texture Value: **0.1**

    Frequencies: **2**

    Contrast: **0%**

    Small Power: **0.5**

    Scale: XYZ **200mm, 200mm, 200mm**

11 Close the Texture Editor, and then close the Graph Editor. Click the Play button.

You'll see the original panning shot of the spiders, but now there's some random movement on the X-axis.

12 Select the camera and open the Graph Editor again. This applies motion to the other camera motion channels.

Tip: To make sure your animation will be displayed as close as possible to the final rendered motion, turn on the Play at Exact Rate option on the General Options panel (**o**).

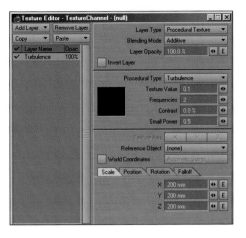

The Texture Editor for the LW_TextureChannel on the camera's position X channel.

Note: You don't have to close the Graph Editor. It can remain open while you work, but you might want to close it to make Layout visible.

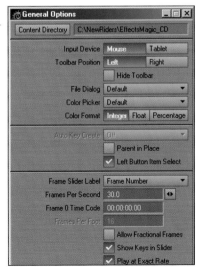

Select the Play at Exact Rate option in the General Options panel.

13 Select the Camera.Position.Y channel from the Channel Bin. Add the LW_TextureChannel modifier, and then double-click it to view its options.

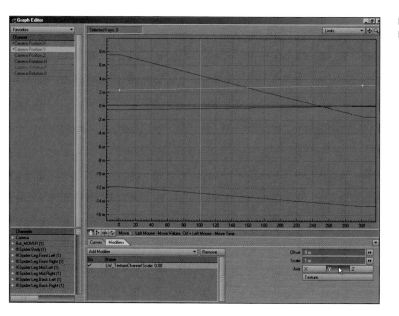

Double-click the LW_TextureChannel modifier.

14 In the channel controls (in the lower-right corner of the Graph Editor), click the Texture button to open the Texture Editor for the Camera.Position.Y channel.

Note: It is not necessary to click an axis for the LW_TextureChannel in the Graph Editor because you are applying procedural textures as motions. The Graph Editor's axis settings are useful for applying an image map as a motion.

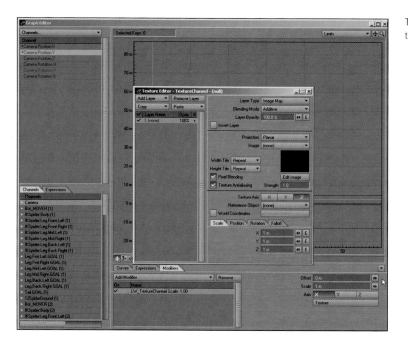

The Texture and Graph Editor for the camera's position Y channel.

15 Set the following parameters:

    Layer Type: **Procedural Texture**

    Blending Mode: **Additive**

    Layer Opacity: **100%**

    Procedural Type: **Fractal Noise**

    Texture Value: **0.8**

    Frequencies: **3**

    Contrast: **0.4**

    Small Power: **0.5**

    Scale: XYZ **2.5m, 2.5m, 0m**

16 Select the Camera.Position.Z channel in the Graph Editor's Channel Bin.

17 Open the Add Modifier drop-down list and add the LW_TextureChannel modifier. Then double-click it and select the Z-axis.

18 From the channel's controls in the lower-right corner of the Graph Editor, click the Texture button to open the Texture Editor for the camera's Z motions. Add the following settings and then close the Texture Editor:

    Layer Type: **Procedural Texture**

    Blending Mode: **Additive**

    Layer Opacity: **100%**

    Procedural Type: **FBMNoise**

    Texture Value: **0.15**

    Increment: **0.26**

    Lacunarity: **2.0**

    Octaves: **4.0**

    Noise Type: **Perlin Noise**

    Scale: XYZ **1m, 1m, 1m**

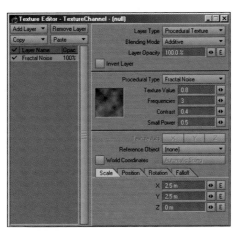

Apply the texture to the camera position Y channel.

Note: Remember that hand-held cameras jitter around all three axes, so you should apply motion to the X, Y, and Z channels of the camera in LightWave.

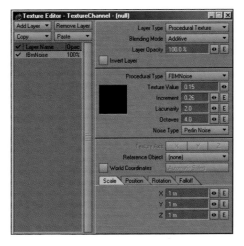

Apply texture motions to the camera's Z motion channel.

19 Close the Graph Editor and return to Layout. Click the Play button to see your hand-held camera in digital action!

> **Tip:** Depending on the speed of your system, it might be better to generate a real-time preview. To do so, open the Preview drop-down list at the bottom-right of the Layout interface and select Make Preview.

PROCEDURAL TEXTURE ZOOMS

You didn't think you were finished, did you? You've come this far and set up procedural textures for the camera's motion channels. But you can go even further and add the same techniques to the camera zoom! Any bad videographer zooms constantly, never knowing to keep the camera steady and still! Mimicking a random zoom in LightWave is easy.

1 Select the camera and open the Camera Properties panel (**p**).

2 Click the E button to the right of the Zoom Factor control.

This takes you to the Graph Editor for the camera zoom.

> **Note:** Clicking the E button for Camera Zoom creates the Camera Zoom channel for the Graph Editor. Once this channel is created, it will always be accessible in the Graph Editor, as long as the envelope is not removed.

3 Select the CameraZoomFactor channel from the Channel Bin, and then select the LW_TextureChannel from the Add Modifier drop-down list.

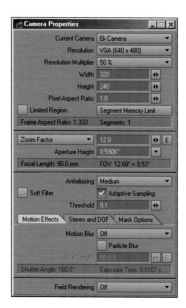

Open the Camera Properties panel.

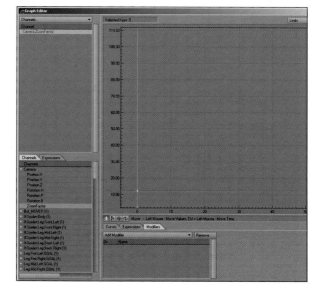

The Graph Editor for the camera zoom.

4   Double-click the LW_TextureChannel listing, and then click the Texture button to open the Texture Editor.

5   Set the following parameters:

Layer Type: **Procedural Texture**

Blending Mode: **Additive**

Layer Opacity: **100%**

Procedural Type: **Ripples**

Texture Value: **3.0**

Wave Sources: **1**

Wavelength: **5.0**

Wave Speed: **0.0**

Scale: XYZ **1m, 1m, 1m**

6   Close the Texture Editor, and then close the Graph Editor. Click the Play button in Layout, or make a preview to see the changes you've just made.

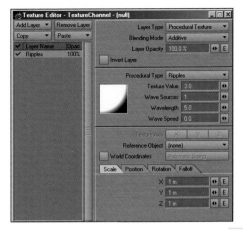

Procedural Texture ripples for the camera zoom channel.

Note: The spider scene might not play back smoothly because of the amount of IK calculations. You can click the Play At Exact Rate button in the Options (**o**) panel to help this. Additionally, you might consider making a small QuickTime or AVI file for playback preview.

HOW IT WORKS

Procedural textures are now implemented as plug-ins, so when a new plug-in is added, your choice of procedurals increases. The procedurals are available everywhere in LightWave [6.5], even Modeler. Along with procedural textures come gradients, which enable you to vary the effects of procedural parameters by varying blending modes.

LightWave [6.5]'s new architecture allows for plug-ins to be everywhere. One in particular is the Texture Editor, and as you've seen here, you can apply procedural textures and computer-generated textures to motion channels. By using a few random patterns such as turbulence and fractal noise, you've told LightWave's camera to adjust or modify its positions over time, based on procedural textures. Essentially, it adds the contour of the three-dimensional procedural texture to the channel.

At first, the concept of textures being applied to motions may seem a bit odd. But in this chapter, you've quickly learned how useful this new feature of LightWave [6.5] really is. As a note, you added procedural textures to motion channels, but you can use image maps as well.

MODIFICATIONS

The variations on this technique are endless. There is the obvious option of controlling other item motions with procedural textures… but you can go further! Use the techniques from this chapter to create random depth of field to simulate a camera lens that constantly comes in and out of focus.

You could use procedural textures for displacement maps to create random fractal landscapes that can rival any landscape-generating program. Use procedurals on lights to create texture effects such as wormholes, vortexes, fire, or smoke. The beauty of LightWave [6.5]'s procedurals is that the Texture Editor panel from which they are applied is identical throughout the program. Once you've mastered using the Texture Editor, you'll know how to apply different textures to different areas of the program. Of course, you can also use procedural textures to actually apply textures to your models.

PHOTOREALISTIC GOLD USING RADIOSITY

"'Tis an old saying, the Devil lurks behind the

cross. All is not gold that glitters. From the tail

of the plough, Bamba was made King of Spain;

and from his silks and riches was Rodrigo cast to

be devoured by the snakes."

—MIGUEL DE CERVANTES

USE LIGHTWAVE'S RICH SURFACING CAPABILITIES TO CREATE REALISTIC GOLD

Photorealistic surfacing can be one of the most difficult and sometimes frustrating tasks in creating a good-looking scene. However, with a little help, you'll not only understand how to achieve the look you need, but you'll also comprehend its creation to the point where you can freely modify it to obtain a different look. This tutorial focuses on just that—creating photorealistic gold for your models, while giving you enough freedom and understanding to be able to create any other metallic surface you're striving for.

Project 10

Photorealistic Gold
Using Radiosity

by Julian Kain

GETTING STARTED

Begin by opening LightWave and loading this chapter's scene from the book's CD.
This scene includes one camera, one spotlight representing the sun, NewTek's apple
object, and an environment object. The environment consists of a flat ground polygon
and a dome-like ball object. Together, these components will allow for realistic shading
and reflection of the apple using radiosity.

1 In Layout, load the **gold.lws** scene from the book's CD.

Take a few minutes to look at the settings this scene includes. First, the Render Options are configured to raytrace both shadows and reflections. This will allow for realistic shadows from the spotlight and reflections from the environment. Second, the Global Illumination panel has been modified to enable radiosity and disable ambient light. Together, these settings will provide for more accurate lighting of the golden apple.

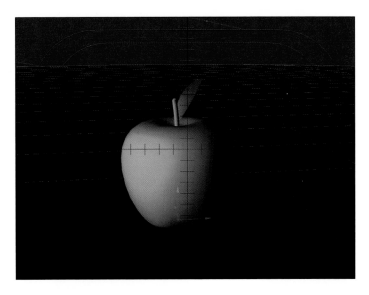

The gold.lws scene loaded in Layout.

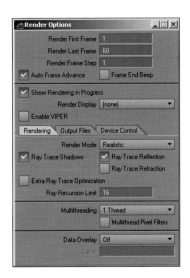

The Render Options panel.

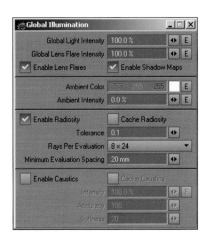

The Global Illumination settings.

2 Click on Cameras/Item Properties to bring up the camera's properties. The default rendering settings have been set to Resolution 640 × 480 and Antialiasing Low.

Because this scene uses a lot of advanced rendering techniques, it will take some time to render. You can enhance the resolution or antialiasing level if you want, but keep efficiency in mind.

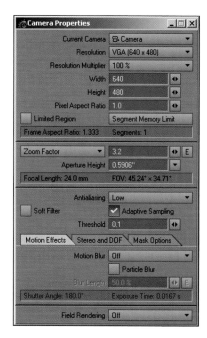

The Camera Properties panel.

BEGINNING SURFACING

Now that you have your rendering environment set up, you need to surface your object. Although you should probably follow these steps the first time, try experimenting with any and all the settings once you feel comfortable.

1 Click the Settings tab and then Surface Editor.

This brings up the Surface Editor, where LightWave's magic and a touch of your own will transform this dull apple into a gold masterpiece.

2 Open the Surface Name window, click the bullet next to Scene in the Surface Name List, and select the surface AppleSkin.

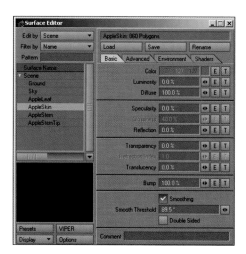

The Surface Editor with the AppleSkin surface selected.

Note: Remember that in LightWave [6.5] you can change multiple surfaces at once! Simply hold the Shift key, select the surfaces, and make any appropriate changes!

3   In the Basic tab, set your surface color to a gold-like appearance: RGB **242**, **177**, **28**.

This will be the color of gold without any reflections or surfacing abnormalities.

4   Click the T button in the Color row to open the Texture Editor for Color, where you will map the gold image onto your object.

5   Set the following parameters:

Layer Type: **Image Map**

Blending Mode: **Additive**

Layer Opacity: **50%**

Invert Layer: **Off**

Projection: **Cylindrical**

Width Wrap Amount: **1.0**

Image: **Color.tif**

The Layer Type allows for different kinds of mapping, including Image Map, Procedural Texture, and Gradient. You will be employing the Image Map, because it gives you more control over the desired look than a Procedural Texture does.

The Layer Opacity is essentially the transparency of the image map over the default color. Because you only want to hint at the surface abnormalities while maintaining a relatively uniformly colored surface, it will be best to mix these surfaces evenly.

The Projection of the image map is the mode in which it is mapped to or wrapped around your object. For flat or complex objects, Planar is usually the mode of choice. If you are surfacing a ball, Spherical is advantageous. Using the wrong kind of projection will cause warping and unwanted stretching. In this case, the apple most closely resembles a cylinder, so that's what you'll use.

Note: The idea is not to map a complex image, but to use one that shows surface abnormalities while maintaining a pure gold feel.

Note: If you are going for a psychedelic, other-worldly radioactive gold, you could select Invert Layer option.

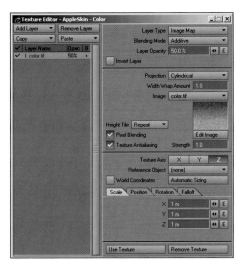

Note: Image Map files can be found on the book's CD.

6   Turn on Pixel Blending and set the Height Tile to
     Reset.

     The Pixel Blending and Height Tile options allow
     for image correction in close-up renders, and repeti-
     tion of the image map to fit the object, respectively.
     Because you will be fitting the image map to your
     object, and since the included images are not seam-
     less, Height Tile should not be used.

7   Set the Texture Antialiasing to On and the Strength
     to **0.35**.

     This will add smoothness to the image. Be careful
     not to overuse it, though; a pitted gold look is
     desired.

8   Set Texture Axis to Y to wrap the texture on the
     vertical axis.

9   Leave the Reference Object and World Coordinates
     options at their defaults.

10   Click on Automatic Sizing to stretch the loaded
     image map to fit your object perfectly.

Note: Pixel Blending is useful when you need your
image map to blur ever-so-slightly upon close examina-
tion. In comparison, Texture Antialiasing supplies a
constant blur regardless of distance.

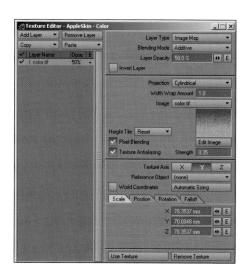

Apply the color.tif image to the
AppleSkin surface.

132

11 Click Use Texture to apply all of the changes you have made.

Notice that the object maintains its true color while also perfectly mapping a surface-abnormality image at half opacity.

COMPLEX SURFACING

The preceding steps outlined exactly how to apply a surface to your object while customizing the procedure to create the beginning of the gold surface. Many of the following surface properties will use these same steps, but with different image maps. The term "mapping method" refers to the texturing procedure you just followed, using the appropriate image map as noted. Now, it's time to delve into more complex surfacing for your object.

1 Open the Surface Editor's Basic tab and set the following parameters:

> Luminosity: **5%**
>
> Diffuse: **60%**
>
> Diffuse Texture (T): **diffuse.tif**
>
> Specularity: **75%**
>
> Specularity Texture (T): **specularity.tif**
>
> Glossiness: **7%**
>
> Reflectivity: **50%**
>
> Transparency: **0%**

Note: Additional uses for luminosity might include brake lights on a car or LEDs on electronic equipment.

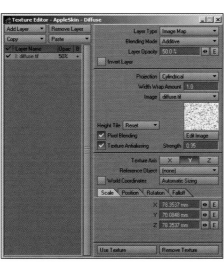

Along with the basic settings, apply the Diffuse Texture.

Translucency: **0%**

Bump: **100%**

Bump Texture: **bump.tif**

Although gold does not emit its own light, a very small Luminosity setting is appropriate; it lends the effect of "shimmering" gold. Because the gold is to be rough and pitted, the Specularity setting is to remain low, and the Image Map (at **50%** opacity, once again) will affect the correct areas' specularity. A relatively large, spread-out highlight is desired for this gold, so a low Glossiness setting is appropriate. The bump map is used quite dramatically to give the appearance of pitted gold.

Note: Reflectivity is a crucial setting, and it can be broken down into two parts: image reflection and raytracing (or the reflection of its surroundings). You will be using raytracing in this rendering, enabling realistic reflectivity. Reflectivity is crucial to creating a photorealistic surface.

2   Set the texture's Opacity to **100%** and change the Amplitude to **1.75**.

Note: Depending on the object you are using, you might want to enable Smoothing, which will use an algorithm to "bend" sharp corners of your object for an overall smoother appearance.

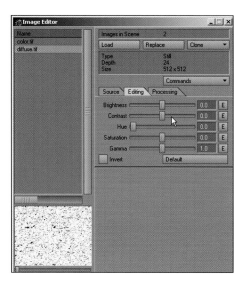

Load the diffuse image in the Image Editor. If you are unhappy with any of the images' contrast settings, edit them directly through LightWave's Image Editor.

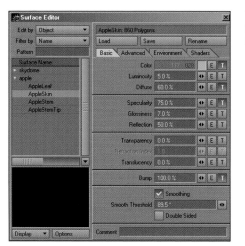

The completed Surface Editor view. With these settings, you've created a realistic reflection on an accurately colored sphere.

MODIFICATIONS

Congratulations! You've successfully created realistic gold surfacing. However, the real beauty of understanding this tutorial is that you can modify the settings with a comprehension of what each will do so you'll be able to create the exact look you are striving for. With the knowledge you've gained, you can create not only other flavors of gold, but other metals. For example, to create gold that is more dull, simply raise the Diffuse, lower the Specularity, and lower the Reflectivity. To create a more pure gold, raise the Diffuse, raise Reflectivity, and possibly lower the Bump Map. Feel free to experiment.

To begin experimenting with creating other metals, simply modify your gold surface in the following ways to create good-looking pitted silver.

1   Change color values to RGB **229**, **229**, **229**.

2   Remove the color texture map.

3   Set glossiness to **25%**.

4   Remove the reflection map.

Note: You might want to change the light to a softer blue or white as a compromise to the surface.

You can also change the lighting scheme to dramatically affect the scene. The following figures show examples of modified lighting.

The same scene with a dark gray-blue skydome and a low-intensity gray spotlight overhead. With Radiosity enabled, this lighting scheme models an overcast day.

Changing the skydome to a lighter blue and the overhead spotlight to a bright yellow-white with Radiosity enabled creates an accurate sunny day lighting scheme.

BUILDING A CAMPFIRE

"Even in a time of elephantine vanity

and greed, one never has to look far to

see the campfires of gentle people."

—GARRISON KEILLOR

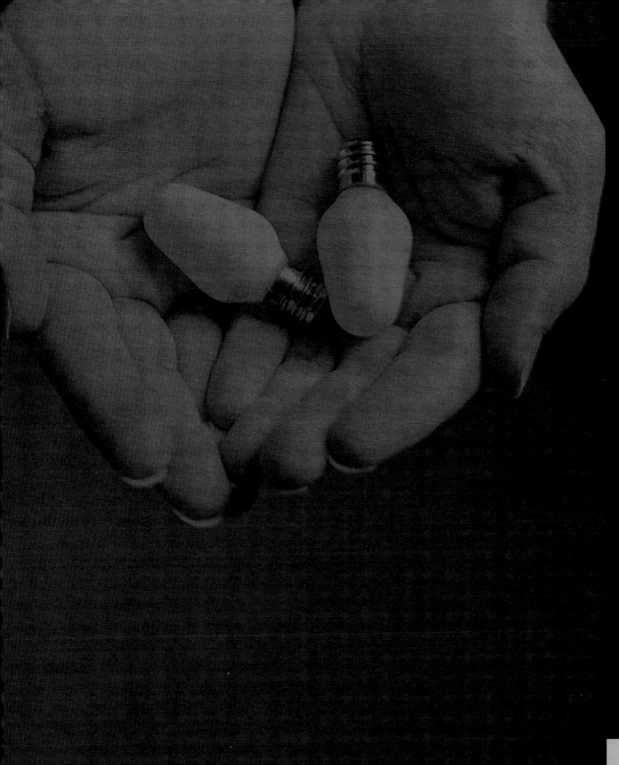

USING POLYGONS, DISPLACEMENT MAPPING, AND VIPER TO CREATE A CAMPFIRE SCENE WITH FIRE

Knowing many different effects is always beneficial to an animator. The more you know, the more ideas you can come up with on your own. And the more ideas you have, the more valuable you will be to your employer or clients.

When you think you might not need to animate a campfire anytime soon, think again. You'll use nothing more than a single light source to create fire with LightWave's Volumetric capabilities. You'll also see how useful LightWave's displacement mapping can be with SubPatched objects. The techniques described in this chapter can be applied to all sorts of animations, from a campfire, to jet propulsion, to stovetop cooking! Read on, and you'll see how cool this technique really is.

Building a Campfire

by Dan Ablan

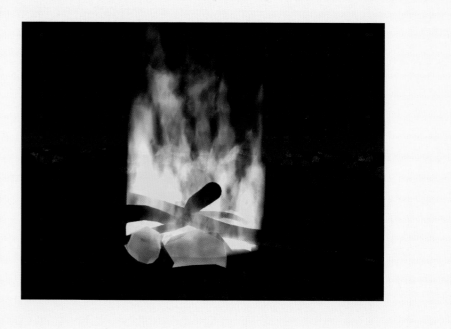

GETTING STARTED

It's always nice if you can build a full scene to demonstrate an effect. To start you off, a partial scene (11campfire_start.lws) is on the book's CD. In this chapter, you will add a realistic ground plane using LightWave's powerful displacement mapping feature. From there, you'll make a cool procedural 3D fire. Are you ready?

1 Load **11campfire_start.lws** from the book's CD.

   It shows a few simple twigs, lava rocks, and a night-time sky. From here, you'll build the ground and the fire.

2 Jump into Modeler by clicking the Modeler button in the upper-right corner of the Layout window.

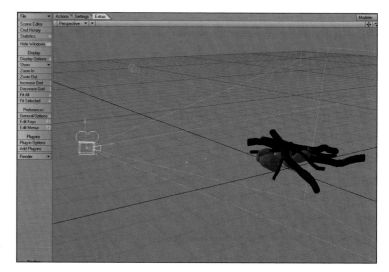

Load the initial campfire scene (11campfire_start.lws) into Layout.

3   Select the Box tool (Shift+x), and in the top view, draw out a flat box that's 25m on the X-axis and 20m on the Z-axis.

4   Press the Spacebar to turn off the Box tool. Press Shift+d to open the Subdivide Polygons box.

5   Select Faceted and click OK.

This creates four polygons for the flat box. That's it. LightWave's subdivision surfaces will do the rest.

> **Note:** You are subdividing this polygon to help keep a rectangular shape when applying a displacement map. However, LightWave [6.5] lets you use SubPatch objects in Layout, which means you can have as little as one polygon in Layout to create a landscape.

6   Press the Tab key to activate SubPatch mode.

Your flat box should now be somewhat rounded on the corners.

7   Press the **q** key to call up the Change Surface requester. Name the new object **Ground** and give it a brownish color (RGB **200, 200, 200**).

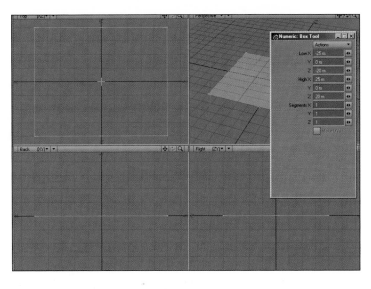

Creating a flat plane with the Box tool is the first step toward creating the ground object.

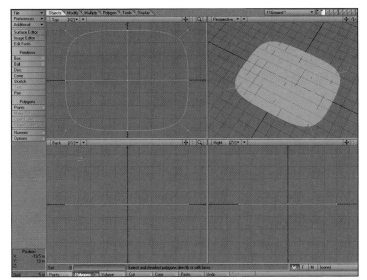

Pres the Tab key to activate SubPatch mode, with which you can attain much greater detail without using additional geometry.

Through the Change Surface requester in Modeler, you can assign a name to the new polygons.

DISPLACEMENT-MAPPED TERRAIN

1   Load the Ground object in Layout, change to
    Perspective view, and zoom out so you can see
    the entire scene.

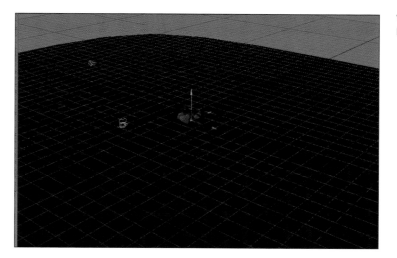

View the Ground object from the
Perspective view in Layout.

2   Go to the Scene Editor and change the visibility of
    the ground object, 11Ground:Layer2, o Front Face
    Wireframe. Then close the Scene Editor.

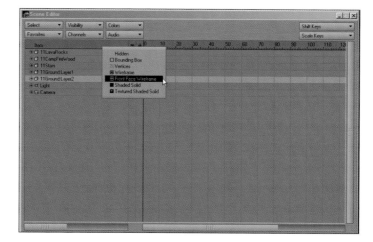

The Front Face Wireframe
visibility option will help you
see the displacement of the
object in Layout.

3 Move the ground object back on the Z-axis about 12 meters, and then adjust your Perspective view. Because the camera and fire are at the front of the ground, it's not necessary to show the ground behind the camera.

Note: Because the ground object is a SubPatch object, LightWave automatically subdivides it in Layout. This enables you to make your landscape more complex.

Note: Remember that if the Render SubPatch Level is set higher than the display level, you will see only a representation of the displacement in Layout. Be sure to render a test frame from time to time.

4 Select the ground object and open the Object Properties panel (**p**).

5 Click the Geometry panel, change Display SubPatch Level to **20**, and change Render SubPatch Level to **60**.

6 In the Object Properties panel, click the Deformations tab, and then click the T button for Displacement Map.

This opens the Texture Editor.

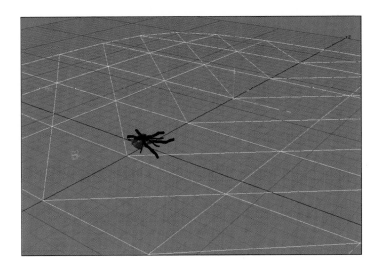

Move the ground object back on the Z-axis and modify the Perspective view to display the change.

LightWave's SubPatch mode allows you to work with a less complex mesh for speed, while setting the render for a higher value.

Note: You can also add additional displacements, such as crumple, on top of the Crust displacement map, which was used to create the landscape. From there, you can surface the landscape with textures, bump maps, and more. Take a look at the final 11Ground.lwo object on the book's CD; it uses the settings in step 2 for Crust displacement, and it has added textures.

7 In the Object Displacement Map window, set the following parameters:

> Layer Type: **Procedural**
>
> Blending Mode: **Additive**
>
> Layer Opacity: **100%**
>
> Displacement: **Y**
>
> Procedural Type: **Crust**
>
> Texture Value: **2.0**
>
> Coverage: **0.65**
>
> Ledge Level: **0**
>
> Ledge Width: **0**
>
> Scale: XYZ **2.5m, 5m, 2.775m**
>
> Position: XYZ **0m, 0m, 12m**
>
> Falloff: XYZ **0%, 0%, 5.0%**
>
> Falloff Type: **Spherical**

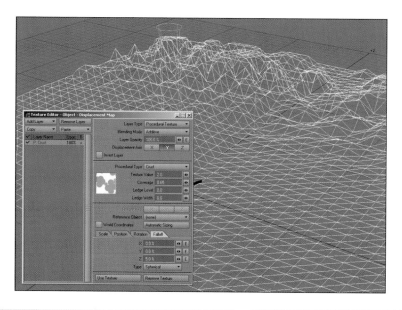

Apply a procedural texture as a displacement map to create a landscape. Subdivision surfaces allow the mesh to be divided, allowing nice displacement.

Note: Notice the positioning of the texture and falloff. They are set to make the displacement happen on the Z portion of the landscape in order to generate a background mountain range.

Note: Depending on the strength of your computer system, you can increase the Display SubPatch Level setting to create a cleaner displacement.

PROCEDURAL FIRE

This next section shows you how to add fire to the twigs, which are now sitting atop the ground object you created.

1 Set the ground displacement and go to the camera view.

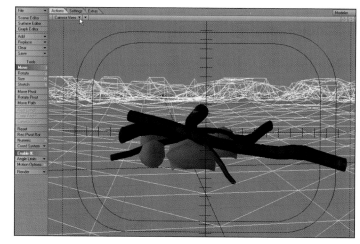

Move to the Camera View and get ready for some fire!

2   From the Actions tab, select Add/Add Light/Add
    Distant Light.

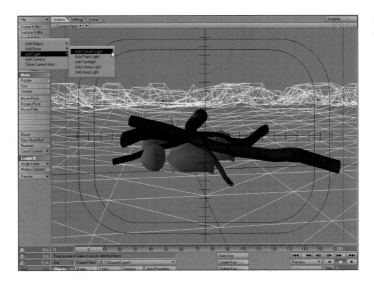

Adding a distant light to
create fire is easy!

3   In the Light Name box, name the light **Fire_Light**.

4   Rotate the Fire_Light object **−90** on the Pitch.

    Because the lava rocks and twigs for the fire are
    centered in Layout at the 0,0,0 axis, that's where
    the light will be centered after it's added.

Name your light when prompted.

5   Move Fire_Light up on the Y-axis 250mm. Create a
    keyframe at frame 0 to lock in the new position.

6   Select Fire_Light and open the Light Properties
    panel (**p**). Click the Volumetric Lighting button.
    Click the Volumetric Light Options button to open
    the controls.

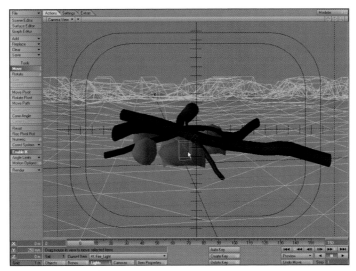

Move the distant light named
Fire_Light slightly and rotate it!

143

7 Click the VIPER button to open LightWave [6.5]'s virtual interactive preview renderer.

You'll see the volume light being drawn.

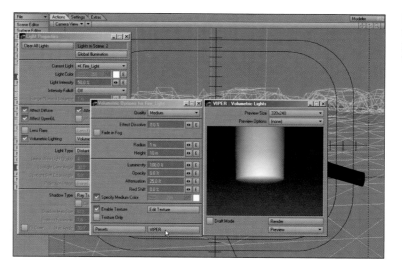

Using VIPER to set up your volumetric light is so easy you'll wonder how you ever worked without it.

8 Set the following volumetric options:

Quality: **Medium**

Effect Dissolve: **0%**

Fade in Fog: **Off**

Radius: **900mm**

Height: **12m**

Luminosity: **600%**

Opacity: **0%**

Attenuation: **25%**

Red Shift: **0%**

Specify Medium Color: **Off**

Enable Texture: **On**

Texture Only: **On**

Set the Volumetric Light options before you apply textures.

Note: When you turn on Texture Only, you're telling the volumetric to display only the textures you apply. None are applied yet, so your volumetric in the VIPER window will go away. Don't worry, though; click the Edit Texture button to reopen the Texture Editor for Fire_Light.

9 In the Texture Editor, change the Layer Type to Procedural. VIPER redraws the volumetric, but with inconsistencies—that's the texture!

Note: You might want to click over to Layout and rotate the camera up slightly before you begin creating volumetric fire. This helps make the full volume visible in VIPER.

10 Click the Falloff tab for the procedural texture, which by default is Turbulence. The volume fades off as it rises. This happens because when a light is added to Layout, it points down the Z-axis. Setting a falloff value of about **20%** on the Z-axis makes the volume light fade even though it's rotated up on pitch.

11 Click the Scale tab and enter the settings XYZ **400mm, 400mm, 1.4m**.

12 Change the Texture Color to RGB **255, 128, 000**.

13 Select Add Layer and choose Gradient. Set the Input Parameter to Previous Layer, and then add three keys to the gradient. Set the following parameters:

   Key 1: **0.35**

   Key 2: **0.5**

   Key 3: **0.95**

This will give you four keys.

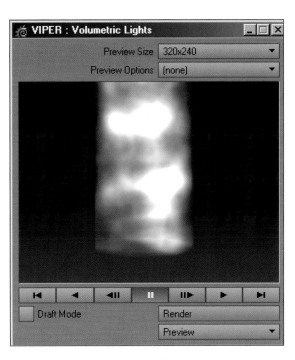

Add a texture to the volumetric light and view the effects in the VIPER window.

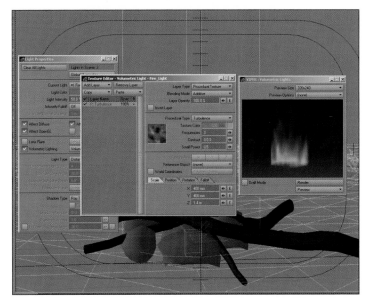

Change a few of the Scale and Texture Color settings to make the volumetric light look more like fire.

14 Change the Alpha of the top first key and the second key to **0%**. Change keys 2, 3, and 4 to the following settings:

> Key 2: RGB **255, 0, 0**
>
> Key 3: RGB **255, 128, 0**
>
> Key 4: RGB **255, 225, 0**

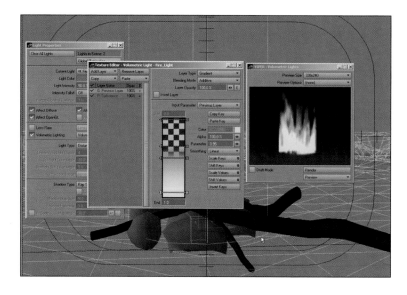

Adding a gradient layer with varying alpha and color keys makes the fire look more realistic, as you can see in the VIPER window.

ANIMATED FIRE

The fire you've created looks pretty good, but it doesn't move—and that sort of ruins the whole effect, don't you think? Follow these steps to animate the fire:

1 Open the Texture Editor and select Turbulence for the Texture Layer.

2 Click the Position tab, and then click the E button for the Z value.

This opens the Graph Editor for the Z-axis (up and down in this case) for the volumetric texture motion.

Note: Directional lights are pointed towards positive Z, by default. Therefore, to move the texture along its local Z-axis, you must animate the Z channel.

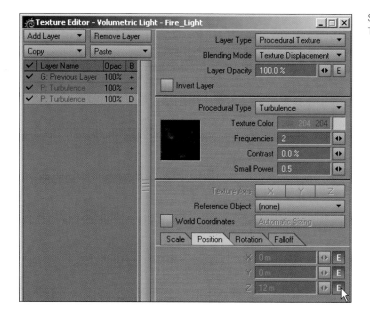

Select Turbulence for the Texture Layer.

3 In the Graph Editor, create a keyframe for the Position.Z texture and set the Value to **6m**. Close the Graph Editor.

4 Select Make Preview from the Preview drop-down list in the VIPER window. In a moment, the preview play buttons appear, and you'll see the texture animated.

Note: You might want to click on Draft Mode first to speed up the preview times.

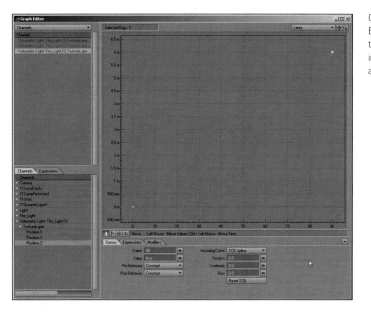

Create a keyframe in the Graph Editor to animate the volumetric texture on any desired axis. In this instance, the Z-axis has a keyframe at frame 90.

5 In the Texture Editor, add another procedural texture layer for the volumetric light. Then click and drag this layer to the bottom of the Layer list. This adds some secondary motion for added realism.

Note: You can also set this procedural to Turbulence, but if you do, change the Blending Mode to Texture Displacement. This will increase render times, but it makes your effect look better.

6 Set Frequencies to **2**.

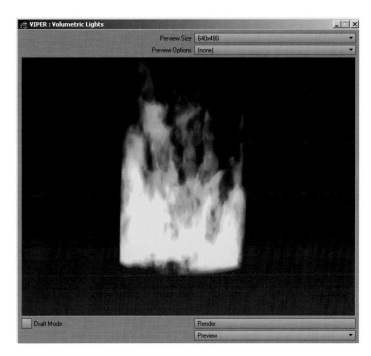

If you don't mind an increased render time, set the new procedural to Turbulence for added realism.

7 Set the Scale to XYZ **600mm**, **600mm**, **1m**.

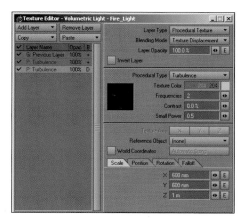

Add another procedural texture and blend it as a texture displacement to add variation in the procedural volumetric flames.

8 Click the E button for the Z position. In the Graph Editor, create a keyframe at frame 90 like you did for the first procedural texture. This time, however, set the Value to **12m**.

9 Close the Graph Editor and make a preview of the flames in the VIPER window. When you're happy with the results, close the lighting panels and return to Layout.

10 Press **F9** to make a full frame render and see how the flames look in the scene. Set the Light Intensity for the fire light to **0%** so only the volumetric is visible in the scene.

11 Animate the camera. Now add some marshmallows, and you're all set!

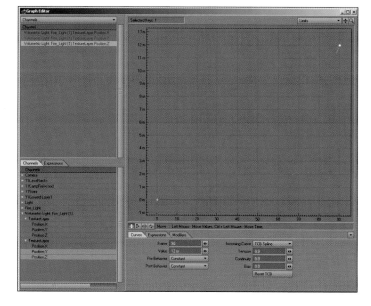

Add keyframes to the second procedural texture with a different value than the first to add motion variation to the volumetric flames.

How It Works

LightWave's procedurals are quite powerful, as you've seen here. What's nice is that once you become familiar with the Texture Editor and with using gradients, you can apply them anywhere, like landscapes or lights! Texture layers in LightWave [6.5] are built on three components: Gradients, procedurals, and image maps. Each of these can be layered and blended in a variety of ways to create many types of effects.

Modifications

Try taking this technique a step further. Add flames shooting out of a rocket ship, or make your own animated flame thrower. Or go the other way and play with the Falloff and Color settings, and you can make smoke with this effect! The possibilities are truly endless, and you can employ the techniques in this chapter everywhere in LightWave, from displacements to lights, surfaces, motions, and even renders. Experiment with this effect; it will help you learn about one of LightWave's most powerful resources.

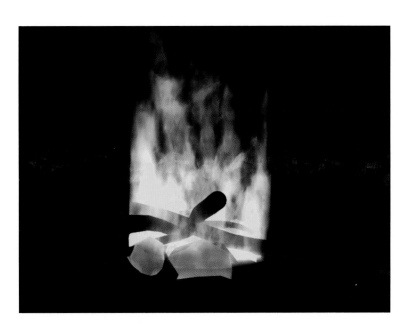

A final scene.

CREATURE WALK
WITH CYCLIST

"You must kill the spider to get

rid of the cobweb."

—MALTESE PROVERB

BRING CREEPY SPIDERS TO LIFE WITH THE CYCLIST PLUG-IN

Automation...it has changed everything, from the industrial revolution, to household appliances, to dry cleaning. It has even found its way into your computer and LightWave 3D. Version 6.5 of this program adds numerous controls to individual motion channels, but those channels still need to be put in motion. What if you could automate motions without using complex expression programming or third-party plug-ins?

You can with Cyclist.

Project 12

Creature Walk
with Cyclist

by Dan Ablan

GETTING STARTED

On the surface, Cyclist seems like a simple control that can be used to turn wheels or gears—which is extremely important. However, there is much more to this motion modifier than meets the eye. The opening spider image in this chapter shows creepy spiders made by Harlan Hill for the book *Inside LightWave [6]*. To take one spider setup and create multiple spiders might seem like a tough scene to accomplish. This not-too-complex inverse kinematics setup enables you to quickly pick up a leg of the spider and move it about, and the entire leg bends and moves along with it. But how in the world do you calculate moving the spider, its distance, speed, and a six-legged walk cycle with an offset? Not so easy…or is it?

1 Load the scene **12spider_ready.lws** from the book's CD. It's the basic spider setup with full inverse kinematics in place.

> **Note:** Although this chapter can't give you all the necessary information on the inverse kinematics setup the spider employs, you can see its hierarchy. Essentially, a null object named Bot_Mover is the master control for the spider. Cyclist uses that null as the Cycle Controller. All other elements of the spider are parented to the null. Be sure to reference *Inside LightWave [6]* (also from New Riders Publishing and Dan Ablan) for more information on complete inverse and forward kinematic setups.

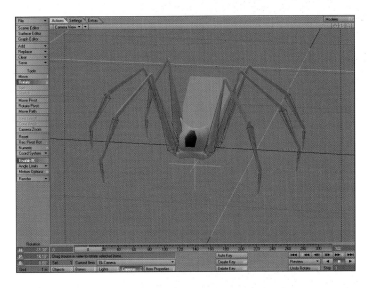

The Perspective view of the single spider object, which was set up with full inverse kinematics for six legs and the body. This sucker is ready to move!

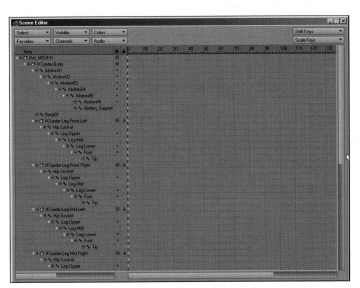

The Scene Editor shows the spider hierarchy.

2 Press **3** on the numeric keypad to switch to a side view.

> **Note:** What's cool about Cyclist is that you only have to make one motion for each leg—and it's the same motion!

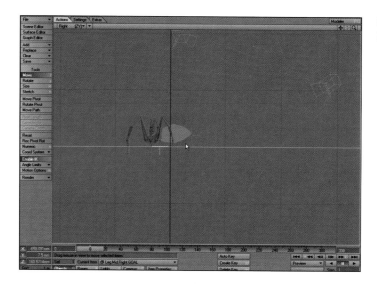

Switching to side view helps you position the leg goals.

3 Zoom in and position the spider so that it fills the frame. Select Leg.Frnt.Right.GOAL.

4 Go to frame 6 of the animation. Press the T button to select Move.

5 Move the front right leg goal up and to the back slightly to the position XYZ –366mm, 165mm, –388mm.

6 Create a keyframe (at frame 6) to lock the position in place. See the small change in leg position at this point? Note that the view has been zoomed in for a closer view.

> **Note:** Make sure you have LightWave's AutoKey feature turned off to follow along with this exercise.

> **Note:** A Goal object is a null that controls the IK setup for the specific leg. Because of the IK, moving the Goal object moves the entire leg. Also, remember you can press the **n** key to activate numeric controls to enter specific values.

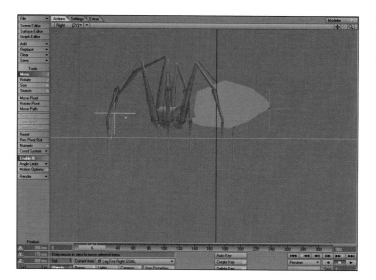

Zoom in on the side view of the spider object to view the small motion path that's beginning to form for the front right leg goal.

7 Move the front right leg goal back to XYZ −342mm, 140mm, −306mm. Create a keyframe at frame 12 to lock the position in place.

8 Set another position for the front right leg goal at XYZ −342mm, 0m, −276mm. Create a keyframe at frame 18 to lock the front right leg goal in place.

9 Press the **f** key to access the Go to Frame panel and go to frame 0. This sends the right leg goal back into its original position so the Cyclist plug-in can perfectly repeat it.

10 Press the Enter key to call up Create Key, and then enter **24**.

With the Go to Frame panel, you can instantly go to any keyframe.

Because you want the last keyframe for the front right leg goal to be the same as the first keyframe (frame 0), you can use frame 0's position to set a new keyframe. Consider this an easy way to copy a keyframe. This will copy the current frame's position, rotation, and scale to the new keyframe.

You've been making keyframes every six frames, with the last being at frame 18. Frame 24 for the right leg goal in the same position as frame 0 now completes the movement.

MOVING MORE LEGS

Although it's going to seem like this is tedious, when you see the control you'll have and realize the time you are saving by setting up these keyframes now, you'll be thrilled when Cyclist is applied. Now that the right leg goal has its movements, set up the next leg goal movements. A spider's legs are going to walk one after the other, moving from one side to another. So the next leg you need to move is the left front leg.

1. Select the Leg.Frnt.Left.GOAL and move it to XYZ 433mm, 180mm, −324mm. Create a keyframe at frame 6 to lock in place.

2. Now move the front left leg goal to XYZ 383mm, 140mm, −239mm. Create a keyframe at frame 12 to lock it in place.

3. Move the front left leg goal down to XYZ 383mm, 0m, −274mm.

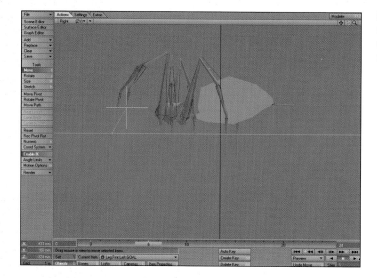

Setting the Leg.Frnt.Left.GOAL into movement with the same keyframes as the Leg.Frnt.Right.Goal. Cyclist will offset them for you.

4. Create a keyframe to lock the new position in place at frame 18.

5. Press the **f** key to call up the Go to Frame panel, and then enter frame 0 to move the front left leg goal to keyframe 0. Create a key for the goal in this position, but at frame 24. This completes the even loop of the front left leg goal.

MORE LEG KEYFRAMES

The spider has four more legs left to keyframe, which you can do on your own.

1. Give each leg five keyframes, each at 0, 6, 12, 18, and 24.

2. Create a continuous motion with Frame 24 in the same position as frame 0.

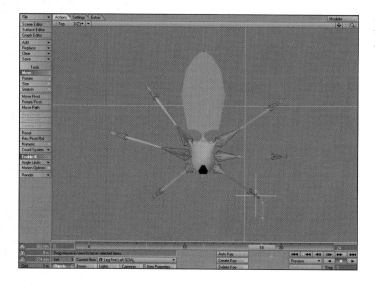

Check the Leg.Frnt.Left.GOAL from the top view. You can see the motion channel's small loop of keyframes.

3 Move and keyframe the goal for each leg only. Move the goals up, then back, then down, then back to the position at frame 0.

Note: A scene has been provided for you with all six leg motions already keyframed. Look for the scene **12sp_legsmove.lws** on the book's CD.

APPLYING CYCLIST

Cyclist is a motion modifier. It is a plug-in that resides within the Motion Options panel for Layout items. You can access the Motion Options panel by pressing the **m** key on the keyboard.

1 Load the scene **12sp_legsmove.lws**. Select the Leg.Frnt.Right.GOAL object and press the **m** key to open the Motion Options panel.

2 Open the Add Modifier drop-down list and select LW_Cyclist.

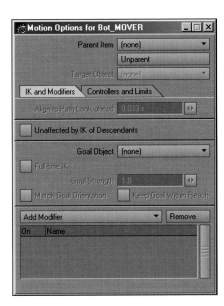

Pressing the m key calls up the Motion Options panel for the selected Layout item.

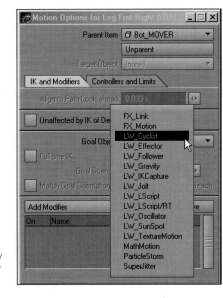

Apply Cyclist to the Leg.Frnt.Right.GOAL by selecting LW_Cyclist from the Add Modifier list in the Motion Options panel.

157

3 Double-click the plug-in in the list to open its control panel.

Double-click the plug-in listing in the modifier list to open the controls for Cyclist.

Note: Across the top of the Cyclist control panel are the Enable buttons. You really don't need to turn any of these off for this animation; just leave them as they are (active).

4 Change the Cycle Frames setting from **0** to **24**. Cycle Frames tells the plug-in what frames you want cycled. Your total keyframe value was 24—for each leg goal.

5 For the Cycle Controller, choose Bot_Mover, the main parent for the full spider.

Specify the Cycle Frames and Cycle Controller.

6 Change the default on Cyclist to Forward Progress by selecting it from the drop-down list.

Setting Cyclist to Forward Progress enables you to control more than just one axis.

Note: By default, the Position X channel is selected. Using Forward Motion for Cyclist does something cool: It tells LightWave to cycle through the defined frames based on its motion progress, both forward and backward.

7   Set the Controller Range from **0** to **.5**. The
    Controller Range tells LightWave how large of
    a range to cycle the motion. This will also help
    you offset each moving leg.

8   Set End Behavior to Repeat. Click OK to close the
    Cyclist control panel. Close the Motion Options
    panel and return to Layout.

9   Go to Perspective view and press the comma key a
    few times to zoom outward.

10 Select the Bot_Mover object and move it on the
    Z-axis to −2.6m. Create a keyframe at frame 90 to
    lock it in place.

11 Move the Bot_Mover back on the Z-axis to 2.5m,
    and then create a keyframe at frame 160.

12 Move it back on the Z-axis to 2.6m and create a
    keyframe at frame 180.

13 Press the **f** key to call up the Go to Frame panel,
    and then enter **0** to bring the Bot_Mover back to
    its original position. Create a keyframe here at
    frame 250.

14 Click the Play button and watch the front right leg
    walk! Notice that when the spider slows down, so
    does the leg! When the spider backs up, the leg walks
    backward! Cyclist rocks!

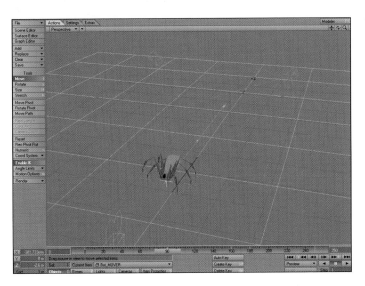

The first keyframe for the
Bot_Mover is at frame 90.

CYCLING OFFSETS

Now you can see the beauty of Cyclist. By moving one null object, the spider character's leg moves in time both forward and backward. Now that you've set up motions for each leg, set up Cyclist with an offset.

1   Select the Leg.Frnt.Left.GOAL and press the **m** key to open the Motion Options panel for it.

2   Add Cyclist by choosing it from the Add Modifier drop-down list.

3   Double-click the Cyclist plug-in in the list to open the Cyclist control panel. Set the following parameters:

> Cycle Frames From: **0** To: **24**
>
> Cycle Controller: **Bot_Mover**
>
> From the drop down list, choose:
> **Forward Progress**
>
> Controller Range From: **0.1** To: **0.6**
>
> End Behavior: **Repeat**

From here, all you need to do is repeat the previous steps for the remaining four legs. All values will be the same, except for the Controller Range setting. Remember to offset each leg with this setting. Use the following settings for the six legs' Controller Ranges:

> Leg.Frnt.Right.GOAL: **0** to **0.5**
>
> Leg.Frnt.Left.GOAL: **0.1** to **0.6**
>
> Leg.Mid.Right.GOAL: **0.2** to **0.7**
>
> Leg.Mid.Left.GOAL: **0.3** to **0.8**
>
> Leg.Back.Right.GOAL: **0.4** to **0.9**
>
> Leg.Back.Left.GOAL: **0.5** to **1.0**

Apply the Cyclist control settings for the Leg.Frnt.Left.GOAL.

Note: The Controller Range was set from **0.1** to **0.6**. You set the range for the first leg goal from **0** to **0.5**. By moving the Controller Range up a notch, you keep the same pace and speed in the motion but offset it slightly.

You can set these up yourself in no time. After you've set up the Cyclist controller for a leg goal, return to Layout and click the Play button to see another leg walk, but this time with an offset.

> **Note:** You can load the **12spider_setgo.lws** scene from the book's CD to see the animation for the Cyclist spider at this point. Use it to compare settings if you like.

ADDING OTHER CYCLIST MOTIONS

The legs look really cool moving at different paces, but in time with the distance of the spider. However, you need to put one more thing into place: the body. The body is stationary on the Y-axis. Right now, only the legs move. But if you've ever watched a spider crawl across your bed, you know his little nasty body bobs up and down, too. With Cyclist, that motion is very easy to set up as well.

1 Switch to a side view in Layout. Then go to frame 0 and select the Tail.Goal object.

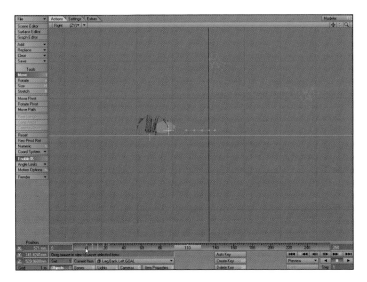

Check out the full Cyclist motion of the spider, with six creepy legs in motion, from the right view in Layout.

2 Move the Tail.Goal object up on the Y-axis from about 55mm to 265mm. Create a keyframe at frame 7.

3 With Tail.Goal still selected, press the F key and go to frame 0. Create a keyframe at frame 14.

4 Press the **m** key to open the Motion Options panel for Tail.Goal. Add the LW_Cyclist modifier.

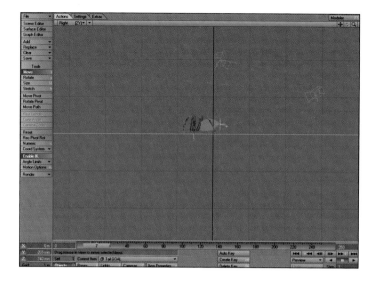

Move the Tail.Goal up slightly on the Y-axis to begin creating a bobbing motion for the spider's tail end.

5 Double-click the LW_Cyclist plug-in in the list to open its control panel. Enter the following settings:

   Cycle Frames From: **0** To: **14**

   Cycle Controller: **Bot_Mover**

   From the drop down list, choose:
   Forward Progress

   Cycle Range From: **0** To: **0.5**

   End Behavior: **Repeat**

Cyclist works well for bobbing the tail end of a creepy spider.

6 Click OK to close the panel, and then close the Motion Options panel and return to Layout. Click the Play button to see how the tail end of the spider bobs with its movements.

Note: You can go one step further with this bobbing motion. If you select the IKSpider.Body object, you can bounce the entire spider with Cyclist while the legs remain fixed—thanks to the Inverse Kinematics chains.

How It Works

Cyclist easily lets you repeat your motions. This example shows just how powerful this simple motion plug-in can be. Once this is set up, you can use LightWave [6.5]'s File, Load From Scene command to create multiple spiders walking about in one scene. Because Cyclist looks to the main parent of the object (the Bot_Mover in this case), if you slow a spider down, the legs slow down as well. Add this all together in one scene, and the result is spiders interacting with one another!

Modifications

If you think about a car driving down a road—slowing down, speeding up, stopping, and backing up—how do you calculate the wheel rotations? Do you just wing it? Or are you a math genius? The answer is Cyclist. You'd think rotating wheels are no big deal—and they're not until the motion can no longer stay constant. Cyclist is perfect for just this sort of thing. You can also try using it on bird wings. Or how about an animal? Are you so bold as to try it on a walking or running human? Imagine having a controllable run cycle that speeds up or slows down on the control of just one null object. Try using Cyclist in all your projects! When you get a chance, load the **12spiders_ohno.lws** scene to see a complete scene with many of these little things crawling around.

VOLUMETRIC
PROJECTIONS

"You know what your problem is, it's

that you haven't seen enough

movies—all of life's riddles are

answered in the movies."

—STEVE MARTIN

CREATING A SMOKY BEAM OF LIGHT WITH VOLUMETRICS

You've seen them before; the lights that streak through logos, making them look extra cool. Maybe you've seen the sunlight streaking through a window on a sunny afternoon. You've probably seen volumetric lighting more than you realize, and perhaps you have added beams of light in your own animations. But taking this useful effect further, this chapter will show you how to take a movie file, project it, and use that movie to color and displace the volumetric light.

Project 13

Volumetric Projections

by Dan Ablan

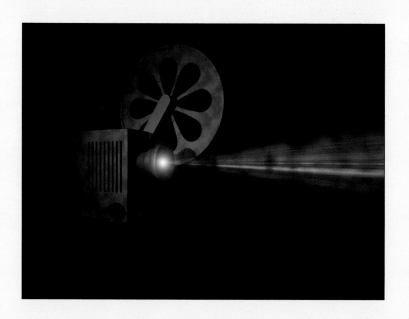

GETTING STARTED

Although this is a really cool effect, neither the setup time nor the render times are too intense. You'll see from the example in the next few pages that this technique can take your animations further by adding yet another touch of realism. You'll learn to project a movie file through a light, add volumetrics to it, and enhance the effect with a little smoky atmosphere. To start, a scene has been provided for you on the book's CD; it's a simple movie projector and screen.

1   Load the scene **13moviestart.lws** from the book's
    CD into Layout.

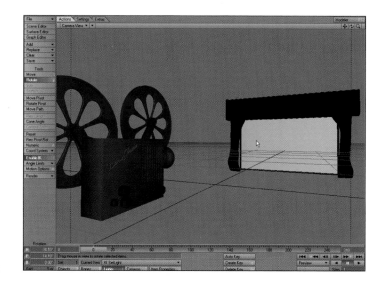

Load 13moviestart.lws in Layout.

2   From the Actions tab, select Add/Add Light/Add
    Spot Light. Name the new light **Projector_Lamp**.

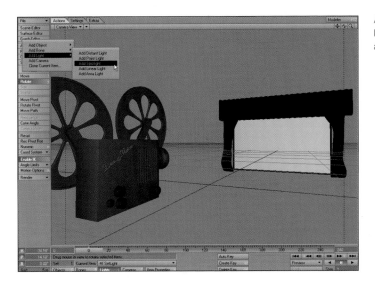

Add a spotlight named
Projector_Lamp to create
a projection light.

3   Position the Projector_Lamp light in front of the
    movie camera lens. Using a combination of side
    and top views helps line things up.

Note: You might want to change the Grid Square Size
for the scene to 1m. This will help you position items
more accurately in Layout.

4   Create a keyframe at frame 0 to lock it in place.

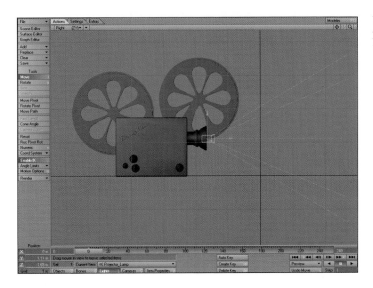

The side view is helpful when
you're positioning items, such as
this light.

PROJECTION LIGHT PROPERTIES

The first order of business when setting up a projection light is to have something project, of course! You'll start in the Light Properties panel and will add a movie file as the projection element.

1 In Layout, select the Projector_Lamp light and open the Light Properties panel (**p**).

2 Make the Light Color more realistic with the following settings:

> Color: RGB **240**, **240**, **210**
>
> Light Intensity: **90%**
>
> Spotlight Soft Edge Angle: **30°**

Leave all other settings at their defaults.

By setting the Spotlight Soft Edge Angle to **30°**, you're setting it equal to that of the Spotlight Cone Angle. This makes for a nice soft transition from the center of the light source to the edges.

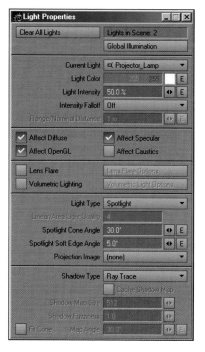

The Light Properties panel for the projector lamp is where all the fun happens.

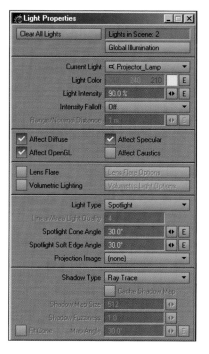

Use color and intensity settings to make the projection lamp look good.

3 Click to open the Projection Image drop-down list, and select Load Image.

Note: Only spotlights can have projection images. This setting will be disabled for all other lights.

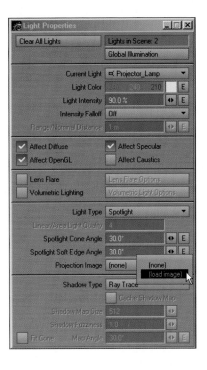

Projection Image allows you to add an image to a spotlight.

4 Load the **citywalkers.avi** movie clips from the book's CD and press **F9** to render a frame. You might need to select All Files in your system requester to see the .AVI file type. LightWave will recognize it.

Note: You can also use the Image Editor to load the movie clip. The Image Editor will allow you to adjust the contrast, brightness, and color values and to set in and out points on image sequences.

Note: There needs to be a change to view the image projection. The first thing is the size of the projection. This is because the image extends onto the curtains, and your moviegoers are not able to see the full projection!

Adding a projection image to a spotlight allows you to project an image or movie file.

5   In the Light Properties panel for the Projector_Lamp light, change the Spotlight Cone Angle to **10°**. The projected image now fits on the screen, but it is a bit narrow for the actual size of the screen so it bleeds off the top. You can fix this by moving the camera down slightly.

> **Note:** At various intervals, you can press **F9** to render a frame and see how your projection looks. Adjust the light and camera positions as you see fit.

Adjust the Spotlight Cone Angle to position the projection on the screen.

VOLUMETRIC EFFECTS

So you have a simple projector object and a movie screen. You've added a spotlight and made it a projection light. The added movie clip is now projected onto the movie screen. Pretty cool. But in a real theatre, you would of course have chairs, people, popcorn, and sticky floors. You'd also have a beam of light coming out of the projector. You can add this to your animation with a volumetric effect.

This volumetric light isn't your ordinary beam of light in a movie theatre. It's actually broken by the images that are projected. Dark areas on the transparent film hold back more light, whereas brighter areas let through more light. LightWave's Volumetrics will work this way for you. Here you use LightWave [6.5]'s volumetric lighting power to add physical volume (a beam) to the projection light.

1   In the Light Properties panel for the Projector_Lamp light, click on Volumetric Lighting. Click the Volumetric Light Options button.

2   Click the VIPER window to open LightWave's virtual preview rendered.

     VIPER will draw a beam of light. Although the VIPER window shows the beam of light, it does not show the projection image.

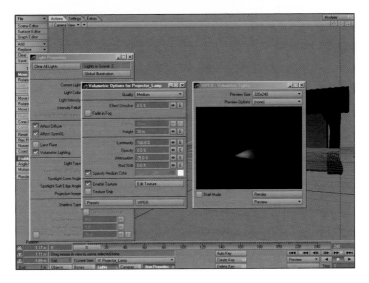

Turn on Volumetric Lighting and use VIPER to create beams of light.

3   Press **F9** to render a frame.

     This shows how, when rendered, the volumetric displays the streaks from the projected movie clip.

A quick render shows that simply turning on Volumetric Lighting for the projected image displays broken beams of light.

4 Go back to the Volumetric Options panel and with VIPER still open, enter the following settings:

>   Luminosity: **200%**
>
>   Opacity: **40%**
>
>   Attenuation: **10%**

5 Press **F9** again to make a quick render and see how your projection looks. You can go further by changing the color of the light or adjusting the values of the volumetric light. Be sure to use VIPER from the Volumetric Light Options panel to see what you are doing in real time. Experimentation is key!

A few changes to the volumetrics help make a brighter beam of light.

ADDED TEXTURES

The projection image looks good, but it will look even better when you see the volumetric move with the changing video clip. But one thing that is not in the volumetric light is the noise or smoky mist you often see in beams of light at a movie theatre. This is easy to set up in the Volumetric Options panel. Remember that you can add textures to just about everything in LightWave. Here you'll add a procedural texture to the volumetric light.

1 Click the Edit Texture button in the Volumetric Options panel, set the values as shown, and then press **F9** for a test render:

>   Layer Type: **Procedural Texture**
>
>   Blending Mode: **Additive**
>
>   Opacity: **100%**
>
>   Procedural Type: **Fractal Noise**
>
>   Texture Color: RGB **78**, **73**, **61**
>
>   Frequencies: **2**
>
>   Contrast: **2.0**
>
>   Small Power: **0.5**
>
>   Scale: XYZ **200mm**, **200mm**, **200mm**

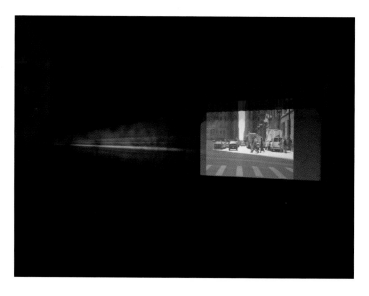

A closer view of the volumetric light now shows fractal noise in the beam.

This opens the Texture Editor for the light. Your scene shows the streaked volumetric projection light, now with some noise. The fractal noise looks good, but it needs to move upward, like dust particles in the air.

2   Click the E button for the Position Y in the Texture Editor for the volumetric light. This opens the Graph Editor.

3   Set a keyframe at 240 and set the value to **6m**. When you render the animation, you'll see a smoky mist traveling upward as the movie plays. Be sure to check the **ch13.avi** on the book's CD to see how this looks.

4   In the Light Properties panel for the Projector_Lamp light, click the E button for Light Intensity to open the Graph Editor.

This adds a little flicker to your projection—the last thing this projection needs. Although the movie clip jiggles the volumetric, you still need the look of the camera's shutter.

5   Click the Modifiers tab, open the Add Modifier drop-down list, and select LW_Oscillator.

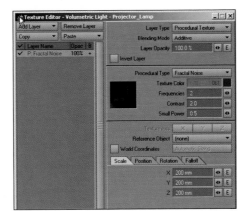

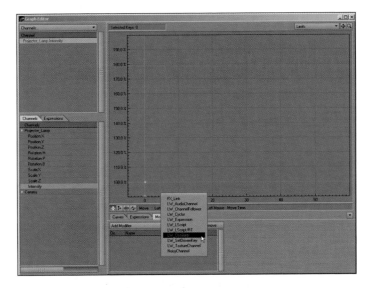

The LW_Oscillator plug-in helps to automate a flickering movie camera.

6 Double-click the Oscillator listing and add the following control panel settings:

Cycle Time: **0.1**

Wave Size: **0.1%**

Offset: **0%**

Phase: **0%**

Damping: **0%**

Start Frame: **1**

End Frame: **240** (or whatever your end frame is)

You can see in the Curve window that the plug-in made a quick ramping up and down, saving you hours of keyframing work.

The only thing left to do is try a test render! You can try offsetting the Oscillator for various effects, or even try adding an additional modifier. Perhaps try adding a texture to the Light Intensity, similar to the smoky volumetric texture you applied earlier. You have lots of options!

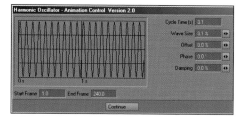

Set a Cycle Time of 0.1 to tell the cycle to change every frame.

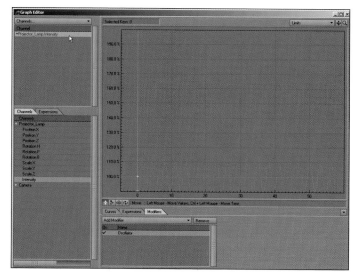

The Graph Editor shows the visible values of the Light Intensity once the Oscillator plug-in has been applied.

HOW IT WORKS

Projection images are easy to set up, and they produce cool and complex-looking effects. Depending on the image or video clip you choose to project, volumetric options added to projected images make for an even cooler-looking effect. LightWave's volumetric lighting is very useful, and this effect is just one of many that can be achieved. The streaking beams within the projection volumetric work by using the dark and light values of the projected image to show or retract more light. This, in turn, changes the parameters of the volumetric light.

MODIFICATIONS

There are so many variations to this effect that it's impossible to list them all here. But a few ideas include using images of branches and leaves to create simulated streaks of light through a forest, and projecting an image of a ghost across a room. You can add to the projection variations with textures such as the one used in this project (fractal noise). Remember, LightWave's Texture Editor allows you to add many procedurals and gradients to volumetric lights, and you can add images as well! With the right video or still image clip, you can add a textured image to the volumetric light of a projected image. The results are neverending. You also don't have to use video clips for projected images. You can render animations and then project them in a new scene—it is a great way to open a demo reel.

To take this project a step further, add a lens flare to the spotlight, with a little lens reflection for good measure. The lens flare will act as a "source" for the light emitting from the projector. You can also add a theatre, seats, and silhouettes of people. And because this light is projected, a person walking in front of the light will have the movie projected on him as well. As long as shadow maps are on, the volumetric light beam will be broken as a person walks through it, as well. Experiment to see what kind of effects you can come up with on your own.

TORNADO

"Cow."

**—JO HARDING,
FROM THE MOVIE *TWISTER***

CREATING A SCARY 3D TORNADO WITH INTEGRATED PARTICLES AND HYPERVOXELS

A number of people have posted questions on the Internet and have requested through email the proper and necessary steps to create a tornado. There are a few methods, some of which are more involved than others. But one of the best ways is to use LightWave [6.5]'s integrated particles and HyperVoxels. The downside to this method is long render times. But once you see the results, you'll know that the rendering is worth the wait.

Project 14

Tornado

by Dan Ablan

GETTING STARTED

In the *LightWave Power Guide* (1996, New Riders Publishing), a tornado was created using polygons and fractal noise transparency maps. LightWave has changed significantly since 1996, and so has computing. The previous method had holes, some literally. The method used for this project creates a completely 3D tornado that you can actually fly around and through!

To start, you need to configure a custom button or two for this project. These interface buttons make it much easier to access the control panels for creating the tornado. Otherwise, you'd have to go through a series of clicks before getting to the necessary panels. By adding the buttons right in Layout, you create an instant link to the plug-in.

ADDING AN INTERFACE BUTTON

In this section, you'll create customized buttons.

1 In Layout, press **F2** to call up the Configure Menus panel. Select the last triangle in the expanded Effects sub-group of the Main menu and click New Group.

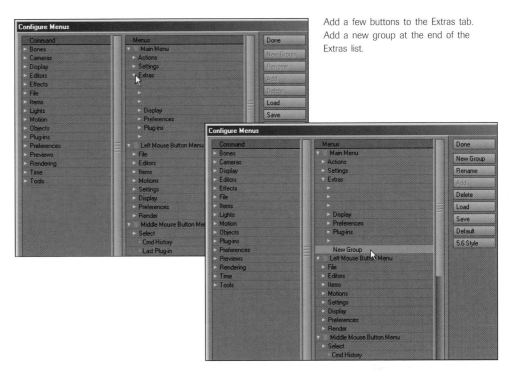

Add a few buttons to the Extras tab. Add a new group at the end of the Extras list.

2 Expand the Plug-ins list in the left column (under Command). Select the FX_Browser plug-in.

Note: This book uses the 6.0 Style menu configuration. If you are using this configuration to follow along with the projects in this book, you'll need to set up a few buttons as described here. Alternatively, you can use LightWave [6.5]'s defaults, which have the buttons already created for you.

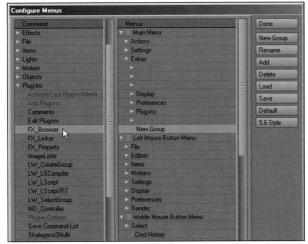

Select the FX_Browser plug-in from the Plug-ins list.

3 Click the Add button.

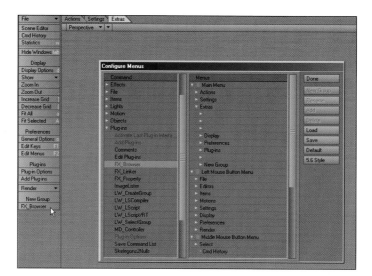

Add the FX_Browser to the new group, and you'll see the button appear in Layout.

4 Repeat this process for the FX_Linker and FX_Property plug-ins. Rename the new group **Particles**.

5 Close the Configure Menus panel, and quit LightWave.

Quitting writes the interface changes to LightWave's configuration file. Restart LightWave Layout.

Note: You can create custom buttons for all your plug-ins if you want. Don't forget that you can also rename all LightWave's buttons through the Configure Menus panel.

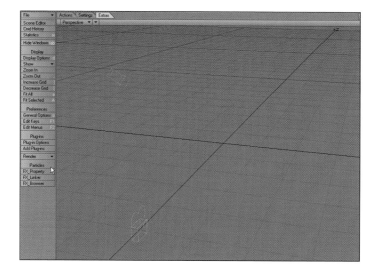

Add a new particle group listing and three plug-in command buttons to Layout.

PARTICLE SETUP

Now that you have made the necessary interface enhancements, it's time
to set up the particle motion for the tornado.

1   Go to the Extras tab, and click the FX_Browser
    button you added.

    The Particle FX_Browser panel opens.

Open the Particle FX_Browser panel.

2   From the Add list, click and select Emitter.

    This adds a particle emitter to Layout.

Choose Emitter from the Add list to
add a particle emitter in Layout.

3   Switch to Camera view in Layout and move the
    camera to XYZ −9m, 121mm, −8m. Rotate
    the camera to H 50.00, P −14.00, B −20.00.
    Then create a keyframe at frame zero to lock
    the camera in place.

4   Change the last frame of the animation to **300** for a
    10-second animation.

5   Select the emitter object and open the Particle
    FX_Property by clicking the button you made, or
    simply click the Property button in the FX_Browser.

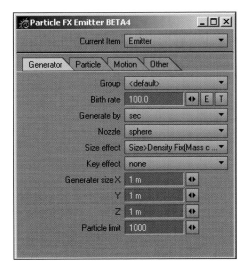

Open the Particle FX_Property panel.

6 Open the Generator tab and set the following parameters:

> Group: **Default**
>
> Birth Rate: **10**
>
> Generate By: **Sec**
>
> Nozzle: **Sphere**
>
> Size Effect: **Density Fix (default)**
>
> Key Effect: **None**
>
> Generator: XYZ   **2m**, **200mm**, **2m**
>
> Particle Limit: **300**

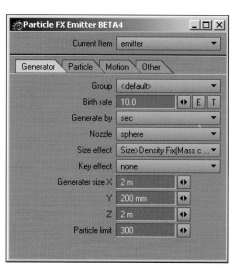

Adjust the settings for the Generator tab for the particle emitter.

7 Click the Particle tab and enter the following settings:

> Particle Weight: **0**
>
> +−: **0**
>
> Particle Size: **0**
>
> +−: **0**
>
> Particle Resistance: **1**
>
> +−: **0**
>
> Life Time: **300**
>
> +−: **13**
>
> Fixed Random: **On**

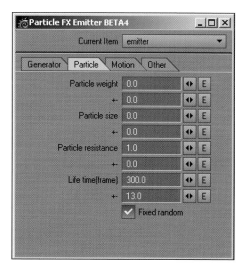

Change the Particle tab settings for the emitter object.

Note: You won't be able to see anything if you render the animation at this point. In order to visually see the particles in a render, you'll need to apply HyperVoxels, explained shortly. You can, however, press the Play button to see how the motion of the particles is coming along.

8 Click to the Motion tab for the emitter object and add the following settings:

Velocity: **100%**

Vector: XYZ **0, 0, 0**

Target: **None**

World Coordinates: **Off**

Explosion: **0**

Vibration: **0**

Threshold1: **510mm**

Threshold2: **3.23m**

Parent Motion: **100%**

There are no settings for the Other tab area values, so leave that one alone.

9 Close the Particle FX_Property panel.

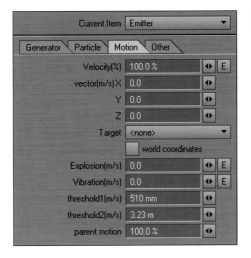

Set the Motion tab settings for the particle emitter.

Now you've set up the necessary particles. But if you play the animation, nothing happens. You need to add some wind to get those suckers in motion.

ADDING WIND

Although the particle emitter is often all you need to generate moving particles (such as the rain particle in Project 8, "Falling Rain and Snow"), this project uses a combination of an emitter and two wind sources. One wind source spins the particles, and the other sucks them up.

1 Select Wind from the Add list.

This will add a wind controller to Layout. When a wind controller is added to Layout, you'll see a clump of points.

Add a Wind controller from the FX_Browser panel.

2 Select the clump of points in Layout and move it to XYZ **5mm**, **2.625m**, **15mm**. Create a keyframe to lock it in place.

3 Open the FX_Property plug-in. On the Mode tab, set the following parameters:

> Group: **Default**
>
> Wind Mode: **Rotation**
>
> Blend Mode: **Add**
>
> Size Effect: **Wind**
>
> Falloff Mode: **Inverse Distance**
>
> Radius: **4.5m**
>
> Power: **200%**
>
> Spiral: **0%**
>
> Doughnut Fat: **50%**

Settings for the Mode tab in the properties panel for the wind controller.

Because the wind controller object is selected, the Particle FX_Property panel shows the controls for wind.

4 Click the Vector tab for the wind controller and set the following parameters:

> Wind: XYZ   **600mm, 0m, 0m**
>
> Turbulence Size: XYZ   **1m, 1m, 1m**
>
> Turbulence Vector: XYZ   **20m, 0m, 0m**

5 Close the FX_Property panel.

The first wind controller is set. The particles are now swirling, but they need to rise up into the sky (which you'll add later).

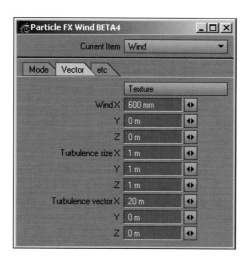

Enter the Vector settings for the first wind controller.

6 Click the FX_Browser button you added to the Extras tab if the panel is not already open. Select Wind from the Add list. Then click Continue to close the FX_Browser.

Add an additional wind controller.

7 Select Wind(2) in the Layout object list and open the FX_Property panel, or click the Property button in the FX_Browser.

8 Open the Mode tab for the wind(2) properties and enter the following settings:

Group: **Default**

Wind Mode: **Cylinder-explosion**

Blend Mode: **Add**

Size Effect: **Wind**

Falloff Mode: **Inverse Distance**

Radius: **5m**

Power: **80%**

Spiral: **60%**

Doughnut Fat: **50%**

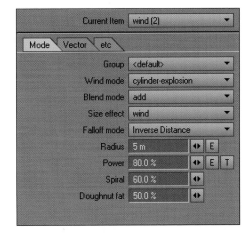

Enter the Mode settings for wind(2).

9 Click the Vector tab in the Properties panel and set the following parameters:

Wind: XYZ   **0m, 3m, 0m**

Turbulence Size: XYZ   **10m, 1m, 10m**

Turbulence Vector: XYZ   **300mm, 300mm, 300mm**

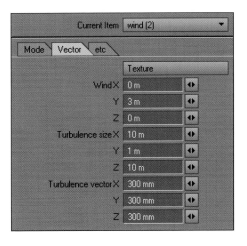

The Vector tab settings for the second wind controller object.

10 Close the Particle FX_Property panel and return to Layout. Select the wind(2) object and move it to XYZ 4mm, 970mm, −33mm. Create a keyframe to lock it in place.

11 Select the emitter object and click the Play button.

You'll see a spiraling tornado-like stream of particles!

You've successfully set up the necessary particle information for a tornado. You can use this technique for all kinds of effects; the particles are simply a base for whatever texture or effect you apply to them. To make a tornado surface, use HyperVoxels 3.0.

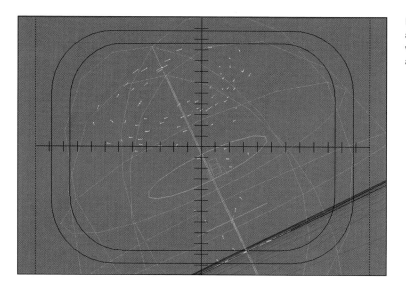

Layout view at frame 250 after the emitter and two wind controllers have been added.

Tornado Surfacing

The great thing about animating a tornado with particles is the amount of control you have. Although the render times are quite high with this project, the results are worth it.

1 From the Settings tab in Layout, click the Volumetrics button to open the Effects panel.

2 Select HyperVoxelsFilter from the Add Modifier. Double-click the HyperVoxels 3.0 listing.

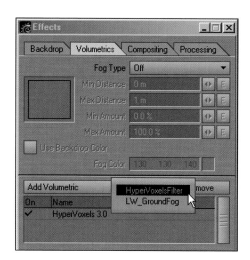

Add an instance of HyperVoxels from the Effects/Volumetrics panel.

186

3 Double-click the Emitter listing in the Object Name list.

4 Change the Object Type to Volume and leave Dissolve at 0%.

5 Click the Geometry tab and set the following parameters:

Particle Size: **2m**

Size Variation: **20%**

Stretch Direction: **Velocity**

Stretch Amount: **500%**

Maintain Volume: **Off**

Align to Path: **Off**

Show Particles: **Off**

User Particle System Color: **Off**

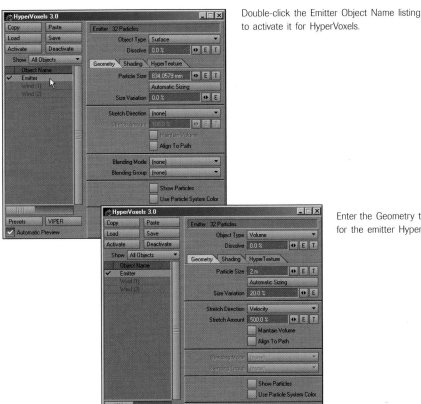

Double-click the Emitter Object Name listing to activate it for HyperVoxels.

Enter the Geometry tab settings for the emitter HyperVoxels.

6 Click the Shading tab. Then on the Basic tab, set the following parameters:

Color: RGB **166**, **174**, **167**

Luminosity: **100%**

Opacity: **100%**

Density: **100%**

Thickness: **20%**

Smoothness: **50%**

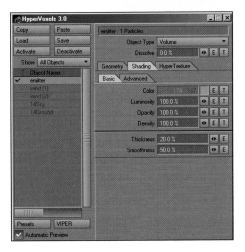

Select the Basic tab settings for HyperVoxels.

7 Click the Advanced tab under Shading and set the following parameters:

- Render Quality: **Medium**
- Near Clip: **1m**
- Volumetric Shadows: **On**
- Texture Shadows: **Off**
- Shadow Quality: **Medium**
- Shadow Strength: **5%**
- Illumination: **Beer**
- Use All Lights: **Off**
- Light1: **Light**
- Ambient Color: RGB **166**, **174**, **167**
- Ambient Intensity: **15%**

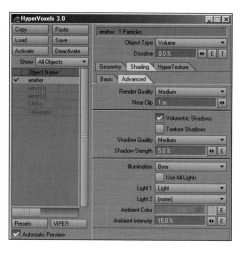

The advanced shading settings for HyperVoxels.

8 Click the HyperTexture tab and enter the following settings:

- Texture: **Turbulence**
- Frequencies: **3**
- Contrast: **0%**
- Small Power: **0.5**
- Texture Amplitude: **85%**
- Texture Effect: **Velocity Translate**
- Effect Speed: **40%**
- Reference Object: **None**
- Scale: XYZ **1m**, **1m**, **1m**

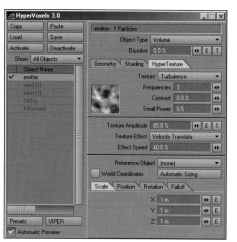

The HyperTexture settings for the HyperVoxels tornado.

9 Open the VIPER window to take a look at the tornado's surfacing.

Remember that this sucker takes a lot of render time, even in VIPER's draft mode.

ENVIRONMENT ADDITIONS

The last thing you need to do to bring the tornado to life (other than render it) is to add an environment.

1   Load the **14Sky.lwo** object and the **14Ground.lwo** object into Layout from the book's CD.

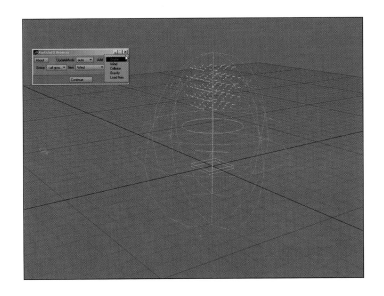

These files are copies of the sky and ground used in Project 8, "Falling Rain and Snow."

2   Change the background from a solid black color to a Gradient Backdrop. Use a medium gray to soft greenish color.

The 14Tornado.lws scene on the book's CD has a complete setup for you to use. In that scene, you'll see that the NoisyChannel modifier was added to the camera in the Graph Editor to simulate a natural hand-held motion effect. You can learn how to do this in Project 9, "Procedural Texture Motions."

HOW IT WORKS

HyperVoxels looks at the particles in a scene and draws a physical volume for them. When the particle motion is controlled through LightWave [6.5]'s integrated particle engine and the right amount of texture is added in HyperVoxels, a convincing tornado is born.

> **Note:** Try adding an additional wind controller at the top of the tornado to make the particles flatten out and become the clouds in the sky. This will make your tornado and sky one complete storm.

MODIFICATIONS

This technique can be used for a variety of animation projects including dust, fire, and smoke. Particles and HyperVoxels make a great combination. Although the render times can be steep with HyperVoxels, the results are often worth the wait. By understanding the different effects you can achieve with HyperVoxels (from solid objects to volumes or sprites), you can easily visualize a scene when setting up the integrated particles.

Another killer application for these particles is to use the FX_Link motion modifier to attach say, a cow or any other object, to a particle or two! Then you can have objects sucked up into the tornado!

DYNAMIC EXPLOSIONS

"If the automobile had followed the same development cycle as the computer, a Rolls-Royce would today cost $100, get one million miles to the gallon, and explode once a year, killing everyone inside."

—ROBERT X. CRINGELY

CREATING KILLER EXPLOSIONS WITH HYPERVOXELS

Explosions—you never know when you'll need them, but it's good to know how to create them. Although many 3D animators use third-party programs to composite and often create explosions, you have the power to create them directly within your scene. The benefit of this is that the explosions are clean and realistic. The downside is that your render times might be increased. Regardless of the method, knowing how to use LightWave [6.5]'s HyperVoxels 3.0 to create killer explosions is a plus.

Project 15

Dynamic Explosions

by Dan Ablan

GETTING STARTED

The techniques used to create the effect in the following pages provide just one way to achieve the desired look. You'll use nothing more than a simple null object and the HyperVoxels feature to create the explosion. A couple of keyframes will make the explosion grow, and you'll shake up the camera using the Jolt plug-in.

1 Open a new scene and switch to Camera view (**6**).

2 Select Add, Add Object, Add Null Object from the Actions tab.

This adds a null object to the scene, which is nothing more than a single point.

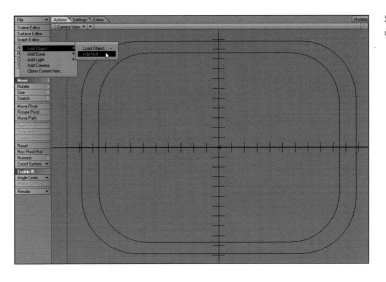

Simply add one null object to create a kick-butt explosion.

3 Name the null object **Explosion_1**.

4 Select a camera and position it at the following coordinates:

Move: XYZ –25mm, 355mm, –5m

Rotate: XYZ 0.0, 12.0, 0.0

Create a keyframe at 0 to lock it in place.

Note: Although not much has happened yet, you've completed enough steps to make this scene save-worthy! You can also reload this scene for future explosion bases.

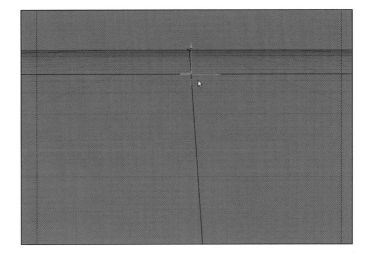

Move the camera back and up to help set up the explosion shot.

5 Select Volumetrics from the Settings tab. Open the Add Volumetric drop-down list and choose the HyperVoxelsFilter option.

6 Double-click the HyperVoxels 3.0 listing to open its control panel. Activate the Explosion_1 null object.

> **Note:** In HyperVoxels, you can hold the Shift key and click an object in the Object Name list to deactivate that object.

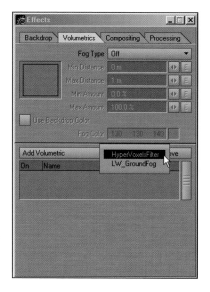

Add the HyperVoxelsFilter plug-in from the Effects/Volumetrics panel.

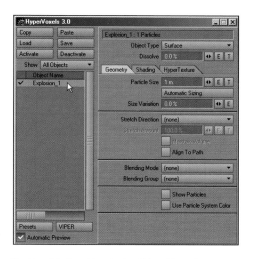

Double-click the object in the Object Name list, or select it and click the Activate button to activate the object for HyperVoxels.

7 Click the VIPER button to open LightWave's virtual interactive preview renderer. You'll see a big ball, which is the null object with the default HyperVoxels settings.

At this point, HyperVoxels is drawing a Surface volume for the null object. Although this is good for blob-like things such as marshmallows, lava (lava lamps especially), and even fluid, it's not what you need for an explosion.

Activate VIPER to see exactly what HyperVoxels is doing. At this point, the default HV settings show just a ball, or Surface volume.

VOLUME OBJECT TYPES

At the top of the HyperVoxels interface is the Object Type field. By default, it is set to the Surface object type, but you also have the choices of Sprite and Volume. The next steps will help you set up soft wispy clouds, perfect for explosions.

1   Select Volume for the Object Type.

A Surface object type will create a solid blob; a Volume object, on the other hand, will create volumetric effects.

Note: Sprite object mode is often faster than Volume mode. A Sprite is essentially a 2D slice of a volumetric HyperVoxel. It can be used for smoke, dust, or perhaps the debris outside of a tornado or secondary smoke from a larger explosion.

Tip: For a speedier setup, you can use Sprite mode for your objects. When you finish with the setup, you can switch back to Volume mode.

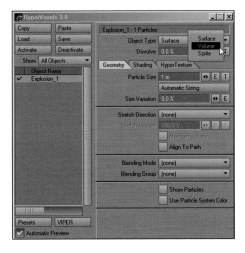

To create cool explosions, use the Volume object type from within the HyperVoxels panel.

Volume objects create a billowing effect that's great for smoke, clouds, or explosions!

2   In the Geometry tab, set the Particle Size to **2m** and the Size Variation to **65%**.

This is the fun part—adjusting the parameters to make the fire come alive. You want the explosion to glow internally and be dark around the edges, almost burning.

Note: Adjusting the parameters can yield all kinds of effects. You can change the colors to blue and aqua to simulate a water splash. Or maybe change the colors to soft grey and more transparent to create a mushroom cloud of exploding smoke.

The Geometry options set the initial size of the HyperVoxel.

3 Click the Shading tab and set the color to RGB **250, 210, 120**.

4 Change Luminosity to **150%**; this will help create the inner glow.

Note: If you set these values at this point, you will be able to see how the explosion is coming along in VIPER. However, when you apply gradients later, these settings will be overwritten.

5 Set Opacity and Density to **100%**. Set Thickness to **80%** and Smoothness to **30%**. These settings help create a fiery smoke look by making the center dense and creating a softer appearance on the outer edges.

6 Open the Texture Editor (**t**) for Color. Change the Layer Type to Gradient. Then create a key and set its Parameter to **14%**. Enter the following settings:

Blending Mode: **Additive**

Layer Opacity: **100%**

Input Parameter: **Local Density**

A Gradient will set up the color shift so that the fiery explosion changes as it expands outward.

7 For the first key, set the following parameters:

Color: RGB   **240, 235, 125**

Alpha: **100%**

Parameter: **0%**

Smoothing: **Linear**

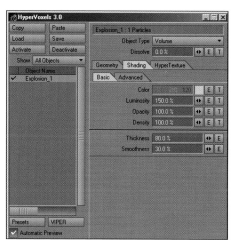

The initial color and shading values for the explosion.

8 For the second key, set the following parameters:

> Color: RGB **215**, **90**, **25**
>
> Alpha: **100%**
>
> Parameter: **14%**
>
> Smoothing: **Linear**

Here you are changing the color based on the density of the HyperVoxels texture. At the lowest density (0%), it's yellow. At the next density level (14%), it's thicker and orange.

9 Click Use Texture to apply these settings.

10 Open the Texture Editor (**t**) for Luminosity. You need to set a Luminosity texture to accentuate the glowing fire.

11 Change the Layer Type to Gradient. Create two keys—one at **12%** and the other at **23%**. Then set the following parameters:

> Blending Mode: **Additive**
>
> Layer Opacity: **100%**
>
> Input Parameter: **Local Density**

12 Enter the following settings for the first key:

> Value: **0%**
>
> Alpha: **100%**
>
> Parameter: **0%**
>
> Smoothing: **Linear**

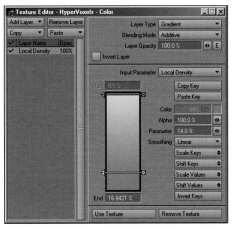

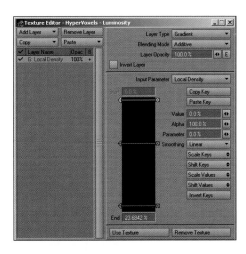

A gradient texture on the color channel helps create a change in the color of the fiery explosion.

197

13 Enter the following settings for the second key:

> Value: **20%**
>
> Alpha: **100%**
>
> Parameter: **12%**
>
> Smoothing: **Linear**

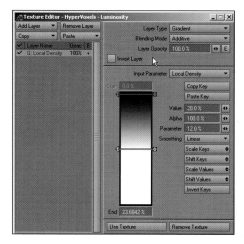

14 Create a third key and enter the following settings:

> Value: **500%**
>
> Alpha: **100%**
>
> Parameter: **23%**
>
> Smoothing: **Linear**

These various settings create a low luminosity in low–density areas and a high luminosity starting at 23% density and beyond. This means the core (the center) is brighter because it is more dense.

15 Click Use Texture to apply these settings.

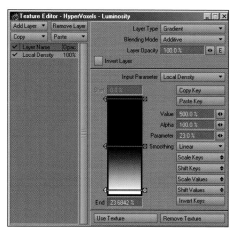

Finish off the glowing fire by adding a luminous gradient.

HYPERTEXTURE SETTINGS

The HyperTexture inside the HyperVoxels panel enables you to set the texture type for the Volume HyperVoxel. This is how you make the explosion billow.

1   Click over to the HyperTexture tab in the HyperVoxels panel and set the Texture type to Turbulence with the following settings:

> Frequencies: **0**
>
> Contrast: **0%**
>
> Small Power: **0.5%**
>
> Texture Amplitude: **125%**
>
> Texture Effect: **Billowing**
>
> Effect Speed: **65%**

Tip: Up to this point, you've only used one null object! To take this explosion further, you can add more null objects with varying HyperVoxels settings. Or take it one step further and use LightWave [6.5]'s integrated particle engine to create a fantastic explosion. Then apply HyperVoxels.

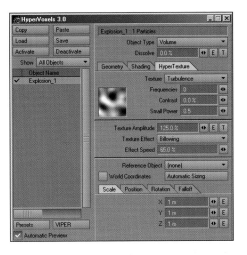

The HyperTexture settings for the explosion, with Turbulence used for a nice random look.

With the color, shading, and texture applied, the explosion looks pretty realistic.

EXPLOSION TIMING

At this point, your explosion is fiery, billowing, and overall pretty cool. But if
you happen to make a preview in the VIPER window (you might want to click
the Draft Mode button), you'll see that the explosion remains the same size
even though it's billowing. This is cool, but a real explosion would start small,
expand outward, and then dissipate—all while billowing. To create this effect,
you have a couple of options. One way is to size and stretch the null object
in Layout.

1   Click over to Layout. Make sure your scene is saved,
    and then select Size from the Actions tab.

2   Select the Explosion_1 object (the null object),
    activate the numeric values (**n**), and enter a value
    of **0, 0, 0**.

3   Create a keyframe at frame 0.

4   Go to frame 100 (**f**), and then press the **n** key
    again for numeric. Enter **8, 8, 8**, and then create a
    keyframe at frame 100.

    Sizing the null object to change from 0 to 8.0 over
    3.5 seconds will make the explosion grow in that
    time frame.

5   Go to frame 0 in Layout. Then press **F5** to open the
    last-used plug-in—in this case, HyperVoxels.

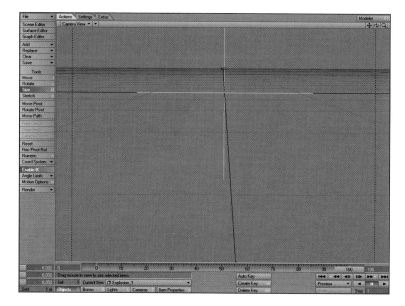

In Layout, size the null object
to change from 0 to 8.0 over
a span of 3.5 seconds.

6 Click the VIPER button to open the preview renderer.

The panel is black because you sized the null down to 0 at frame zero.

7 From the VIPER window, select Make Preview.

Your billowing, exploding fireball grows from small to large in 3.5 seconds. Within a second, the fireball fills the frame. The larger the fireball explosion becomes, the more engulfed you are in the animation. But because the null explosion object size goes from 0 to 8 in 100 frames, you have room to dissolve it out.

Tip: You might want to use Draft Mode to speed up the preview, or even better, you can switch to Sprite mode in the HyperVoxels panel.

8 Open the Graph Editor for Dissolve by clicking the E button for Dissolve in the HyperVoxels panel.

Note: When working in the Graph Editor, you can use the left and right arrows on your keyboard to move between selected keyframes. Note that if you have been adding or changing values in the input fields, you might need to press the Escape key first.

The explosion null is scaled to 0 at frame zero, and that value is reflected in the VIPER window, which shows a black screen.

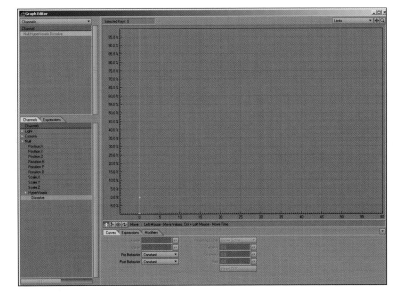

You can set a dissolve envelope for the explosion to make it fade off at a specific interval.

9 Create two keyframes—one at 25 and the other at 95. Set the Value at frame 25 to **0%** and the value at frame 95 to **100%**. This will completely dissolve the explosion from frame 25 to frame 100. Hold the Shift key and double-click in the curve window to select all keyframes. Set the Tension to **1**.

This helps adjust the curve slightly to make the transition smooth. This eases the dissolve in and out.

10 Make another preview in VIPER. The explosion continues to grow larger as it dissolves out.

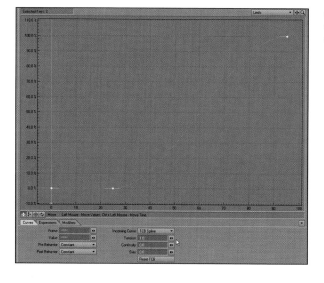

A Tension setting of 1 helps the dissolve envelope ease in and out of keyframes.

11 You can add more to the dissolve if you think it is too clean or too smooth. In the HyperVoxels panel, click the T button for Dissolve and set the following parameters:

Layer Type: **Procedural Texture**

Blending Mode: **Additive**

Layer Opacity: **100%**

Procedural Type: **Turbulence**

Texture Value: **95%**

Frequencies: **6**

Contrast: **0%**

Small Power: **0.5**

Scale: XYZ **500mm, 500mm, 500mm**

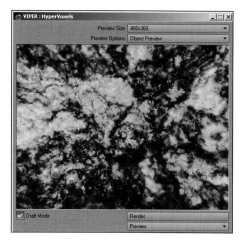

This enables you to set a Texture on the dissolve! Now your dissolve will have some randomness as well.

12 Click Use Texture, and then close the HyperVoxels panel.

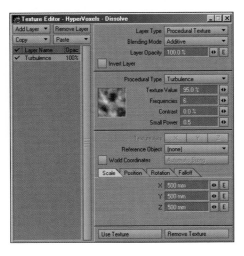

Add a turbulence texture to the dissolve envelope to help randomize the effect.

Tip: Additionally, you can add a TextureChannel to the dissolve envelope.

CAMERA SHAKE

The final stage in creating an explosion of this magnitude is to shake the camera a bit. This helps add to the feeling that the explosion is powerful. You'll apply a motion modifier for the camera. Although you could choose from many modifiers, the perfect one for an explosion is Jolt, from master programmer Bob Hood.

Note: Be sure to check out the awesome chapter on Lscript programming written by Bob Hood, in *Inside LightWave [6]*.

1 In Layout, select the Camera.

2 Open the Motion Options panel (**m**). From the Add Modifier drop-down list, add the LW_Jolt plug-in. Then double-click it to open its control panel.

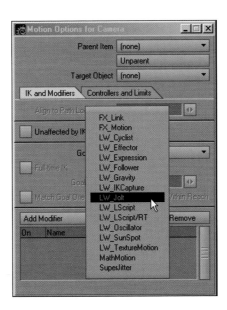

Add the LW_Jolt plug-in from the Add Modifier drop-down list.

3 Make sure the Jolt Keys listing reads 0, and then click the Create Key button.

The explosion begins right at frame zero, so that's where you want to "jolt" or shake up the camera. Once the keyframe has been created, the other commands become active.

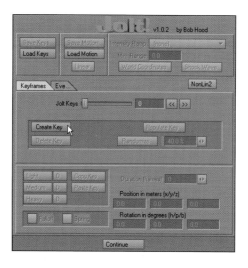

Create a keyframe at frame zero to begin jolting the camera around.

4 Click the Heavy setting in the bottom left corner of the Jolt panel and set the following parameters:

Duration: **55**

Position: XYZ **0.01, 0.05, 0.2**

Rotation: HPB **0.1, 0.2, 1.2**

Falloff: **On**

Spring: **Off**

This sets the initial values to work from.

5 Close the Jolt panel, close the Camera Motion Options panel, and save your scene. Click the Play button in Layout to see the camera with the Jolt motions.

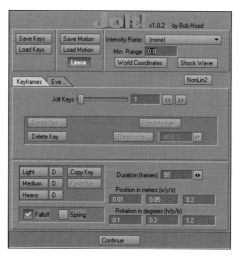

Set the Jolt parameters to make the camera jiggle and move, starting when the explosion begins and lasting for 55 frames.

From here, you can really go places. The effect described is the tip of the iceberg. One simple null object has been transformed into a killer explosion. Now imagine applying the HyperVoxels to more than just one null! You could animate particles in LightWave [6.5]'s particle engine and create a huge mushroom cloud explosion. Change the variables in HyperVoxels from Volume to Surface, make the settings more water like, and create a spray of water. The possibilities could go on and on, but instead of reading about it, go do it!

Note: If you switched HyperVoxels to Sprite mode for speedier previews earlier, be sure to switch back to Volume mode.

HOW IT WORKS

Using LightWave [6.5]'s powerful HyperVoxels 3.0, you can generate Volume-, Surface-, or Sprite-based objects on points. One simple null object in a scene is all you need to get going. LightWave's rich Texture Editor can be used for the color, luminosity, motion, and even dissolve, as you've seen here.

MODIFICATIONS

This effect shows just one null object set to an explosion. You used the Jolt plug-in to add a shaky camera effect. From here, you can manually keyframe the camera every 10 frames or so for additional motion. You'll see something like this in the final scene (15Explosion.lws) on the book's CD.

But you can go so much further with this. For example, use LightWave's integrated particles or Particle Storm to create smaller offshoot explosions that happen after the main explosion.

You can use more null objects for additional explosions, or to set up streaks of smoke and fire that shoot out from the main explosion. Add an additional null with almost identical parameters as the main explosion, but with an offset to get a fiery secondary motion. Honestly, the possibilities are endless—all it takes is more render time.

You can play with the color gradient and add some blue at 0% for additional detail. You might also try changing the speed of the explosion, making it grow more rapidly at first and then fade off. Finally, spend some time and make a library of different explosions for future projects!

OCEAN SURF

"No one can see their reflection in

running water. It is only in still water

that we can see."

—TAOIST PROVERB

ALL AT SEA OVER OCEANS

Seawater is a dynamic entity—a fluid, ever-changing medium. It literally reflects the world around it, while it flows with waves and ripples.

This tutorial will teach you how to make a realistic-looking seawater surface, and you'll learn about Motion Envelopes, and the SkyTracer and Oscillator plug-ins, as well as how to make and animate the necessary textures and objects.

Project 16

Ocean Surf

by Gary Whitley

GETTING STARTED

Before you start, make sure that you have the SkyTracer and Oscillator plug-ins installed from the LightWave directory on your hard drive (Programs/Plugins/Effects/SkyTracer.p and Programs/Plugins/Animate/ Oscillator.p), as they will be needed later.

Lighting this scene is straightforward, since there is only one light source—the sun. You will use a Distant Light to represent the sun, and Ambient Intensity to provide scattered fill, just like in the real world.

1 Load the scene **Seawater_basic.lws** from the CD.
This will load the basic setup and most of the objects
and settings required for the scene. We'll be building
the rest, and making other adjustments, as we go
along.

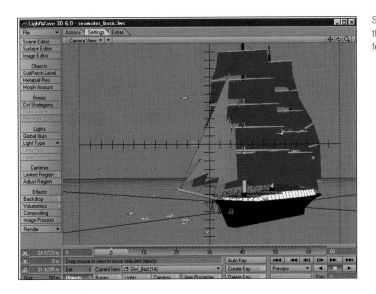

Seawater_basic.lws provides
the ship, some birds, and a
few other basics.

2 Set the Ambient Intensity level to **25%** in the Global
Illuminations panel (Settings/Global Illum). Ensure
that Radiosity and Caustics are turned off, to speed
up the preview renders.

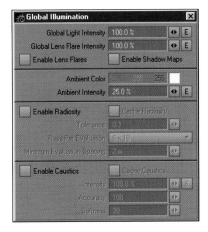

Set the Ambient Intensity to 25%.

3 To represent the sun, you'll use a Distant Light. Open the Light Properties panel (**l**, **p**) and set the following values for the default light:

> Light Color: RGB **255**, **241**, **215**
>
> Light Intensity: **100%**
>
> Shadow Type: **Ray Trace**
>
> Turn on Affect Diffuse, Affect Specular, and Affect OpenGL.

4 Position the light to**:**

> XYZ **−670mm**, **210mm**, **560mm**.

Select the light, press **t** (to select Move), then **n** (for Numeric), and enter the following coordinates in the Position settings**,** to put the light quite low in the sky, as it would be near to sunrise or sunset.

You will also need to orient the light to point toward the ship.

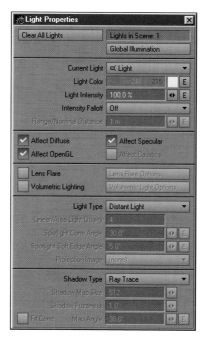

Use these settings for your main light while building the SkyTracer object.

Note: These settings will only be used temporarily, and will be changed after the SkyTracer model has been made in the next section. The pale orange light will give a more pleasing color to the sky, which you will be making using SkyTracer. After the sky object has been made, the light color will be changed back to white to complete the project.

5 With the light still selected, press **m** (for Motion Options) and select the GW_ship object to be the target object for the light. Press Enter twice to set the light into position.

Position the "sun" by typing in its X, Y, and Z coordinates.

A New Sky...

The way an ocean looks is really a reflection of the things around it—light and sky, weather, and the effects of the seasons. To make the seawater look realistic, it needs to reflect the sky; you'll use LightWave's SkyTracer plug-in to generate a sky object, ready-mapped with images, to put into the scene.

Note: The color of sky is influenced by the color of the distant light in the scene, which is why it was set to a pale orange color in the previous section. This should give us an early evening or early morning look. Other light colors could be substituted to give dull, rainy-looking skies, tropical noon, and so on.

Note: By experimenting with different colors and brightness levels for the distant light, coupled with SkyTracer's wide range of cloud type and cover options, it is possible to simulate different weather and lighting conditions—for example, a pale, grayish light coupled with a higher percentage of nimbus-type cloud cover can provide a dull, rainy-looking sky. Make the light redder and add ore haze for a sunset-type effect.

By making variations in the light color and strength, and the amount and type of cloud, haze, and other SkyTracer settings, a variety of different skies can be created for use as backdrops or render-warped objects.

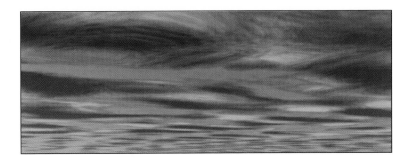

1 Open the Image Process panel (Settings/Image Process). Then open the Add Pixel Filter list and select SkyTracer.

2 Double-click the SkyTracer line below the Add Pixel Filter button to open the SkyTracer window.

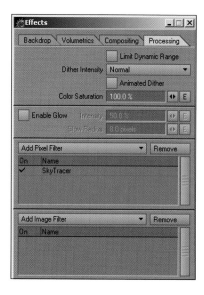

Open the Image Processing panel and add the SkyTracer pixel filter.

3 Click on the Render Warp Images button in the top-left of the SkyTracer window.

This option will make a LightWave scene, composed of a cubic object complete with ready-mapped SkyTracer images to make a seamless sky. It will provide a realistic surrounding and will also be reflected by the surface of the sea.

Note: There are other ways to provide a sky for such scenes, but consideration has to be made for both reflections and camera movement.

Although it is possible to use SkyTracer to render a sky background for each frame of the scene, it will not reflect off the water, as skies made this way cannot be seen by raytracing.

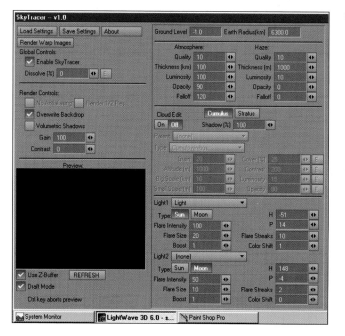

Click the Render Warp Images button.

Note: Another possibility is to cubic map a single SkyTracer image onto a cube, but there are then problems with how the "corners" render in the background.

It might also be possible to use a rectangular plane mapped with a SkyTracer (or other) image, but you should consider how the camera might move within the scene, as the edge of the sky may soon become inconveniently apparent.

4 Change the Base Name to Seawater and set the save directory to somewhere convenient on your hard drive. Click on the arrow-head to the right of the Base Name input box to set the save path.

5 Choose a format for the render output from the Image Type list.

JPG makes much smaller files, but the final output quality will not look as good as BMP, for instance. Note: You might need to add the BMP Input-Output plug-in before you can save BMP files.

6 Click OK and wait.

You should see a series of five images being drawn one after the other in the preview window. After the images have been rendered, an Info dialog box appears, to tell you that a new object and scene have been created.

7 Click OK, and exit the SkyTracer window.

A new object called LW_Sky.lwo will be created in your default Object directory.

8 Reverse Step 1 and remove the SkyTracer pixel filter item from the Image Process panel.

9 Load the new sky object (called **LW_Sky.lwo**) using Add from the Actions toolbar.

Note: Before completing Step 5, you may find it useful to set your Content Directory to where you want the files to be saved. Use the **o** key to access the General Options panel and make the necessary adjustments.

To set the save directory, click the right-pointing arrow button to the right of the Base Name box.

Note: For best results, TIF or TGA RGB files should be used. From there, you can import the RGB sequence back into LightWave for additional compositing and effects. Remember—garbage in, garbage out!

10 Resize the new object to be a 1 km cube, centered at XYZ **0, 0, 0**.

You can do this by first selecting Size (**h**) and then Numeric (**n**) and entering **5000** for X, Y, and Z values.

The previously rendered images will be mapped onto the cube to simulate a naturalistic sky background.

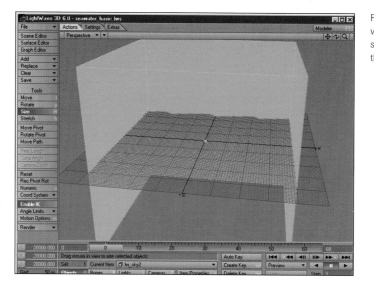

Resize the LW_Sky object to make it very large compared to the ship. The ship is the tiny speck in the center of the layout window.

11 Return to the Light Properties panel (**l, p**) and set the light color to white (RGB **255, 255, 255**) and the light intensity to **150%**.

Although the previously set light settings made for good skies, they were little dark for our overall purpose.

Note: Although I hate to say this, I have found using SkyTracer to be a baffling experience at times, principally because it never quite seems to do what you ask it when it comes to sorting out the names or locations for the images it makes, so you may still have to tell Layout where the SkyTracer image files are located when you load the LW_Sky object.

I have found SkyTracer to be the cause of a lot of frustration, but it is worth using for the stunning results it produces. Persevere until you get the right results.

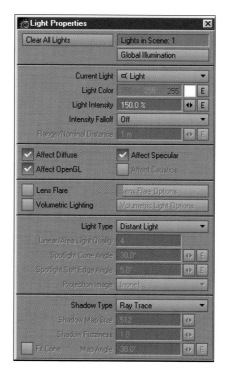

Reset the lighting to white and 150% intensity, now that the SkyTracer images have been made.

AND A NEW SEA

You might have noticed that there's no sea below the ship at the moment. That's because you'll need to make it first. If you're in a rush or feeling lazy, the object already exists (SeaPlane.lwo) and you can simply add it to the scene. Or you can create it yourself using the following steps, in which you will make a new multi-polygon object to represent the surface of the ocean, and apply textures and motions to it to make it look realistic.

1   Open Modeler and make a large, subdivided plane by selecting Box (**x**), opening the numeric panel (**n**), choosing Active from the Actions list button. Setting the following:

Low: XYZ **-500m, 0m, -500m**

High: XYZ **500m, 0m, 500m**

Segments: XYZ **70, 1, 70**

2   Click on the Polygons button at the bottom of the Layout window (Ctrl+h) to select polygon selection mode, and then triple the polygons in the object (press **t** or select the Polygon tab, then Triple). Then flip all the resulting polygons so that their normals are all pointing upward if they are currently upside-down (press **f** or select the Polygon/Flip).

These steps will make the object appear to be solid and will give it enough polygons (around 20000) to let it flex smoothly when a displacement map is applied.

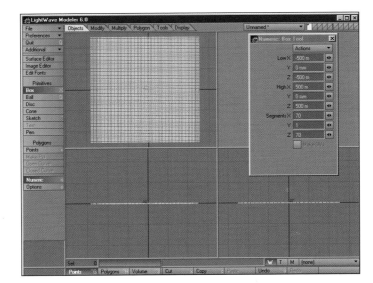

Make a segmented, tripled plane to represent the ocean surface.

3   Click on the Polygon button at the bottom of the
    Modeler screen (or use Ctrl+h) and then press **q** to
    call up the Change Surface panel. Name the surface
    of the new seawater object as "Seawater." Uncheck
    the Make Default button and click OK, or just press
    an Enter key.

4   Save the new object as SeaPlane.lwo, and return to
    Layout and Add the SeaPlane object to the scene.

    It should fit exactly into the X and Z dimensions of
    the sky object.

    Although the environment surrounding the seawater
    contributes heavily to the way the sea looks, we also
    need to give the object a variety of different surfaces
    and textures in order to achieve a good seawater
    appearance and animation.

5   Open the Surface Editor panel, select the Seawater
    texture, and make the following basic settings:

    Color: RGB   **0**, **128**, **192**

    Luminosity: **20%**

    Diffuse: **39.5%**

    Specularity: **68%**

    Glossiness: **40%**

    Reflection: **65%**

    Transparency: **0%**

    Translucency: **0%**

    Bump: **130%**

    Next, we'll add some variation to the basic surface
    color of the ocean object.

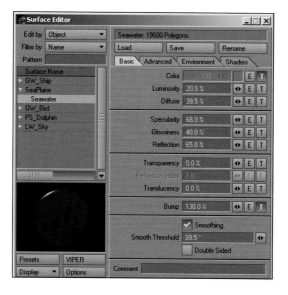

Set up the basic texture properties.

6 Click the T button to the right of the Color setting in the Surface Editor to open the Texture Editor for Color. Change the Layer Type to Procedural Texture and the Procedural Type to Turbulence. Then make the following additional settings:

Texture Color: RGB **0, 210, 210**

Frequencies: **3**

Contrast: **0%**

Small Power: **2.0**

Select the Scale tab and set X, Y, and Z to **5m** each. Click Use Texture to close the Texture Editor window.

These Scale settings make the texture larger and more in keeping with the scale of our objects. Leave the other settings as they are.

The basic sea surface (left) and Using Turbulence for the color texture (right).

Adding a Crumple-textured bump map raises up the surface into a wave-like texture (left).
The final surface (right), with the map still there but subtle.

Use a displacement map to add real motion to the sea surface, though this will only really be fully visible when the scene is animated.

7 Click Use Texture to return to the Surface Editor window.

In order to give that characteristic choppiness to moving water, adding a Crumple surface as a Bump Map will break up the object's planar look to give the impression of wavelets and less-smooth surfaces.

8 Click the T button to the far right of the Bump box, opening the Texture Editor for the Bump texture. Change the Layer Type to Procedural, and then the Procedural Type to Crumple. Now make the following additional settings:

Texture Value: **100%**

Frequencies: **4**

Small Power: **0.75**

9 Select the Scale tab and set X, Y, and Z to **20m** each.

Note: If you want more detail, try making this **5m** instead.

Click Use Texture to close the edit window and then close the Surface Editor panel.

As well as the "minor" surface break-ups caused by the Bump Map, there are also the larger swells to be considered—the ones that run across the oceans, breaking as waves when they finally hit the shore. By Displacement Mapping the seawater object with a ripple texture, all its polygons will behave as if they were actually affected by those swells, rising and falling as the peaks and troughs pass.

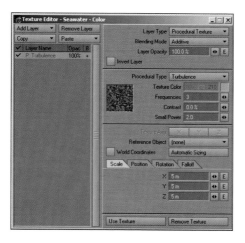

Modify the color setting to a turbulent procedural texture to give the seawater surface a more realistic look.

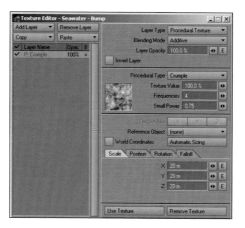

Use Bump Mapping to break up the smooth ocean surface.

10 Select the SeaPlane object, and then Item Properties (**p**). Click the Deformations tab, and then the Displacement Map button. Set the following parameters:

Layer Type: **Procedural**

Procedural Type: **Ripples2**

Texture Value: **1.0**

Waves Sources: **3**

Wavelength: **0.5**

Wave Speed: **0.01**

Scale: XYZ   **20m**, **500m**, **30m**

Position: (see the Animation Envelopes section following)

Click Use Texture to close the edit window and then close the Object Properties panel.

11 To see the effect of the displacement map on the ocean object, create an animated wireframe preview. Set the Maximum Render Level to Wireframe (use the Camera View button to access Maximum Render Level).

12 Click the Preview button and then Make Preview. This will make an animated wireframe sequence. When it has completed rendering, the Preview Playback Controls panel will pop up and you can play the preview back to see the result. If you have been successful, you'll see the waves moving.

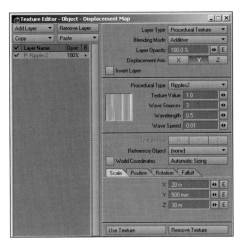

Use Displacement Mapping to add swells to the ocean.

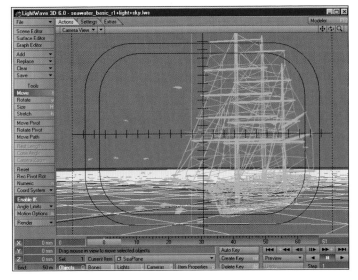

Make an animated wireframe preview to check the motion of the displacement-mapped waves.

219

ANIMATION ENVELOPES

To bring the seawater to life during an animation, you need to animate the surface textures you've just made. You'll need to adjust the motion envelopes of the various surfaces to make this happen. For simplicity, you'll make all the motion envelopes the same—with one exception for the displacement map.

You'll be making changes to the motion envelopes for Color Texture, Bump Texture, and Displacement Mapping by adding keyframes to hold the new motion distance values. Then, when the sequence is animated, the textures will vary throughout the animation by morphing from keyframe to keyframe.

1 Open the Surface Editor, select the Seawater surface, and then select the T button to the right of the Color selection.

The Texture Editor window opens for the surface color. You have already set most of the properties for the Color Texture and Bump Texture in the previous section. Now you need to set the motion envelopes to make the textures move.

2 Click the Position tab and then click on any of the E buttons to the right of the X, Y, and Z data fields, to access the Graph Editor.

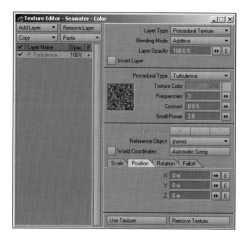

Use the Texture Editor to set the motion envelopes.

3   In the Graphic Editor, click on the add key button (because we will be adding keyframes to set the new values). Then use the left mouse button and click on the graph at frame 60, setting up the values given below for the X, Y, and Z position channels.

X: = **1m** at Frame **60**

Y: = **0m** at Frame **60**

Z: = **1m** at Frame **60**

Exit the Graph Editor and then click Use Texture to close the edit window.

Note: To change channels, select from the list at the left of the panel. You may find it easier to set the value roughly with the mouse, then correct it by typing into the Value box located below the graph area.

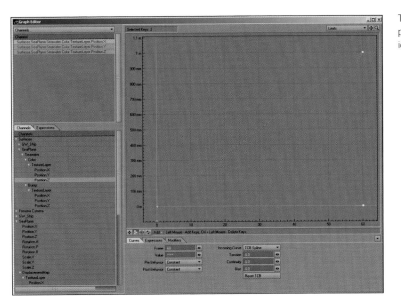

The Color and Bump texture position envelopes share identical values.

4   Repeat Steps 1–3 for the Bump Texture.

The route to the Displacement Map settings is slightly different, and is accessed through the Object/Properties route described earlier, when we set the original displacement settings.

5   Open the Displacement Map panel. Click the Position tab and then click on any of the E buttons to the right of the X, Y, and Z data fields to access the Graph Editor:

X: Frame = **60**   Value = **1m**

Y: Frame = **60**   Value = **–100m**

Z: Frame = **60**   Value = **1m**

Exit the Graph Editor and then click Use Texture to close the edit window.

Now try a test render to see how the project is progressing.

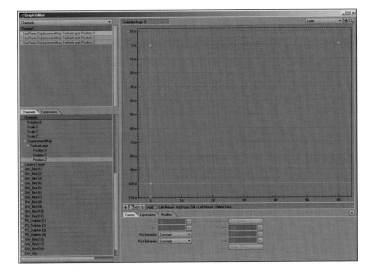

Use the position envelope settings to animate the displacement map.

6 Go to the Camera Properties panel (**c**, **p**), choose a resolution and multiplier to preview at, decide whether to use anti-aliasing settings, and to what extent.

The larger the image, and the higher the anti-aliasing settings, the longer the preview will take to render. If you're not sure, try the following settings:

Resolution: **VGA (640 x 480)**

Resolution Multiplier: **50%**

Anti-Aliasing: **Low**

7 Close the Camera Properties panel and press **F9** for a preview render.

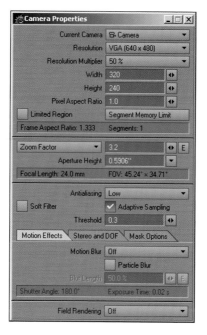

Choose how you would like to see your preview rendered and press F9 to see the results.

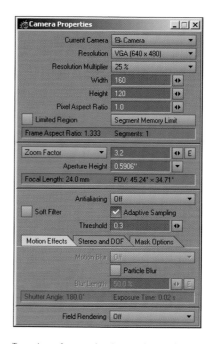

To make a faster animation preview, reduce the image size and turn off anti-aliasing.

You might also like to make an animation preview to check that the motion of the ocean is to your liking. For speed, adjust the Camera Properties to a lower resolution, and maybe even select a Limited Region to render. Then select Settings/Render/Output Files tab and set the animation file rendering output to AVI (you may need to install the relevant input/output plug-in from the plug-ins directory to do this), make sure that Auto Frame Advance and Save Animation are both enabled, and render all 60 frames of the project.

Note: Refraction is what happens when light passes through the surface of a transparent object and is deflected or bent by the change of density at the air/object interface.

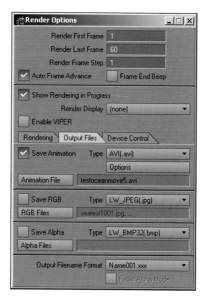

Set up the animation output name, file type, and other parameters and make a test animation.

Note: Since this is water, why isn't it transparent in this tutorial? Well, in this instance it doesn't need to be—you never get into a situation where you need to see through it, so you can save rendering time by turning off transparency.

But, if you need to, you can increase the transparency levels in the Surface Editor (this depends on the characteristics of the water you're modeling) and also apply Ray Trace Refraction to the final render (using Settings/Render/Rendering tab), if you need the realism —and have the rendering power.

ADDING BIRDS AND MAMMALS

To make your renders even more credible, why not add some real life to the scene? The oceans support a rich variety of life—so put some into your pictures. The bird object took only a few minutes to build (after a little bit of research) and the dolphin was recycled from a friend. They don't need to be elaborate models, just to be lifelike enough for our brains to be convinced that they are seeing the real thing.

Note: None of the birds nor animals in this scene have motion paths, so don't be surprised that they don't move when you make test animations. You could always set up their motions yourself.

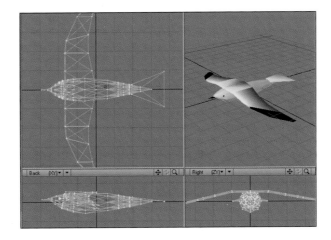

Objects don't have to be elaborately modeled to work successfully in a scene.

ROCKING THE BOAT

Since the water is moving, then the boat will move too. Although the boat isn't set to move in a forward direction in this project (you can make it do that if you want), it will still roll, pitch, and yaw in the waves. LightWave has a plug-in that can help us achieve this motion quite easily—Oscillator.p.

Make the following settings and then render a wireframe preview animation to test the results.

1   Select the ship object and then open the Motion
    Options panel (**m**).

2   Click on the Add Modifier button and select
    LW_Oscillator. A new Oscillator item is added
    to the list below the button.

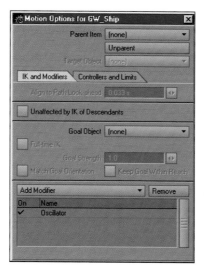

Select the ship object and open
the Motion Options panel.

3   Double-click the new Oscillator item. The
    Harmonic Oscillator Animation Control
    panel opens.

    Set the Start Frame to **1** and the End Frame to **60**.

    Make the following settings for Y Position, Heading
    Angle, and Bank Angle, and leave all the other
    settings at their defaults:

    Y Position
    Cycle Time(s): **1**
    Wave Size: **100 mm**

    Heading Angle
    Cycle Time(s): **1**
    Wave Size: **200 mm**

    Bank Angle
    Cycle Time(s): **1**
    Wave Size: **200 mm**

    When you've made the settings, exit the Harmonic
    Oscillator panel with the Continue button, and then
    close the Motion Optons panel.

Oscillator provides a simple way of imparting
wobble and travel to an object.

Note: Each item needs to be Enabled (by using the
Enable button in the panel) before its settings can
be changed.

ADDING REFLECTION

There is just one more thing to do, and that is to make the hull of the boat moderately reflective, to catch the light moving off the water.

There's something not quite right here.

1 Open the Surface Editor, find the SmoothHull surface, and set Reflection to **30%**.

Now the boat will look more lifelike, and we don't have to increase our rendering time by using a procedural method such as Caustics.

But by making the ship's hull moderately reflective, it appears that light reflected from the water is playing upon its surface.

FINAL RENDER SETTINGS

Now that we've set the scene, we need to decide how we wish to render it.

Feel free to choose your own settings, or use these instead:

1 Open the Camera Properties panel (**c, p**) and make the following adjustments:

Resolution: **SVGA (800x600)**

Resolution Multiplier: **100%**

Antialiasing: **Enhanced Medium**

Adaptive Sampling: **On**

Threshold: **0.3**

Leave all the other settings as they are.

2 Open the Render Options panel (Render/Render Options) and set it up as follows:

Auto Frame Advance: **Off**

Show Rendering In Progress: **On**

Render Mode: **Realistic**

Ray Trace Shadows: **On**

Ray Trace Reflections: **On**

Leave all the other settings as they are.

You can also choose to use LightWaves's Radiosity feature to make your scene look even more realistic, though your rendering times will be increased as a result.

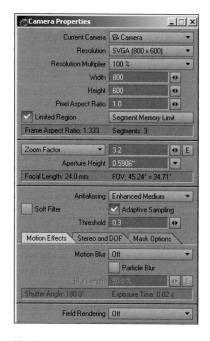

Use these suggested camera settings.

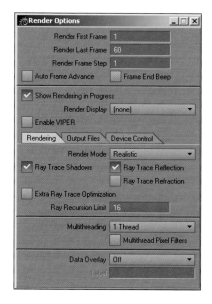

Set these render options to generate the final image.

Note: Radiosity is the way that light is scattered and diffused around a scene as it is reflected from one surface to another. Producing this effect requires a lot of extra calculation by LightWave, and so the rendering times will be somewhat longer when radiosity options are enabled.

3 To activate Radiosity, go to the Global Illum panel, enable Radiosity using the check box, and set the following parameters:

Enable Radiosity: **On**

Cache Radiosity: **On**

Tolerance: **0.3**

Rays Per Evaluation: **6×18**

Minimum Evaluation Spacing: **2m**

The completed scene is on the CD and is called Seawater_final.lws.

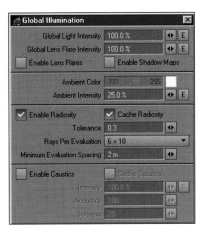

For increased realism (and longer rendering times), turn on Radiosity.

If you've completed the project successfully, it should look something like this (left) or like this (right) if you choose not to use radiosity settings.

Use the FastFresnel shader plug-in to add impact to the specularity and reflectiveness of the seawater surface, though at the expense of increased rendering times.

227

MODIFICATIONS

With a little thought and experimentation, you should be able to adapt some of the core elements of this tutorial for use in other situations or environments.

For instance, make some changes to the SkyTracer settings and lighting color and strength and you could make an alien sky (however you might imagine that to be) for your interplanetary space-drama, or something more mundane, such as a wet day in the tropics.

Adapt the way that the seawater surface is textured and displacement mapped by using other procedural textures and different colors, and you could be on the way to making a hot lava pool undulating menacingly in its crater, or even flowing down the side of a volcano.

Increase the size of the displacement mapping effect to change the height of the waves (but remember that the smoothness of this effect depends to a large extent on the number of polygons comprising the object to which the displacement is applied; more polygons = more smoothly rendered, less-faceted, surfaces) and make a calmer or stormier sea.

Change the settings once more again and you might have the appearance of vast fields of wheat blowing in the wind, or low-lying fog billowing along a valley bottom.

As usual, experimentation is the key, and the more you play, the more you'll learn how to adapt the myriad features of LightWave to your style of 3D animation.

UNDER THE
OCEAN

"Water, water, everywhere,

And all the boards did shrink.

Water, water everywhere,

Nor any drop to drink."

–SAMUEL TAYLOR COLERIDGE

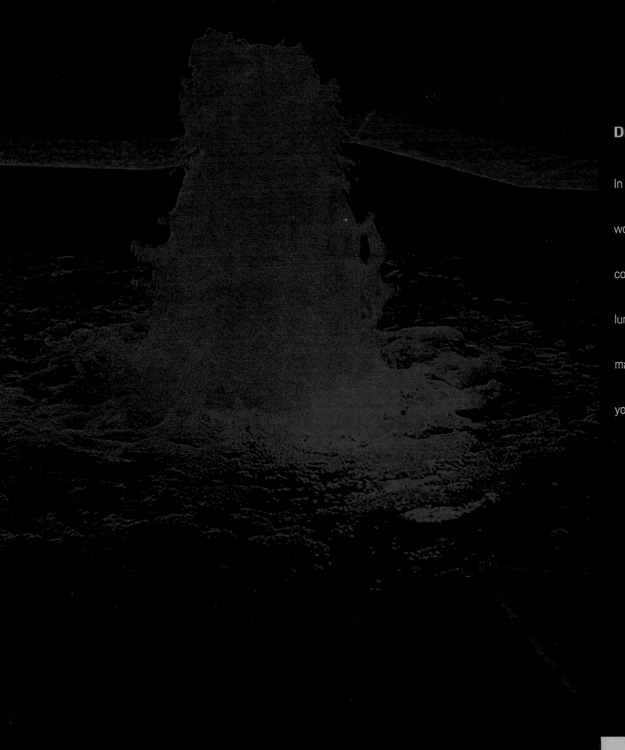

DESIGNING A DEEP-SEA ENVIRONMENT

In stark contrast to the airy, sun-lit surface

world, the depths of the oceans are dark,

cold places where the only light comes from

luminescent animals and the artificial lights of

man and his machines. This project will show

you how to model such an environment.

Project 17

Under the Ocean

by Gary Whitley

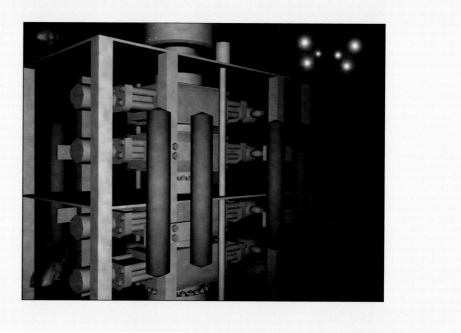

GETTING STARTED

By the time you complete this project, you'll have used a range of LightWave 6 tools, including lens flares, fog, particle objects, parenting and targeting objects, and gradient backdrops.

You will need to have the prims.p plug-in installed for this project. You'll find prims.p in the Programs/Plugins/Model directory of the LightWave install on your hard drive.

To get started, load the scene **underwater_basic.lws** from the CD. This loads most of the scene's objects into place, but not the main lighting or other effects, which will be used to produce the characteristics of an underwater environment. The completed scene is also on the CD and is called underwater_final.lws.

After the scene is loaded, you'll make adjustments to lighting, fog, lens flares, and glow settings to impart a suitably "deep" look to our images. You'll also add an extra object to simulate particles.

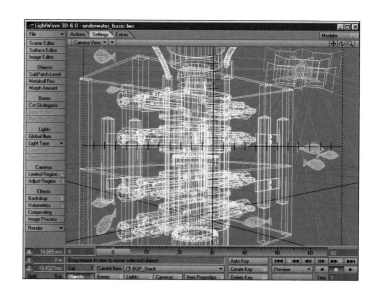

This unlit wireframe view shows where items are located, but not how they might appear when rendered.

LIGHTING THE SCENE

Because sunlight never reaches the ocean depths, you'll have to provide your own lights if you want to see anything more than a few self-illuminating fish. It will take several steps to achieve this:

1 Open the Global Illuminations panel (Settings/ Global Illum) and set the Ambient Intensity level to **0%** since there is no ambient light present at the depth being illustrated. Ensure that Enable Radiosity and Enable Caustics are turned off at this stage, which will help speed up the preview renders during the project.

   For the main lighting you'll use two spotlights—one on each side of the camera and parented to it. This will simulate the POV (Point Of View) of an ROV (Remote Operated Vehicle). If you parent the lights to the camera, they will always remain with the camera if it is moved.

2 Add a new spotlight (Actions/Add/Add Light/Add Spotlight) and call it Spot_1.

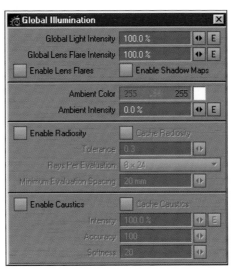

Turn off Ambient Intensity since no light from the surface reaches the deep ocean floor.

3 Open the Light Properties panel (**l** then **p**) and make the following settings for the new spotlight:

> Light Color: RGB **255, 255, 225**
> Light Intensity: **100%**
> Intensity Falloff: **Linear**
> Range/Nominal Distance: **20 m**
> Spotlight Cone Angle: **30°**
> Spotlight Soft Edge Angle: **10°**
> Shadow Type: **Ray Trace**

Turn on Affect Diffuse, Affect Specular, and Affect OpenGL.

To make this light move when the camera moves (as it would in the real world because the lights are attached to the camera unit), you need to make the camera the parent object for the light.

4 Make sure the new light (Spot_1) is selected, and then select Motion Options (Settings/Motion Options, or press the **m** key). Now set Spot_1's Parent Item to Camera.

5 Position the new spotlight just to the left of and at the same height as the camera, and then make sure it is pointing in the same direction as the camera. Press the Enter key twice to make the new light position permanent.

Now you need to make another identical spotlight to go on the other side of the camera.

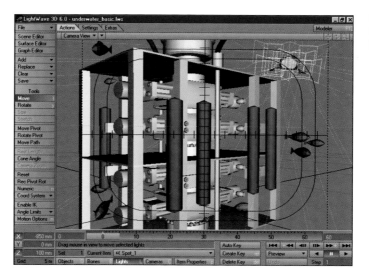

Change the view to Shaded Solid so you can see how the lights affect the scene.

Use these settings for your first spotlight.

6 Clone one copy of Spot_1 (use Actions/Add/ Clone Current Item), rename it Spot_2 (use Actions/Replace/Rename Current Item to do this), and drag this new light to the right-hand side of the camera, parallel with the first spotlight. Press Enter twice to set this light's new position.

Now that the camera is the parent of the two spotlights, whenever it is moved or rotated, the lights will mirror any moves the camera makes.

7 Move the camera back to its original position in the scene, making the following adjustments to the camera's position:

> X: **−5.96 m**
>
> Y: **2.14 m**
>
> Z: **−7.15 m**

Did you notice that the camera is still pointing at the sub-sea object? That's because there is already a target object in position for the camera to aim at. This isn't strictly necessary because you could simply rotate the camera to any view you desire; however, setting a camera target helps when the camera is being animated and ensures that the camera stays locked on to the desired view.

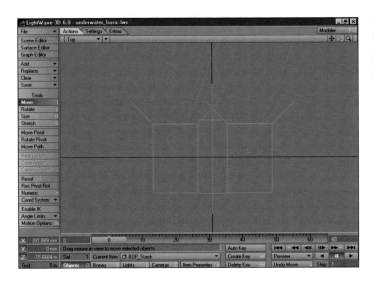

The two spotlights are positioned on either side of the camera. (Note that the other items in the scene have been hidden for the sake of clarity).

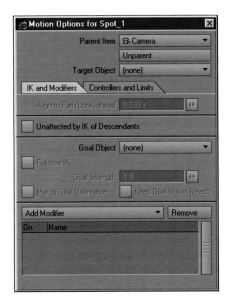

Set the camera to be the parent of the new spotlight.

Note: The camera can be set to target any object, but it is more efficient to add a new null object (Actions/Add/Add Object/Add Null) and name it "Camera Target." The current Camera Target is already positioned at these settings:

> X: **−0.54 m**
>
> Y: **2.05 m**
>
> Z: **−0.22 m**

To make the camera track the target object, you would use the Motion Options (Settings/Motion Options, or press the **m** key) and set the new Camera Target object as the Target Object for the camera. This ensures that the camera will always point where it is told.

8 So that you can get an idea how the new lights you've added will affect the scene, change the preview mode to Shaded Solid.

9 Open the View drop-down menu and set the Maximum Render Level to Shaded Solid. Try a test render to see how the project is progressing.

10 Go to the Camera Properties panel (**c** then **p**) and choose a resolution and multiplier to preview at. Decide whether to use anti-aliasing settings, and if so, to what extent. If you can't decide, use the following settings:

> Resolution: **VGA (640 × 480)**
>
> Resolution Multiplier: **50%**
>
> Anti-Aliasing: **Low**

11 Close the Camera Properties panel and press **F9** for a preview render.

Note: The larger the image is and the higher the anti-aliasing settings are, the longer it will take to render your preview.

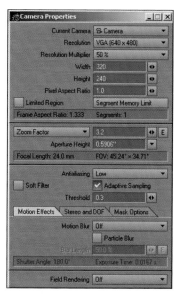

Try these settings for your preview renderings.

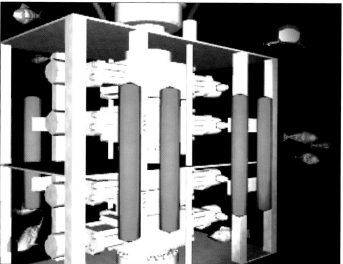

The image before background colors are added.

BACKGROUND COLORS

Although the deep oceans are dark, some subtle color variation will be visible in the background when you light the scene. To produce this, you need to set up a gradient backdrop, as described in the following steps:

1 Select the Backdrop tab in the Effects dialog box (Settings/Effects) or press Ctrl+b.

2 Enable Gradient Backdrop and set the colors as outlined here:

> Zenith Color: RGB **0, 40, 80**
>
> Sky Color: RGB **0, 0, 72**
>
> Ground Color: RGB **0, 0, 72**
>
> Nadir Color: RGB **0, 0, 40**

Leave the other settings as they are. The scene will have a dark blue background that becomes blacker with depth.

Make the background a gradient of very dark blues.

3 Try another test rendering (**F9**) at this stage, and you'll see the subtle difference the new background gradient makes.

A colored gradient backdrop adds more realism, but the image still looks rather harshly lit.

FOG-BOUND

Although it may seem a little strange, one of the keys to creating underwater scenes is to apply a fog effect, which reduces visibility with distance from the camera and blurs objects into the background. To achieve this you need to use the Volumetric Effects options. Follow these steps:

1 Select Volumetrics (Settings/Volumetrics).

> **Tip:** You can also set up your keyboard shortcuts so that you can use the **v** key to go to the Volumetrics tab.

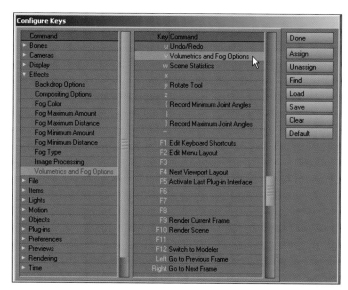

You can create a keyboard shortcut for the Volumetric settings by pressing F1 and setting the assignment.

2 Make the following adjustments:

> Fog Type: **Linear**
>
> Min Distance: **1m**
>
> Max Distance: **18m**
>
> Min Amount: **0%**
>
> Max Amount: **70%**
>
> Use Backdrop Color: **On**

These settings apply fogging to any object between 1 and 18 meters of the camera. Beyond this, objects will disappear into the fog.

Enable Use Backdrop Color to ensures that any fog-affected objects will fade into the background and look more realistic.

You will be able to monitor how the changes you make to the fog settings actually affect the scene, since the fog effect will be applied to the Shaded Solid preview and any lights and objects it contains.

Set up fog volumetrics to give a more realistic underwater look.

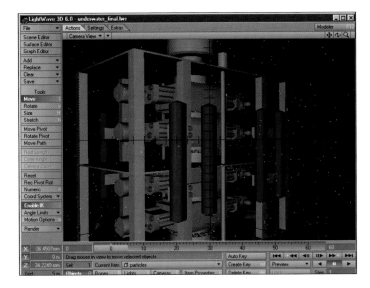

The effects of the fog will be evident when the Shaded Solid preview is selected.

3   Once again, check to see how you're doing with a test render (**F9**).

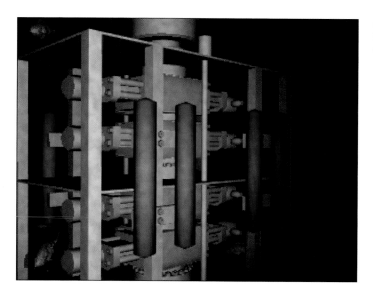

By adding fog, we add depth, and the objects begin to fade away with distance.

LENS FLARES

A crucial part of creating deep ocean scenes is to add lens flares to any light sources that are visible to the camera. In this case, you need to add lens flares to the lights attached to the ROV in the top right-hand corner of the scene. Incidentally, you may have noticed that the ROV object is rather crudely modeled; this is deliberate, as it will never get closer to the camera than in this shot. And because it will be mostly obscured by fog, it can be a simple model, which will save both memory and rendering time.

Six lights, in three pairs, are already attached to the ROV object. Two are slightly more yellow than the other four white lamps. To provide some variation, each light has its own lens flare settings, as described here:

ROV_yellow 1 and 2   Flare Intensity: 100   Flare Dissolve: 0

ROV_white 1 and 2   Flare Intensity: 60   Flare Dissolve: 0

ROV_white 3 and 4   Flare Intensity: 100   Flare Dissolve: 0

The following settings have also been applied to each ROV light's lens flare:

Fade Off Screen: On

Fade In Fog: On

Fade Behind Objects: On

Central Glow: On

All the other options remain unchanged.

240

In case you are wondering how to make these various lens flare settings, here's a basic run-down of the procedures required:

1 Open the Global Illumination panel (Settings/Global Illum) and select Enable Lens Flares.

2 Select a light from the ROV object (for this exercise choose the ROV_yellow(2) light).

Open the properties for this light (press **p**) and make sure Lens Flare is enabled.

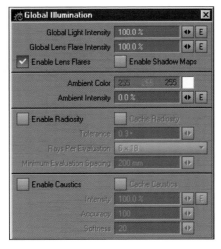

For lens flares to have any effect, they must be globally enabled.

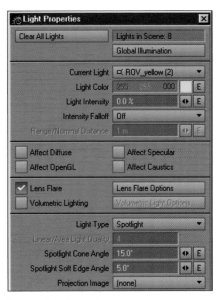

To make lens flares affect an individual light, Lens Flares must be enabled for that particular light.

3 Click the Lens Flare Options button to the right of the Lens Flare check box. A new panel will open. Enable the following options: Fade Off Screen, Fade In Fog, Fade Behind Objects, and Central Glow.

Tip: When setting lens flares for multiple lights, you can open the Lens Flare Options panel and select the light to be flared from the main interface. You could also cycle through your lights using the up and down cursor keys and then make the changes you require.

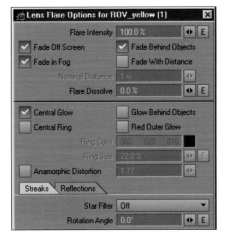

These Lens Flare settings give a more acceptably blurred look to distant fog-affected lights.

For reference, each ROV light also has the following lighting characteristics:

Light Intensity: **0%**

Lens Flare: **On**

Light Type: **Spotlight**

Spotlight Cone Angle: **15°**

Spotlight Soft Edge Angle: **5°**

Shadow Type: **Ray Trace**

Tip: If you set the light intensity to **0%**, all you see will be pure lens flare, which is fine in this case because the ROV will never be seen closer to the camera and doesn't need to cast light from that distance.

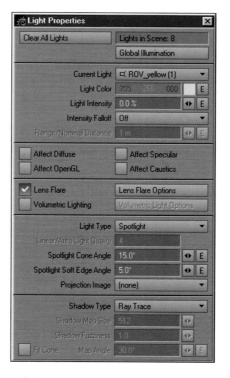

The ROV lights are all variations on a simple spotlight.

4   Check to see how the lens flares look by making another test render.

Lens flares from the ROV vehicle lights impart even more depth and realism.

PARTICLE TRICKS

If you study photographs and video images taken in the deep oceans, you will often see many illuminated specks. These could be minute animals, or they could be minerals or other particles suspended in the water, like dust in sunlit air. These particles are lit by the POV ROV's spotlights and show up as a multitude of tiny bright spots in the image. To simulate them, you need to generate an object composed of many individual points that can be rendered as part of the scene.

1   Open Modeler and set the extent of the top view to be approximately **40m** across.

2   Start the LWSprayPoint tool (Objects/Additional/LWSprayPoint).

3   First use the numeric options (**n**) to pop up the numeric panel for LWSprayPoint, and then click on the Actions button and select Activate from the resulting drop-down menu. Then set Rate to **10** and Radius to **5m**.

4   Use the new circular object to spray points around the Top or other views by clicking on the crosshair in the center of the circle and dragging it around with the mouse. Aim to make a roughly spherical object with approximately 1000–1200 points in it, which will fill the viewing area.

    This creates the water-borne particles.

5   To find out how many points you have made, select Tools/Statistics (**w**).

6   Rename (**q**) the object's surface **Particles** and save it as **myparticles.lwo**.

Note: For this task, you'll use the LWSprayPoint tool (which is one of the plug-in tools you loaded at the start of the project as part of prims.p). The great thing about LWSprayPoint is that it makes an entire object from single-point polygons, which provide the specks for the scene in Layout.

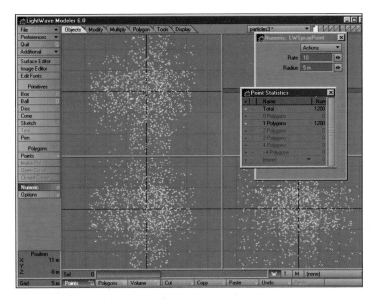

Use Modeler's LWSprayPoint tool to create an object made of single point polygons, which will give the effect of particles.

7 Return to Layout and load your new object (or just use the particles.lwo object from the CD), placing it centrally in the scene.

To improve the appearance of the particles, you need to make them glow, as well as blend them into the image.

8 Open the Surface Editor, set the Edit By option to Scene, and select the surface named Particles.

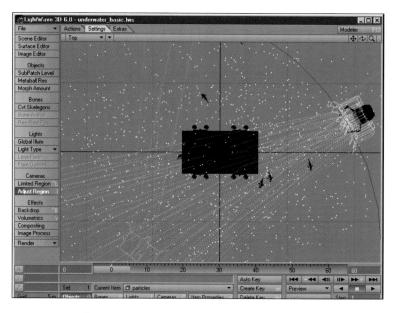

Load the particle object into the center of the scene.

9 Set Luminosity to **100%**. The other settings remain unchanged.

10 Select the Advanced tab in the Surface Editor and set Glow Intensity to **100%**.

11 Open the Image Process dialog box (Settings/Image Process) and set the following parameters:

Enable Glow: **On**

Intensity: **20%**

Glow Radius: **3 pixels**

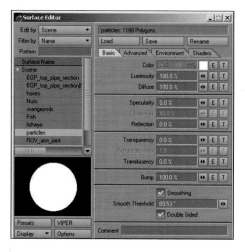

Luminosity helps the particles to shine brightly when illuminated.

Make Enable Glow active in the Image Process panel.

12 Do one more test render to make sure everything has turned out okay. Don't worry that you can't see many of the particles you just made; this is a subtle effect to add realism and depth to the image.

The particles will add subtlety and realism to the image.

FINAL RENDER SETTINGS

Now that you've set the scene, you need to decide how you want to render it. Feel free to choose your own settings, or you can follow these steps:

1 Open the Camera Properties box (**c** then **p**) and make the following adjustments:

> Resolution: **VGA (640 × 480)**
>
> Resolution Multiplier: **50%**
>
> Antialiasing: **Enhanced Medium**
>
> Adaptive Sampling: **On**
>
> Threshold: **0.3**

Leave all the other settings as they are.

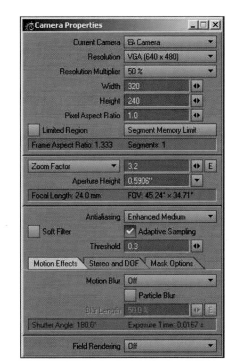

Use these camera settings.

2 Open the Render Options panel (Render/Render Options) and set it up as outlined here:

Auto Frame Advance: **Off**

Show Rendering in Progress: **On**

Render Mode: **Realistic**

Ray Trace Shadows: **On**

Ray Trace Reflection: **On**

Leave all the other settings as they are.

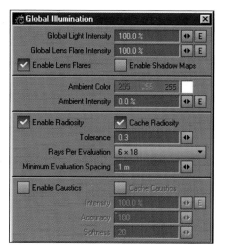

Set these render options to generate the final image.

You can also choose to use LightWave [6.5]'s new Radiosity feature to make your scene as realistic as possible, although your rendering times will be noticeably increased if you do. To activate Radiosity, open the Global Illumination panel, mark the Enable Radiosity check box, and set the following parameters:

Cache Radiosity: **On** (optional)

Tolerance: **0.3**

Rays Per Evaluation: **6 × 18**

Minimum Evaluation Spacing: **1m**

For added realism, use Radiosity.

So there you are; the project is complete. For comparison, there is also an image rendered using radiosity. Notice that in the figure with radiosity, the lighting is more lifelike, and light is scattered more realistically throughout the image (though at the cost of a greatly increased rendering time).

If you've completed the project successfully, you should see something like this.

MODIFICATIONS

Although this project was about the creation of a deep underwater scene, you could easily modify it to represent shallow water, a foggy land environment, or even one in space. By changing the lighting colors, backdrop color, fog levels, and lens flare settings for the various lights, you could simulate all kinds of other environments. Oh, and don't forget to put the fish away somewhere safe if you're heading off into space! They tend to blow themselves apart otherwise…

You'll be able to modify some of the techniques you've used here for other situations. Lens flares are useful for all sorts of effects, such as car headlights in fog, airplanes flying at night, or alien ships landing. But remember that lens flares are just that—artifacts caused by the lens elements of an optical device such as a film or video camera.

You could use a particle object coupled with some downward movement and object jitter (using the SuperJitter plug-in effect) to make rain or a sort of snow-falling effect.

And you could dirty up the surfaces of the sub-sea or other objects using procedural and/or image-mapped textures to make rusty-looking wrecks or rocky surfaces, for example. Thicker fog will make for murkier waters, and different kinds of wildlife can represent different ocean environments.

SPACE LIGHTING

"It's human nature to stretch, to go, to

see, to understand. Exploration is not

a choice, really; it's an imperative."

—MICHAEL COLLINS,
GEMINI AND APOLLO ASTRONAUT

PORTRAYING LIGHT ACCURATELY

This project takes you through the process

of lighting a space scene. "But there's no light

in space," you say. Ah, there's the rub! So

how's it done?

Project 18

Space Lighting

by Phil South

 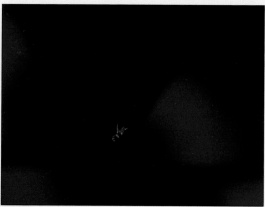

GETTING STARTED

Few TV dramas set in space portray the light accurately. In space, there is no shadow detail because all the light comes from one direction. There is only one light source—the local star (the sun)—and unless the light source is right behind the space vehicle, at least half of it will be in deep shadow, rendering it invisible against the blackness of space.

In this project, you'll use a nebula to pick out the black shadow areas of a space ship, and you'll use fill lighting to add detail to the dark areas of the ship.

Basically, you are cheating a little—well, actually a lot. As I've said repeatedly, there is no light in space, or at least not very much. Realistic space lighting is a strong light coming from one direction and no detail at all in the shadows. The blackness of space and the blackness of the shadows are the same color, so they merge together. While you're in space, this isn't a problem because you are inside the ship (hopefully).

In a 3D environment, it means you can't make out the shape of anything. If you're doodling about at home, none of this matters, but if you're doing visual effects for film or TV, you need to see what's going on in the frame.

We define the outline of the ship using a luminous nebula. Nebulae are clouds of gas in space. Although they are not very numerous in space, we will conveniently site a nebula near our scene to pick out the shape of our ship. The one in this example is a little bit bright and highly colored. A more subtle coloration would probably be easier on the eye.

Finally, you imitate the "light" coming from the nebula by shining a couple of lights up under the ship so that as you move around it, the shadow areas are filled with soft colored lights. Although it's not realistic, it is artistic and is a flexible enough technique to be applied to any space scene.

MODELING THE NEBULA

To prepare for this project, start Modeler, and load randomstars.lwo from the CD. This is a big ball of single point polygons that simulates stars when the camera is inside.

You need to make a big ball that is bigger than the stars and can enclose them completely. You do this so the stars are inside the nebula object and appear to shine through the luminous gas of the nebula. Follow these steps:

1   Go to a new layer and put the stars in the background layer.

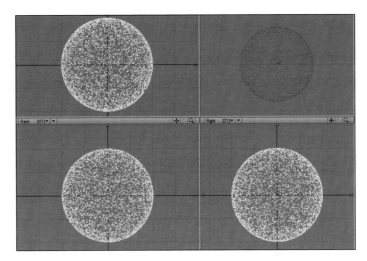

The randomstars.lwo model is a sphere made of stars.

2   Draw a ball with the Ball button in the Objects menu, and then make it a little larger than the stars. Flip the polygons inward (because you'll be looking at it from within, of course) and name the surface **nebula**.

3   Save the object as **nebula.lwo**.

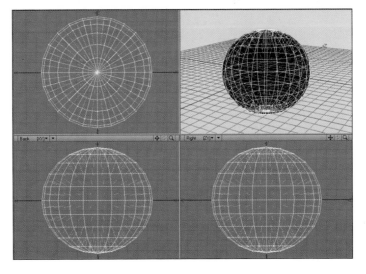

Make the nebula object a ball that's larger than the stars object, with its surface normals pointing inward.

NURBing the Ship

The space ship will be a simple SubPatched object. SubPatch objects allow you to make smooth shapes from coarser, more blocky polygons by using the polys as a control cage for a spline-based object. This is described in more detail in the LightWave manual.

1 From the book's CD-ROM, load **spaceship_blocky.lwo**, which contains the ship, created in simple block form.

2 Press the Tab key to activate SubPatch mode. Then "cast it in stone" by pressing Ctrl+d to freeze the SubPatch curve and create polygons. Save the object.

Note: You can also save the object without freezing the curves. LightWave [6.5] allows you to load SubPatched objects directly in Layout.

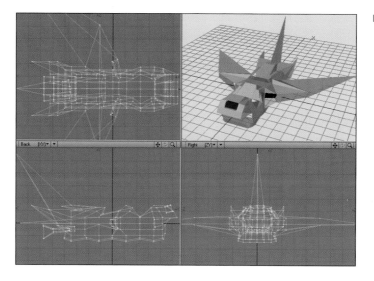

Load the file spaceship_blocky.lwo.

3 In Layout, texture the Airintake and Default Surfaces using the following settings:

> Airintake
>
> Color: RGB **0, 0, 0**
>
> Diffuse: **100%**
>
> Default (the hull of the ship)
>
> Color: RGB **122, 122, 122**
>
> Diffuse: **100%**
>
> Specularity: **100%**
>
> Glossiness: **10%**
>
> Smoothing: **On**

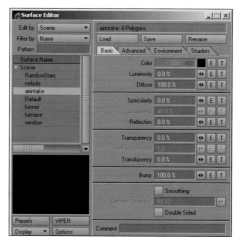

It pays to make your own textures from scratch, but this will do for a demonstration.

You need to set the diffuse value of the surface. To do so, you will use a diffuse map that varies the diffuse setting across the surface depending on the density of the bitmap at that point.

4 Click the T button next to Diffuse to open the Texture Editor, and then enter the following settings:

> Layer Type: **Image Map**
>
> Blending Mode: **Additive**
>
> Layer Opacity: **50%**
>
> Projection: **Cubic**
>
> Image: **genericpanels.tga** (located on the LightWave CD in the Images/Space directory)
>
> Scale: XYZ **1m, 1m, 1m**

Apply the same textures for Specularity.

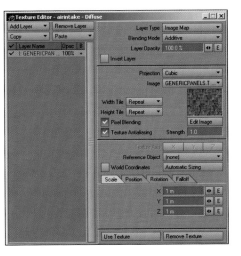

Apply a cubic diffuse texture map for the airintake surface.

5 Texture the following surfaces in either Modeler or Layout, as you did for the airintake surface:

> Funnel (exhaust):
>
> Diffuse: **45%**
>
> Specularity: **85%**
>
> Glossiness: **10%**
>
> Smoothing: **On**
>
> Furnace:
>
> Luminosity: **200%**
>
> Window:
>
> Diffuse: **100%**
>
> Specularity: **25%**
>
> Glossiness: **10%**
>
> Reflection: **12%**

Note: These settings an vary, depending on the look you're after. Feel free to experiment with different variations. For example, try using the same specularity settings for a Glossiness texture.

6 To add a little frost to the glass, make a specular texture map. For the Window, click the T button next to Specularity and enter the following settings:

Layer Type: **Procedural Texture**

Blending Mode: **Additive**

Layer Opacity: **100%**

Procedural Type: **Fractal Noise**

Texture Value: **80%**

Frequencies: **3**

Contrast: **1.0**

Small Power: **0.5**

Scale: XYZ **5mm, 5mm, 5mm**

Now you can put it all together. You have a star field, a spaceship at which to point the camera, and a nebula to pick out shadow details.

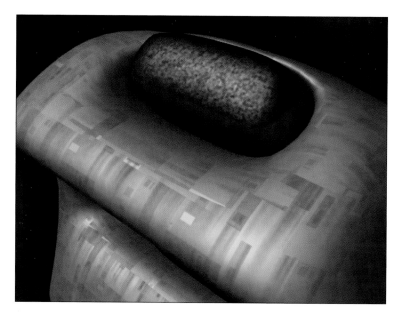

Add a fractal noise map to the specular channel to frost up the window.

MAKE A SCENE

Start building the scene and putting some lights in it. The following steps tell you how:

1 In Layout, load all the objects—first the ship, and then the nebula and random stars.

Whoa, what happened there? Everything vanished. Well, actually, no, it didn't—it just got smaller.

This is a common problem with adding objects to Layout. By default, LightWave moves the camera a safe distance from any newly loaded object to give the viewer a clear shot of the object. If you load an object that is big, like the stars object (which is 10,000 kilometers in diameter), anything small that was already loaded, like the ship, will shrink so small it doesn't even occupy a single pixel on the screen.

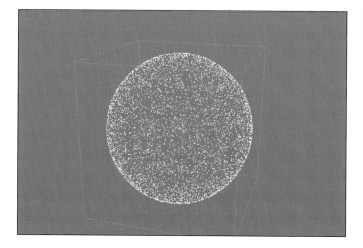

Everything will vanish if you forget to keyframe the camera.

The trick to adding objects to a scene and not losing your way like this is to add a keyframe to the camera and the object when you load the small objects. If the keyframe is added, the camera won't move when new objects are loaded. You may also need to adjust the grid size to alter the clipping distance (the closest point the camera will see). To do so, you simply adjust the grid size using the **[** and **]** keys.

Now that you have everything loaded, you can add the nebula texture.

When the grid size is adjusted, everything is placed normally in the frame.

2 Load the image map **nebula.jpg** with either the Image Editor or the Load Image tool in the Surface Editor.

Nebula.jpg is a simple airbrushed purple and blue cloud. It was created in PhotoShop, and although this one is very simple, you could spend a whole lot of time on it, tweaking it this way and that. The key thing to remember is to use a lot of detail, but don't smother it—know when to stop.

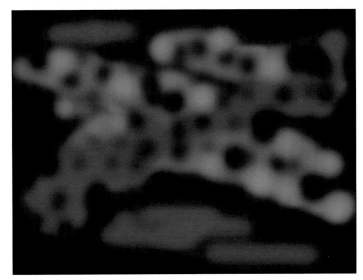

The nebula is loaded into Layout.

3 Map the nebula texture into the nebula object. To do this, open the Surface Editor and choose the Nebula surface. Click the T button next to Surface Color and select the Texture Image of "nebula.jpg." Then, click the T button next to Color and enter the following settings.

Layer Type: **Image Map**

Blending Mode: **Additive**

Layer Opacity: **100%**

Projection: **Spherical**

Width Wrap Amount: **2**

Height Wrap Amount: **1**

Image: **Nebula_map.jpg**

Texture Antialiasing: **Off**

Scale: XYZ **220km, 220km, 220km** (Yes, that's 220 kilometers; these objects are big.)

4 Go to the Object Properties for the nebula, click the Rendering tab, and turn off all the shadow options. Click off all three: Self Shadow, Cast Shadow, and Receive Shadow.

You must turn off all shadowing options for the nebula because if you don't, the shadow cast by the nebula object will cut out all the rays from the main light into the scene.

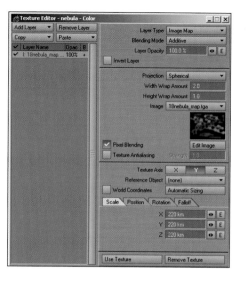

Apply a spherical color texture map with the 18nebula_map.tga image.

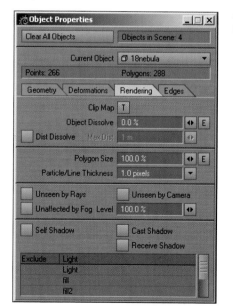

Shut down all the shadows to let the light through.

CHEATING WITH LIGHT

You have to cheat because good cinematography needs light, and in space, there is none. There is no reflected light unless you are really close to a planet, and even then it's a pretty muted fill light. The shadow detail is missing because there is no light other than the sun, so only the stars that it blots out define the outline of the ship. This would be realistic, but it lacks any kind of mood. Therefore, you need to define the black shadowed areas of the ship with something. Before you get to that, however, you'll start with the lighting. Follow these steps:

1   In the Lights panel, change the name of the default Light to **Key Light**. Ramp up its Intensity to **150–200%**. There is no atmosphere to dilute the rays out here in space. Finally, give it a very slight yellow tint, something like RGB **255**, **255**, **207**. Set the Light Type to **Distant**.

2   Make a new distant light by clicking Add Light. Name the new light **Nebula Light**. Drop its intensity to **25–35%** and set its Shadow Type to Off. Make the color blue, like RBG **0**, **0**, **255**. Then, use Clone Current Item to make another light, but make this one more purple, like RGB **255**, **0**, **255**.

3   Go to Global Illumination and turn Ambient Intensity down to **0%**.

This is the most important part of lighting a space scene because there is no light other than the sun. (Well, in this case there is, but this isn't reality—it's fantasy.)

4   To use the fill lights to emulate the light coming from the nebula, you have to angle them correctly. Have the main or Key light stay where it is by default (pointing down and slightly into the scene).

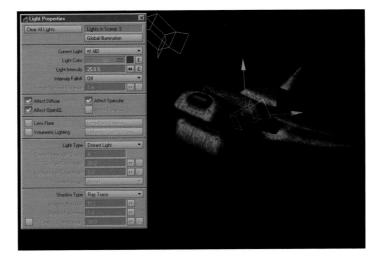

Cheat the blue light coming from the nebula by using extra lights in the scene.

5 Rotate the first blue fill light so it points up at the shadow areas of the ship.

Unless you have an expensive OpenGL card, you will have to guess on this and do some test renders. Looking through the light using the Light View is a good idea.

Now you have a space ship, a nebula, and stars that shine through like little diamonds. You may want to ramp up the color of the stars so they're closer to white; the default value is a little gray.

Use the fill lights to fill in all those shadows.

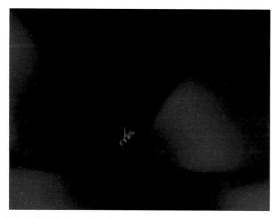

The finished shot takes the camera down toward the ship.

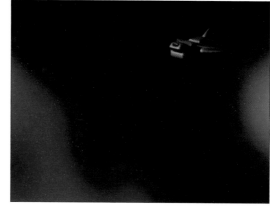

MODIFICATIONS

There are many ways you can reapply these ideas:

■ You could replace the nebula with a planet if you are getting tired of nebula or if the effect is getting stale.

■ You could make your ship pass in front of the sun and use a lens flare to pick out the edges.

■ Use other larger spaceships in the shot to pass behind or even (by using Radiosity or more cheating lights) to cast subtle light on the ship as they pass.

■ You could have the ship shine lights on itself, like the USS Enterprise and certain airline aircraft do. Having headlights and lights shining onto the body of the aircraft makes for better visibility and decreases the likelihood of collisions—and it looks pretty cool, too. Try it out.

SMOKE PLUMES

"Shall we play a game?"

—JOSHUA,
FROM THE MOVIE *WARGAMES*

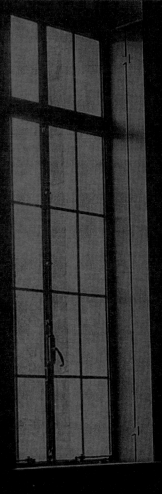

USING DEFORMED POLYGONS FOR SMOKE EFFECTS

There are many ways to create smoke effects in LightWave, but most require that you relinquish a lot of render time. It's sometimes easier to fall back on a more traditional effect using deformed polygons, which cuts render time and provides you with a usable effect, especially if you're going for a more stylized look. Project 11, "Building a Campfire," can be modified to create procedural smoke, so this chapter will show you how to create smoke with polygons.

Project 19

Smoke Plumes

by Phil South

GETTING STARTED

There are many new ways to make smoke plumes—like columns of smoke that trail up into the sky—using technologies like Particle Storm and HyperVoxels, all of which involve some kind of processing. Processing time can be expensive and time consuming. But what if you could create effective and convincing smoke plumes that save both time and money? Smoke plumes can be done with simple shapes using no particles and merely employing a displacement map and surface attributes to create a smoke-like effect.

What you are going to do in this project is modify the Hummer.lws scene that comes with LightWave to produce a scene depicting a smoking Hummer tire on a landscape.

MODELING THE TUBE

First you have to make a segmented tube. That will be your plume of smoke, and it must be segmented so it will bend when you deform it.

1   In Modeler, use the Disc tool to make a tube
    4 meters in the Y-axis with a 350mm radius.

2   Give the tube 40 segments in the Y-axis and 32 sides.

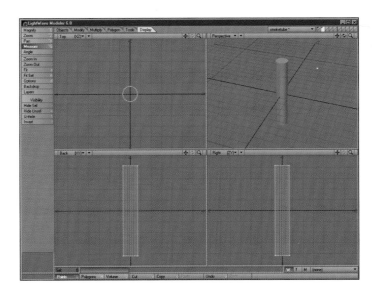

The basic smoke tube is a tall, thin cylinder made with the Disc tool.

3   Taper the tube using Taper 1 by a factor of about
    36% so the top is only 250mm (use the Measure tool
    to verify this). Name the surface "smoke" and save
    the object.

This is a very simple shape, but its complexity comes from what happens to it in LightWave Layout. Load Layout and move on to the next stage.

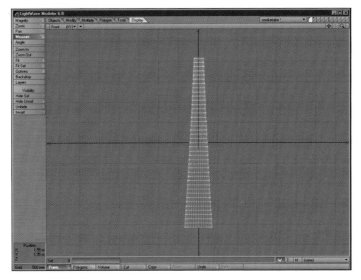

Taper the top of the tube so it is narrow at one end.

MODIFYING THE HUMMER SCENE

What you are going to do is take a picture of a heavily armored Hummer and make it look like the Hummer has met with a horrific accident—say all its missiles exploded at once before launch, and all that's left is this one smoking tire. Tragic, but highly amusing. The lighting isn't quite right, so you'll move the sun into position as well.

1 Load the **Hummer.lws** scene from the LightWave/Scenes/Vehicles directory, which was installed when you installed LightWave 3D.

2 Delete all objects associated with the Hummer itself, except for one tire. Delete all the parented nulls, everything except the one tire.

> **Note:** Remember, you can select more than one item at a time in LightWave [6.5]. In the Scene Editor, hold the Ctrl key to make multiple selections, and delete.

3 Delete the camera move keyframes, position the camera at XYZ −4.2259, 1.9, 5.8801, and then rotate it to XYZ −214.30, 4.50, 0.20.

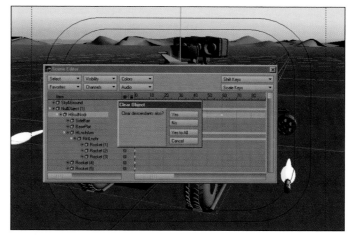

If you delete the HbodNodr object, you can delete all the child objects at once.

4 Rotate the main light, The Sun, around to the following settings:

Light Rotate = HPB **88.60, 62.40, 0**

This gives the scene the appearance of being a little later in the day. Adjust the colors of the lights, too.

5 Make the light called The Sun a white color, using RGB **255, 255, 255**.

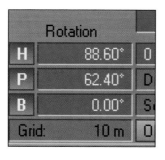

It is much more precise if you use the numeric option to type in the figures when rotating objects.

6   Make the Fill Light kind of pinkish: RGB **241**, **207**, **180**.

7   Take the remaining tire and put it on the landscape in front of the camera at XYZ –281.151mm, 0, –2.2497mm. Then rotate it to XYZ –0.40, 5, –93.30.

8   Position the smoke tube above the tire. Load the smoke tube object and place it above the tire at –350.633mm, 2.2m, –2.3365mm.

9   Before you close and save the scene, set the maximum number of frames to **120** in the Scene Editor.

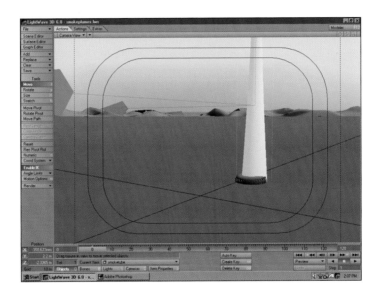

The finished scene, before surfacing the tube.

SURFACING THE SMOKE

Now for the interesting part. So far, it's all been very simple; the complexity comes from the surfacing. A part of the surface is actually a deformation of the polygons using a displacement map.

Displacement Mapping, unlike other types of surface mapping, actually distorts and moves around the polygons of an object. That's why you had to give the original tube so many segments. If an object is displacement mapped and doesn't have enough polygons, either it will try to bend and won't, or it will distort and break down the polygon edges and cause rendering errors.

1 Choose the tube object and bring up the Displacement Map Texture Editor. You can find the Displacement Map panel under the Deformations tab, within the Object Properties panel.

2 Change Layer Type to Procedural Texture, set the Procedural Type to Fractal Noise (if it isn't already), and change the Scale to XYZ **200mm**, **4.15m**, **200mm**.

When you close the panels and look at the Layout view, you will see that the smoke tube now wiggles a little up and down its length, making it look a little more smoke-like.

The tube is good, but it's not quite right. With the default settings and the changes you made, it's now a wiggly tube. But the effect is not really turbulent enough.

3 Open the Displacement Map settings for the tube object, and enter the following settings:

Texture Value: **0.6**

Frequencies: **9**

Contrast: **0.3**

Small Power: **0.6**

Making the displacement more extreme makes the tube a lot more turbulent, but those settings skate a thin line between making it busy and making it broken-looking.

You now need to do something about the color and transparency of the smoke tube. At the moment, it looks like matte plastic or rock, and as you may know, smoke is a little more transparent than that.

Wiggling the tube polygons with the displacement map imitates the movement of a column of smoke.

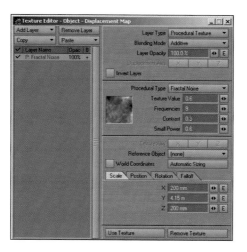

Alter the settings to a more extreme level for more turbulent smoke.

4   Make the basic color of the tube white (RGB **255, 255, 255**).

5   Click the T button at the side of Texture Color and make the following changes:

   Layer Type = **Procedural Texture**

   Procedural Type = **Fractal Noise**

   Texture Color = RGB   **202, 202, 202**

   Frequencies = **3**

   Contrast = **2.0**

   Small Power = **0.5**

6   Click the Scale tab at the bottom of the panel and set the scale of the texture to XYZ **300mm, 1m, 300mm**. Click Use Texture.

   This creates a light gray color that, because of the fractal noise nature of the texture, is weaker and stronger up and down the tube.

7   Back at the main Surface Editor, enter the following settings:

   Luminosity = **75%**

   Diffuse = **25%**

   Transparency = **65%**

   Smoothing = **On**

8   Click the T button next to Transparency, and set the following parameters:

   Layer Type = **Procedural Texture**

   Procedural Type = **Fractal Noise**

   Texture Value = **80%**

   Frequencies = **3**

   Contrast = **3.0**

   Small Power = **0.5**

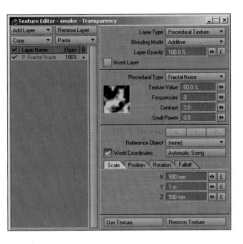

Add a fractal noise texture to the color channel to color the tube unevenly.

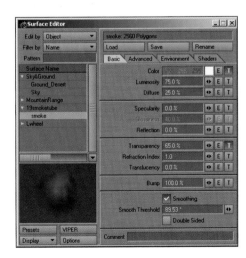

267

9 Click the Scale tab at the bottom of the panel and set the scale of the texture to XYZ **500mm**, **1m**, **500mm**. Then click Use Texture.

The color is nearly right, but you'll have to add another procedural color texture to the color channel to add a slightly sooty-black look to the smoke. I don't know if you've ever set fire to a tire (I won't tell if you don't), but they burn with pretty blackish smoke.

10 Go back and click the T button next to Color. Click Add Layer/Procedural. On the new layer, add the following settings:

> Layer Type = **Procedural Texture**
>
> Procedural Type = **Fractal Noise**
>
> Texture Color = RGB **41, 41, 41**
>
> Frequencies = **3**
>
> Contrast = **2.0**
>
> Small Power = **0.5**

11 Click the Scale tab at the bottom of the panel and set the scale of the texture to XYZ **300mm**, **1m**, **300mm**. Then click Use Texture.

The preceding steps added to the complexity of the texture, added "holes" in the smoke, and created colors that also have holes.

12 Click the Shaders tab and choose Add Shader/Edge_Transparency. Double-click on the shader and set it to Edge Transparency = Transparent. Then close the Surface Editor.

Now you have some pretty convincing smoke pouring off the tire. However, if you animate the scene and show it as a video…. Although the smoke looks cool, it's just standing there. You need to animate the smoke if you want it to look good.

268

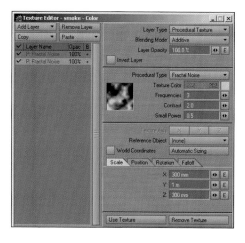

Now your tube is transparent and colored with fractal noise to give a smoke-like appearance.

Add a black fractal noise channel, and already it looks more smoky.

ANIMATING THE SMOKE

You create the animation of the smoke by moving the textures up the column while keeping the column still. As long as you put no keyframes in for the smoke tube, the column will stay put. But you have to actually move the displacement map and the color and transparency textures upward to get the effect you're looking for. Back to the Texture Editor:

1   Click the T button next to Color and click the Position tab. This presents three more sliders and E buttons.

The E stands for envelope. You're going to make an envelope to move up the texture during the shot. Through trial and error, I determined that the perfect distance for the texture to rise during this shot is 3 meters. Nice and slow.

2   Click the E button next to the Y-axis to enter the Graph Editor. Click the Add Keyframe button and click around the 120 mark on the graph to make a keyframe at 120. You probably won't get it exactly right, so just click the graph and then adjust the figures in the Frame field by hand. Click the Value field and type **3m**. Then close the panel.

3   Click the other layer and do that again. (This texture color has two layers—dark and light, remember?) Click the E button next to the Y-axis and make a keyframe at frame 120. Click the Value field, and this time type **6m**. Then close the panel. You could cut and paste the channel and modify the height in the Y-axis.

One layer moves up 3 meters during the shot, and the other moves up 6 meters. The colors not only move up, they shift past one another during the shot.

If the colors of the texture are moving up, it's a perfect shot, right? No. You need to do the same thing to the displacement map, which also has to

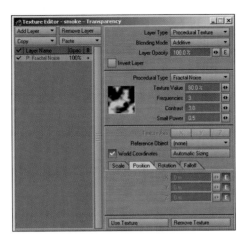

Make an envelope that moves the texture through the polygons.

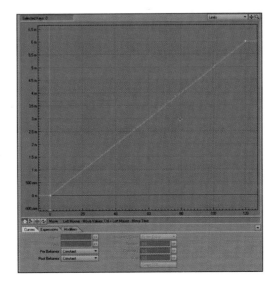

Use the Position motion graph to move the texture up the tube during the shot.

move up if you want the smoke to move as if it's being diverted by air currents, like the kind of rising air you get in the desert.

The colors move up 3 meters and 6 meters. If you move up the displacement map by this amount, it will follow the colors and look a bit odd. Instead, offset it a bit at 5 meters.

4   Click on the Objects button and click Item Properties. Then click the T button next to Displacement Map to open the Texture Editor.

5   Click the E button for the Graph Editor next to the Y-axis and make a key frame at frame 120. Click the Value field and type **5m**. Then close the panel. (You could also cut and paste as before.)

You're almost there, but there is still one more element left: the Transparency channel.

6   Open the Surface Editor and click the T button next to Transparency to open the Texture Editor.

7   Click the E button next to the Y-axis to enter the Graph Editor, and make a keyframe at frame 120. Click the Value field, and this time type **4m**. Close the panel. (Or paste the channel again and alter the figure as before.)

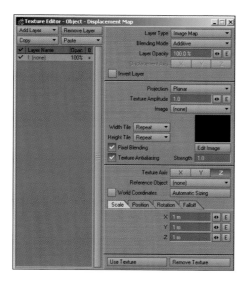

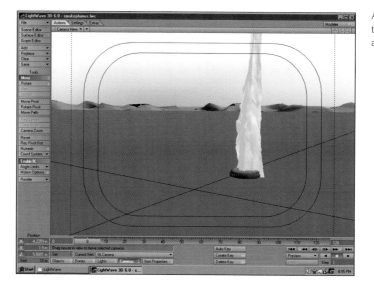

After you add the motion in the texture, the smoke rises as it should.

Now you have all the textures, colors, displacement, and transparency moving upward slowly and gently at 3, 4, 5, and 6 meters through the duration of the 120-frame shot.

HOW IT WORKS

Obviously, the displacement map makes the tube weave back and forth like smoke or water. Moving the displacement map upward during the shot makes the ripples move as though they are being blown gently from beneath, like rising air coming off the hot desert floor. The colors move in a similar way but at a different speed, so the interaction of all the moving texture elements makes the sum effect more complex than the parts that make it up.

MODIFICATIONS

The principles that make up this effect are simple and yet quite powerful. You can use the same techniques to make curtains of water, water pouring from a jug, cloth tubes like sleeves on a washing line blowing in a breeze, and many other things.

A good source of displacements for this kind of animation is, of course, the Motion Designer plug-in that comes with LightWave [6.5]. You can set up the basic circumstances of the animation and then let Motion Designer take care of the math. Once the animation is calculated, you simply apply it to the displacement channel of the object using the MD_Plug plug-in, and it renders without having to calculate the movement again.

Motion Designer could also make you some wicked deformations for your smoke. It might look like cloth, though, so take some time to learn how Motion Designer works its magic.

Also, you could try adding a little HyperVoxels fire to the effect. Just use a little ripple of fire around the edges, though, because this is more realistic; you don't want it to detract from your smoke.

271

FAKING
RADIOSITY

"Je ne veux pas que mes

ongles soient arrachés."

—FROM THE BOOK *FRENCH FOR CATS*
BY HENRY BEARD

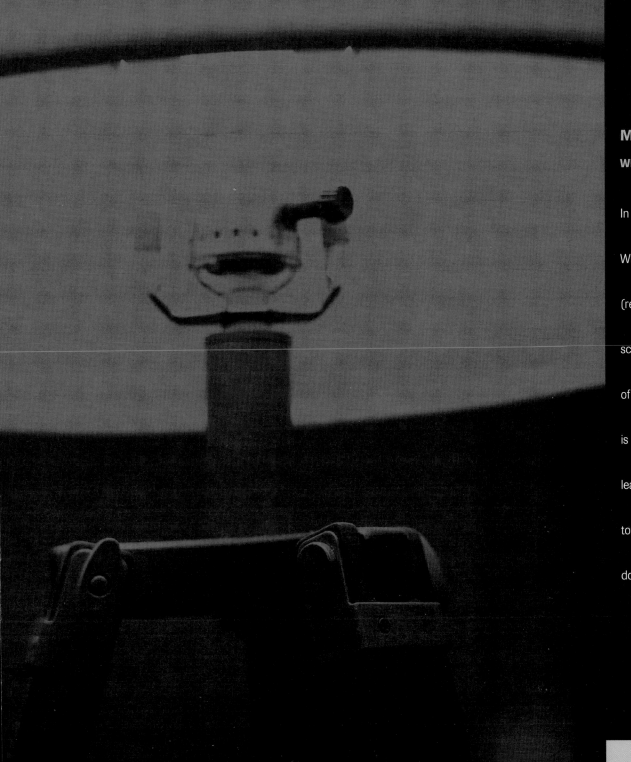

MAKE A FLASHING POLICE LIGHT WITH FAKE RADIOSITY

In this effect, we are going to fake radiosity.

Why would you want to do that? Well, radiosity

(reflected light bouncing around inside a

scene in a realistic fashion) is a key component

of making a scene look "real". Photorealism

is a sort of holy grail in 3D graphics, and

learning how to do it the hard way is a key

to understanding how it works when you

do it automatically.

Project 20

Faking Radiosity

by Phil South

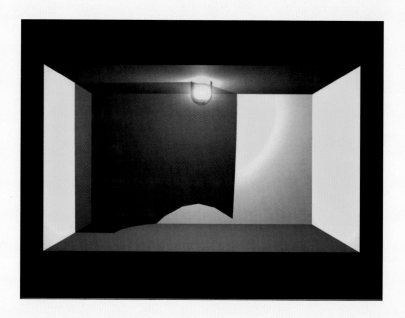

GETTING STARTED

In this chapter, you are going to make an old-fashioned police light, the kind that has a small reflective shade rotating around a bulb. You're going to put this in a room and rotate it to show how the light plays around the room, and then you're going to add lights to fill in the shadows and provide a fake radiosity that moves just like it would in real life.

Although real calculated radiosity has been added to LightWave [6.5], for a considerable period of time in LightWave's history, this excellent feature was unavailable to LightWave animators. In the olden days of about two years ago, we had to simulate radiosity by placing lights to provide "reflected" light where there was none. Although it could be argued that this is a redundant technique, it could also be argued that all techniques are useful in certain animation circumstances. It could certainly be the case that you might want to save a few clock cycles by faking radiosity instead of calculating it (because, of course, any calculated effect will require computationally more processor power than one for which the circumstances are preset). That being said, let's see how this applies to the real-life example.

MODELING THE LIGHT

Although the files needed to render this scene are on the book's CD, the objects are pretty simple, so you might as well model them instead of loading them.

In Modeler, you first make a cover for the light. You're going to make it 250mm radius and about 500mm in the Y-axis. Here's how you build it:

1   Make a point on the Y-axis at 290mm.

2   Make the following points at 0 on the Z-axis:

X = **250mm**,	Y = **–35mm**
X = **242mm**,	Y = **–100mm**
X = **216mm**,	Y = **–160mm**
X = **177mm**,	Y = **–212mm**
X = **125mm**,	Y = **–250mm**
X = **70mm**,	Y = **–277mm**
X = **0mm**,	Y = **–285mm**

3   Make points on the X-axis at 250mm and Y at 290mm.

4   Press the **p** key to make the polygon.

5   Lathe the polygon around the Y-axis at 0mm to form the cover. Name the surface glass and save the object as lightglass.lwo. This is the cover of the light, the glass through which the light will shine. Now you need to make the shade.

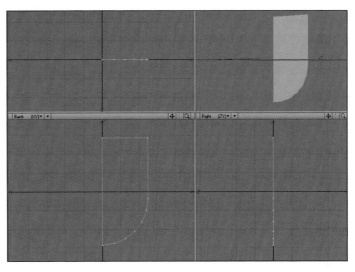

Make a straight line and a curve ready for Lathing.

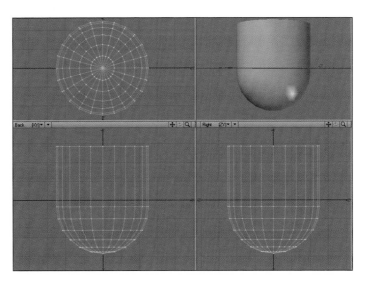

Lathe and save the cover.

6 Make a ball using the default ball settings with a radius of 200mm. Delete the polygons from the top and bottom and more than half from one side. Give it a surface of light shield and save it as **light_shield.lwo**.

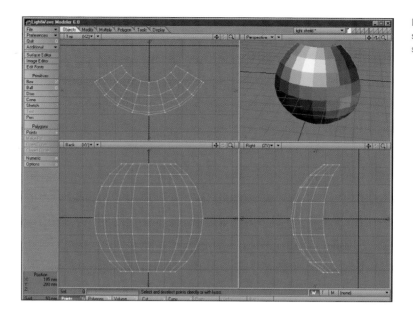

Delete the polygons on one side of a ball to make the shade.

MODELING THE ROOM

Finally, you will make the room where you will be casting this light. It's a simple box with its polygons flipped inward. Obviously, this means that you'll be able to see the room from within, but the walls won't be visible from outside.

1 Make a box with the proportions 6m, 6m, 6m. Flip the polygons inward by pressing the **f** key.

2 Select the ceiling polygon and give it a surface of **ceiling**.

3 Select the floor polygon and give it a surface name of **floor**.

4 Select the walls and give them a surface name of **walls**.

5 Save the whole box as **radiosityroom.lwo**.

Note: You could make the polygons double-sided, in which case you'll be able to see inside the box only if you place the camera inside the walls. If the sides are single-sided and face inward, you'll be able to place the camera outside the walls and still see the room within.

Note: If you're feeling lazy, just give the whole object a surface of room.

The surface names and textures shouldn't affect the experiment, but it would be as well if at least the walls and ceiling were plain and light colored.

Anyway, the box is built. So wiping the sweat from your brow after that mammoth feat of modeling (you did great, kid), you can move along to the meat and potatoes of this tutorial—the Layout.

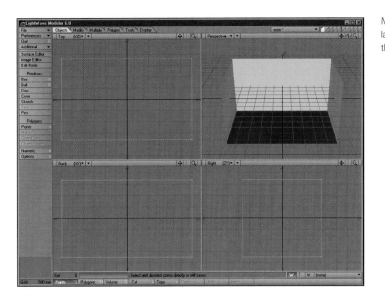

Make the box slightly rectangular and position the ceiling near the origin.

ORGANIZING THE OBJECTS

As I said, the surface textures of the room and the light don't really matter too much in this case, but for the sake of argument, color and texture them anyway. The wall should be a kind of matte white. The light glass should be glass (of course), and the shade could be some kind of metal (although that's not so important because you won't really see it well enough to know what it's made of). Switch to Layout for these next steps.

1 Make the light's glass surface look like glass:

Color: RGB **200**, **200**, **200**

Specularity: **100%**

Glossiness: **60%**

Reflection: **4%**

Transparency: **100%**

Smoothing: **On**

Double sided: **On**

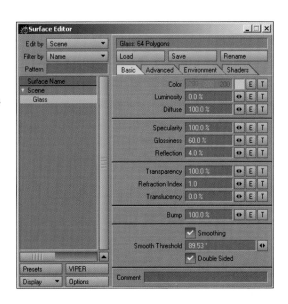

Set up hte basic surface properties for the glass portion of the light.

2 Click the Environment tab and select Reflection: Ray Tracing and Refraction: Backdrop.

3 Click the Shaders tab and add an Edge Transparency shader. Set it to Opaque.

4 Make the light shield surface look like metal by applying these settings:

> Color: RGB **200, 200, 200**
>
> Diffuse: **35%**
>
> Specularity: **100%**
>
> Glossiness: **10%**

5 Turn on both Double Sided and Smoothing.

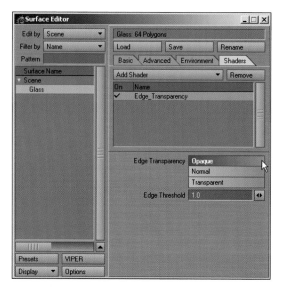

Add the Edge Transparency shader to the glass surface, and doulbe click the listing to open the controls. Select Opaque.

6 Make the walls and ceiling of the room a matte white with a hint of sheen:

> Color: RGB **255, 255, 255**
>
> Specularity: **20%**
>
> Glossiness: **5%**

Note: The best way to go about this would be to make the objects so they are all in place around the origin where they would be in the finished scene. Then when the objects are loaded into Layout, they should all be in place. It's good practice to model objects in the right scale and in the right position with relation to themselves and the origin.

7 Position the items as follows in Layout:

- Load all the objects into Layout.

- Move the light glass up in the Y-axis until it intersects with the ceiling.

- Move the light shield up in the Y-axis until it is inside the glass.

Note: Ambient light is a bit of a cheat in LightWave. Although you have radiosity in LightWave [6.5], you still have to put up with the Ambient light effect, which effectively turns off the modeling and shading. Therefore, your best bet is to turn off Ambient lighting. If you were lighting this room on a sound stage, you'd start with a single light and go from there.

8 In the Global Illumination panel, turn the Ambient light setting down to **0%**.

9 Open the Light properties panel and change the default light to a point light. This should be with the default settings.

10 Select the shield and rotate it either by hand or by using the numeric option. Set the heading to **360°**. Make a keyframe at the end of your shot so the shield makes at least one full turn during the take. Set the duration of the shot to **250 frames**.

To make the light fitting work, you rotated the shield, thus covering up the light from the point light as it goes around. You can make this rotation fast (like a police car) or slow (like a cargo elevator) and either blue or yellow as you please. The point is that you rotate the shield around its axis 360° or more during the shot.

11 Turn on Ray Trace Shadows in the Render panel. (You can also turn on reflection and refraction if you anticipate being up-close on the glass at any point in the shot.)

12 Render the scene.

You will notice that as the shield goes around the lamp, the area behind it is black. There is no shadow detail, no radiosity, nothing. Without radiosity, the light rays from any light source hit the first surface they come to and stop like an air pistol pellet in a peach. How do you get the light rays to bounce? Well, you can't unless you turn on radiosity, but the point of this tutorial is to not do that, so… you'll add more lights to the scene.

13 Add two more point lights to the scene and parent them to the shield.

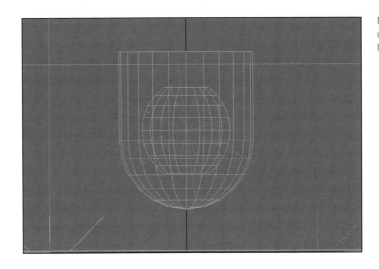

Move the light up in the Y-axis until it's at the center of the light glass.

Note: You can alter the duration of the shot from 250 frames, but be careful. If you set it too short, you'll miss it, and if you set it too long, you'll nod off.

Note: If you want the light to go around more times, set it to 720°, or 1440°, or any multiple of 360°.

14 Position light 2 to the rear of the shield and to the right with the coordinates XYZ 490mm, −490mm, −560mm.

15 Position light 3 to the rear of the shield and to the left with the coordinates XYZ −510mm, −510mm, −560mm.

16 Render the scene.

This looks a lot better, but you will notice two things. First, the lights are perhaps a little too bright, and second, they cast shadows. The brightness thing is solved easily by turning the lights down a little.

17 In the Light properties panel, turn lights 2 and 3 down to about **20%**.

18 Turn Shadow Type to Off for lights 2 and 3.

19 Turn off Affect Specular for lights 2 and 3. The lights affect the specularity of any objects they shine down on.

Now you have a room that is lit by three lights—only one of which is visible—and the shadow detail of the room is a lot better without the nasty processing overhead of radiosity. In addition, you have the oily self-gratification of doing things the hard way. Good work. With determination like that in the face of a seemingly pointless (and frankly arduous) task, you could get into the Marines. Or at the very least you could be in the first *Karate Kid* movie.

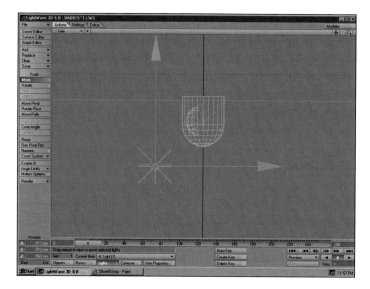

Position the new lights carefully behind the shield to cast light into the shadow of the shield.

How It Works

Clearly, you save a lot of render time by adding lights instead of just blindly rendering radiosity every time. For scenes that move lights around, radiosity isn't really your best option because it has to be cached to reduce errors. Using carefully placed lights is the best way to cover the largest variety of scenes, but not without the most amount of effort. Nothing worth doing is easy to do.

Simply put, the lights you placed behind the shield send light out behind it, throwing fill light into the shadow and making the scene look more realistic. The reason you use more than one light (you could add more) is to make the "reflected" light move a little. Reflected light, especially light that bounces off walls, moves around
a bit as the light bounces off other walls as the light source moves. The best way to simulate that is to have a couple of lights moving around with the main light. They operate against one another, and the light they cast ebbs and flows just like light that is really reflected off walls.

You might also want to add some colored lights to simulate the way reflected lights take on the color of the surfaces they are reflected from.

Modifications

You can use this technique in a number of ways to add realism to your scenes. You could parent a light to the side of a light-colored spacecraft so that it faintly illuminates a space station as it passes, simulating the sunlight reflected from its hull. You could stick a light under a table in a room to simulate light reflecting from the walls and floor shining underneath the legs. (Although tables almost always cast shadows, it is not pitch black underneath.) Fill any shadow in your scenes with reflected light and see the scene come alive.

In outdoor scenes, and especially scenes in which you are adding 3D elements to live action backgrounds, lighting is of crucial importance, and using many lights to simulate the radiosity caused by the HUGE bright light of the sun is the key to great compositing. Learn how to position lights for the most subtle and effective radiosity simulation, and you have the ability to mimic almost any lighting conditions when creating special effects for movies and video. I told you this technique would be worth learning!

FIXED PROJECTION COMPOSITING

"It's 106 miles to Chicago, we've got a full tank of gas,

half a packet of cigarettes,

it's dark, and we're wearing sunglasses."

—ELWOOD BLUES

"Hit it."

—JAKE BLUES, FROM THE MOVIE, *THE BLUES BROTHERS*

ANIMATE CHICAGO WITH STILL IMAGES

Every once in a while, you need to do
something cool to enhance an animation or
video project. Often, you don't have access to
expensive compositing software, or perhaps you
don't have the time to learn complex third-party
imaging tools. LightWave 6.5 has a feature
called "Fixed Projection" that enables you to
animate through real images. It's really an
illusion, a "magic" trick if you will, which allows
you to composite images with simple polygons
and move through them. The result is an
animation through still images. These images
can be of people, objects, buildings, or
whatever else you can think of. For this
project, you'll use a building scene from
downtown Chicago.

Project 21

Fixed Projection Compositing

by Dan Ablan

GETTING STARTED

All right, so maybe the opening image is a bit misleading; it is a 3D animation, just not 3D buildings. There is software on the market today that allows you to use photographs to model objects. Those same photos are then used as image maps. So a picture of a street suddenly becomes an animation of a street. Because of size limitations in the images used, you can't implement much animation, but enough for a cool effect. Note that it's a good idea to animate on just one axis, as you do in this example.

For this effect to work, you need to do a little image manipulation in a program like Adobe Photoshop. Using the Rubber Stamp tool, areas of the image next to the building were painted over the building to simulate its removal.

During the course of the animation, the building in the foreground will move towards the camera, and the background image (the one painted in Photoshop) will become more visible. The more that is painted out, the more you can reveal. Get it?

The original image from a digital camera.

The same image with portions of the foremost building crudely painted out in Photoshop.

IMAGE POLYGONS

First, you create and manipulate the images. The next step is to create a polygon that will be used to mask, and then become the building.

1   Open LightWave Modeler and press the **d** key to call up the Display Options panel. Click the Backdrop tab.

2   For Viewport, select 3, which is the bottom left quad in Modeler.

> **Note:** You should be working with the modeler configuration menus provided on the book's CD.

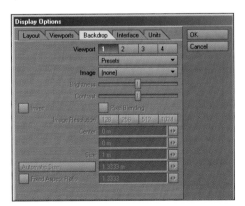

The Backdrop tab of the Display Options panel.

3 Load the **HuronSt.tga** image from the book's CD.

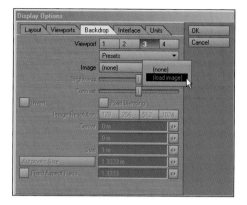

Load an image into Modeler's backdrop.

> **Note:** Depending on the speed of your system and the amount of video memory you have, you might be able to increase the Image Resolution for display.

4 Click OK to close the Display Options panel, and the image appears in the bottom left view.

5 Move the mouse over Viewport 3, the one with the backdrop image. Press the **0** key on the numeric keypad to bring that view into full frame.

Pressing **0** again returns the view to Quad mode.

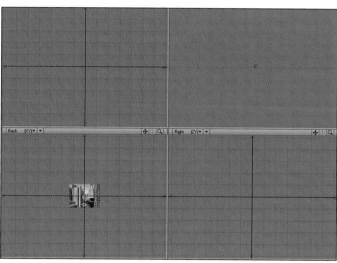

HuronSt.tga appears in the Viewport.

6 Press the period key about 7 times to zoom in toward the image.

Tip: Instead of using the period key to zoom, you can use the Viewport Zoom feature.

Note: For visual clarity of this project, the Brightness and Contrast settings for the backdrop image have been decreased so you can see the points and polygons better in print.

7 Select the Points command from the Objects tab, and begin making points around the building to the front left of the image.

Make the backdrop image full frame.

Decrease the brightness and contrast of the backdrop image so the points and polygons are easily visible.

8 Continue creating points around the building, making the last point at the lower-left corner.

Begin making a polygon of the foremost building by creating points around the perimeter.

9 Press the **p** key to make a polygon.

10 Press **q** and change the surface name of this polygon to **va_building**.

Note: Make sure your polygon is facing the camera (the negative Z-axis); otherwise, it won't be visible in Layout unless you turn on Double Sided.

That's it for Modeler. The beauty of this technique is that you don't need anything more than a flat polygon to represent your buildings. Be sure to go further with this technique and make polygons for the other buildings in the shot. For time, this effect will introduce you to the technique of Fixed Projection with just one flat polygon.

Adding a few simple points makes a polygonal shape of the building.

FIXED PROJECTIONS

The method of Front Projection Image Mapping (FPIM) has been included with LightWave for years. But LightWave [6.5] brings an added feature called Fixed Projection. Essentially, FPIM allowed you to add the same image to a polygon as you did to a backdrop, and the software would match the image position. This is excellent for compositing, or better still, for making dinosaurs walk behind photos of real buildings.

The Fixed Projection technique takes FPIM a step further, allowing you to move around the scene while it "sticks" the image to the polygons.

1   In Layout, load the **HuronSt.tga** and
HuronSt_bg.tga images from the book's CD.
Load them through the Image Editor (Settings tab).

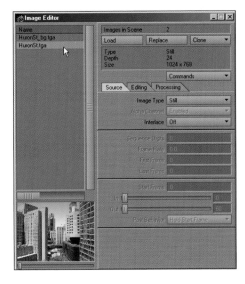

Load the two images in the Image Editor.

> **Note:** Remember that you can hold the Shift key to load both images at once.

2   Switch to Camera View (press **6** on the numeric keypad).

3   Click the Backdrop button from the Settings tab. Then click the Compositing tab and for Backdrop Image, select the HuronSt_bg.tga image.

Remember, you are placing the image with the painted out buildings as the background layer.

> **Note:** Remember that the background image in Layout doesn't move. It can't have a light cast onto it, nor can it receive shadows. It's just there!

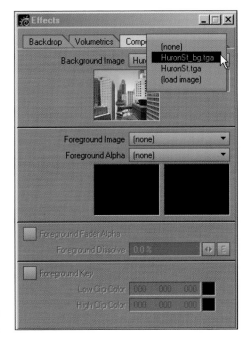

Place the HuronSt_bg.tga image in the background in Layout.

4 Select Add/Add Object/Load Object from the Actions tab. Load the building polygon you created in Modeler.

The object on the CD is 21VaBuilding.lwo.

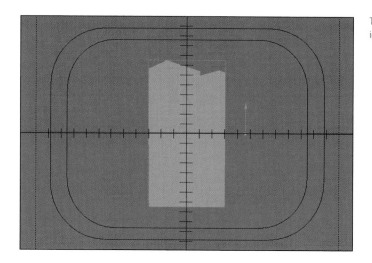

The flat polygonal object loaded into Layout.

5 Press the **d** key to call up the Layout Display Options panel. Select Background Image for the Camera View Background. Close the Display Options panel.

The color image appears in the backdrop in Layout.

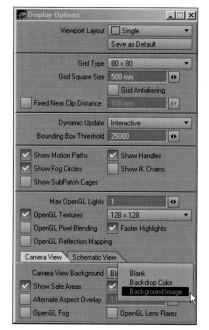

Set the Camera View Background to show the background image.

The color image is now visible in the background.

6 Select the 21VaBuilding.lwo object and move it toward the camera and to the left so it lines up with the building it is based on.

Note: If you have trouble lining up the polygon building with the background image, you can temporarily put the non-painted image in the background for reference. Once the polygon is aligned, replace the painted image in the background.

7 Create a keyframe at frame zero to lock it in place.

8 Open the Surface Editor and select the Va_Building surface. Click the T button next to Color.

This opens the Texture Editor for Color.

9 Set the following parameters:

Layer Type: **Image Map**

Blending Mode: **Additive**

Layer Opacity: **100%**

Projection: **Front**

Fixed Projection: **On**

Image: **HuronSt.tga**

Width Tile: **Reset**

Height Tile: **Reset**

Pixel Blending: **On**

Texture Antialiasing: **Off**

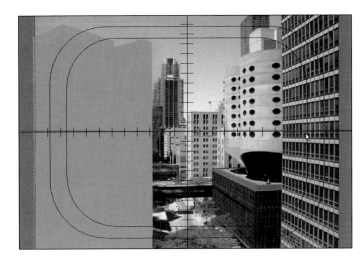

Move the flat polygon over the backdrop image.

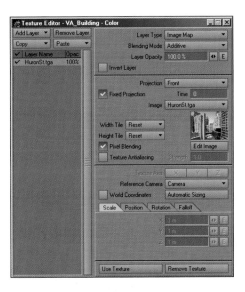

Enter these settings in the Texture Editor for Color.

10 Press **F9**.

You'll see the image mapped on the building polygon. It's dark however, and it doesn't match the backdrop image.

A render shows that the image of the background is now mapped on the polygon, but it appears dark.

11 In the Surface Editor, change Luminosity to **65%** and Diffuse to **40%**.

The camera's position at 9 is XYZ −407.315mm, −1.5058 mm, −2.5365m.

12 Move the camera in to approximately −2m on the Z-axis. Then move it up about 50mm. Create a keyframe at frame 180 to lock it in place.

Note: You might need to adjust the building polygon if any of the front projection map bleeds off the edges. Simply move the building object to line up with the background image more closely.

Note: Be sure to view the file fixed.avi on the book's CD for the final animation.

A luminosity boost brightens the image to make it match the backdrop.

How It Works

What you've done here is used two images and a simple polygon to create a false 3D dimension. Although only one building was demonstrated here, you can repeat these steps to map the street and other buildings, leaving the horizon and distance of the image as the background image. The final result will look as if you're flying through the buildings. When it's done properly, people often mistake this effect for real video. This tutorial does not truly demonstrate the full potential of Fixed Projection, but it gives you the basis for more complicated effects.

The technique is simple, and the results are wide ranging. It uses two images—one original image and one with buildings partially painted out. A polygon is mapped with LightWave's Front Projection Image Mapping and told to be "fixed." When that polygon is moved, the image attached to it stays with it. What's behind the polygon is the image with the painted-out buildings. The result looks as if you're moving past the buildings.

The real power of Fixed Projection is evident when the object is 3D (a box) and roughly follows the contours of the buildings (in this case). So when you truck in, you see more of the building's sides and less of the front. What Fixed Projection does then is automatically stretch and squeeze the image mapped to the polygon surfaces to fill it in based on your perspective. This gives you the impression that you are viewing more or less of the sides.

Modifications

There are so many variations to this cool effect that it's really just a matter of experimenting. The image used for this project can be taken further by using other images as polygonal templates. Applying the same front projection mapping on those polygons would add to the fly-through effect.

Taking it a step further, this is a great way to simulate the ever-popular, frozen-in-time look. Very expensive video equipment is most commonly used to create the look you see in commercials every day, but you can do it in LightWave with Fixed Projection settings. For example, take a photo of friends at a table, posed with reactions on their faces so the shot looks "frozen." Move them out of the way and take the exact shot of the table (this will save you the trouble of having to paint them out). Make polygons over the images of the people as you did for the building. Apply the front projection maps with the Fixed setting and animate over the empty table background shot. Very cool stuff.

APPENDIX A

"*The important thing is this: to be able at any moment to sacrifice who we are for what we could become.*"

—CHARLES DUBOIS

WHAT'S ON THE CD-ROM

This appendix is a brief rundown of what you'll find on the CD-ROM accompanying this book.

BROWSING THE CD-ROM

If you browse to the CD in Windows Explorer, you will see two directories called "Movies" and "Projects". The "Movies" directory contains both AVI and QuickTime files. The "Projects" file contains objects, scenes, and images used to create or further illustrate the projects in the book.

If you have "AutoPlay" turned on, your CD will load automatically. Simply click on the navigation buttons on the left to access the information or project files you're looking for.

ACCESSING THE PROJECT FILES FROM THE CD

Many projects in this book use pre-built LightWave [6.5] files that contain pre-set parameters and other important information you will need to build the final project. In many cases, several LightWave [6.5] files are available to show the project at various stages of completion. The LightWave [6.5] files have a .lwo extension. Several of the projects also come with additional files, such as ready-made images and textures.

All the files for a project are conveniently located in the CD's Projects directory. The Project directory contains subdirectories for Images, Objects, and Scenes, within which you'll find directories for the individual projcects. To access the project files for Project 10, Photo Realistic Gold, for example, you'll find the images in the Projects/Images/Chapter10 directory, the objects in the Projects/Objects/Chapter10 directory, and the scenes in the Projects/Scenes/Chapter10 directory.

We recommend you copy the project files to your hard drive, but that is not absolutely necessary if you don't intend to save the project files.

READ THIS BEFORE OPENING THE SOFTWARE

By opening the CD package, you are agreeing to be bound by the following agreement:

You may not copy or redistribute the entire CD-ROM as a whole. Copying and redistribution of individual software programs on the CD-ROM is governed by terms set by individual copyright holders.

The installer and code from the author(s) are copyrighted by the publisher and the author(s).

This software is sold as-is, without warranty of any kind, either expressed or implied, including but not limited to the implied warranties of merchantability and fitness for a particular purpose. Neither the publisher nor its dealers or distributors assumes any liability for any alleged or actual damages arising from the use of this program. (Some states do not allow for the exclusion of implied warranties, so the exclusion may not apply to you.)

WINDOWS 98/95/NT INSTALLATION INSTRUCTIONS

Insert the CD-ROM disc in to your CD-ROM drive.

From the Windows 98/95/NT desktop, double-click on the My Computer icon.

Double-click on the icon representing your CD-ROM drive.

Double-click on the icon titled **START.EXE** to run the CD-ROM interface.

> **Note:** If windows 98/95/NT is installed on your computer and you have the AutoPlay feature enabled, the START.EXE program starts automatically whenever you insert the disc into your CD-ROM.

INDEX

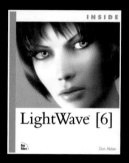
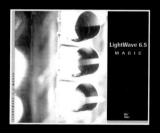

THE NEW RIDERS

PROFESSIONAL LIBRARY

Inside 3D Studio MAX 3: Modeling,
Materials, and Rendering
Ted Boardman and Jeremy Hubbell
0-7357-0085-0

Inside 3D Studio VIZ 3
Ted Boardman and Jeremy Hubbell
0-7357-1002-3

Inside Adobe Photoshop 5.5
Gary David Bouton and Barbara Bouton
0-7357-1000-7

Inside Adobe Photoshop 5, Limited Edition
Gary David Bouton and Barbara Bouton
1-56205-951-3

Inside Adobe Photoshop 6
Gary David Bouton, et. al
0-7357-1038-4

Inside AutoCAD 2000
David Pitzer and Bill Burchard
0-7357-0851-7

Inside LightWave 3D
Dan Ablan
1-56205-799-5

Inside LightWave 6
Dan Ablan
0-7357-0919-X

Inside trueSpace 4
Frank Rivera
1-56205-957-2

Inside SoftImage 3D
Anthony Rossano
1-56205-885-1

LightWave 6.5 Magic
Dan Ablan, et. al
0-7357-0996-3

Maya 2 Character Animation
Nathan Vogel, Sherri Sheridan, and Tim Coleman
0-7357-0866-5

Net Results 2: Best Practices for Web Marketing
Rick Bruner
0-7357-1024-4

Photoshop 5 & 5.5 Artistry
Barry Haynes and Wendy Crumpler
0-7457-0994-7

Photoshop 5 Type Magic
Greg Simsic
1-56830-465-X

Photoshop 5 Web Magic
Michael Ninness
1-56205-913-0

Photoshop 6 Effects Magic
Rhoda Grossman, et. al
0-7357-1035-X

Photoshop 6 Web Magic
Jeff Foster
0-7357-1036-8

Photoshop Channel Chops
David Biedny, Bert Monroy, and Nathan Moody
1-56205-723-5

<preparing web graphics>
Lynda Weinman
1-56205-686-7

Rhino NURBS 3D Modeling
Margaret Becker
0-7357-0925-4

Secrets of Successful Web Sites
David Siegel
1-56830-382-3

Web Concept & Design
Crystal Waters
1-56205-648-4

Web Design Templates Sourcebook
Lisa Schmeiser
1-56205-754-5

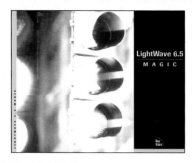

LightWave 6.5 Magic

Each New Riders Magic book has been created with you, the computer graphics professional, in mind. Complete effects, adaptable solutions, time-saving techniques, and practical applications. Buy your favorite Lightwave, 3D Studio MAX or Maya book online today.

LightWave 3D Workstation with Dual 1Ghz Processors

Lightwave 3D workstation online and choose from a wide selection of hot 3D OpenGL cards including Nvidia Quadro2 MXR, Intense 3D Monster 4210/4110, ELSA Gloria II and IBM Fire GL2 plus plugins and monitors.

NewTek LightWave

Breakthrough rendering technology, advanced character animation and new modeling paradigm makes LightWave the established leader. Buy Lightwave, 3D Studio MAX or Maya Online from IntelliStations.com today!

Books, Videos, and Training

Check out intellistations.com for all of the latest books, videos and training classes that are available for Lightwave, 3D Studio MAX and Maya.

intellistations.com

The Ultimate Internet Resource for Video, Film, 3D and Creative Graphics Professionals.

Buy Online via our Secure Ordering system for VISA, MC and AMEX

Build your Video/3D Dream Machine with our **Online Configurator**

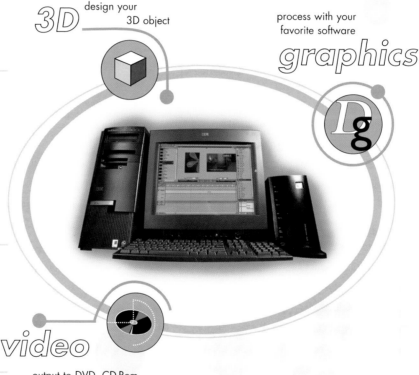

3D design your 3D object

process with your favorite software

graphics

Dg

video

output to DVD, CD-Rom Web/Streaming media, or any other tape format

IntelliStations.com is your source for Digital Content Creation tools that will allow your projects to be done on time, every time. The one you really want for video editing, 3D animation, web design/graphics, and more.

Our knowledgeable technical production engineers will also ASSIST you with INTEGRATION of your IntelliStations.com system with your professional production equipment.

If you have questions while building your dream system you can call us 24x7x365 at 1-800-501-0184 for assistance from one of our IntelliStations.com DCC specialists. Ask about our no money down and creative financing programs.

Check out CGchannel.com, our content provider for 3D reviews, demos and more!

IBM Business Partner

SONY Authorized Professional Reseller

NewTek

CG channel.com

Solutions from experts you know and trust.

www.informit.com

OPERATING SYSTEMS

WEB DEVELOPMENT

PROGRAMMING

NETWORKING

CERTIFICATION

AND MORE...

**Expert Access.
Free Content.**

New Riders has partnered with **InformIT.com** to bring technical information to your desktop. Drawing on New Riders authors and reviewers to provide additional information on topics you're interested in, **InformIT.com** has free, in-depth information you won't find anywhere else.

- Master the skills you need, when you need them

- Call on resources from some of the best minds in the industry

- Get answers when you need them, using InformIT's comprehensive library or live experts online

- Go above and beyond what you find in New Riders books, extending your knowledge

As an **InformIT** partner, **New Riders** has shared the wisdom and knowledge of our authors with you online. Visit **informIT.com** to see what you're missing.

THE LIGHTWAVE [6.5] MAGIC CD

The CD that accompanies this book contains valuable resources for anyone using LightWave, not the least of which are:

- Project files: All the example files provided by the authors enable you to work through the step-by-step projects.
- Other: Movie files in MOV and AVI format, and Web resources.

ACCESSING THE PROJECT FILES FROM THE CD

The majority of projects in this book use pre-built LightWave files that contain preset parameters, artwork, audio, or other important information you need to work through and build the final project.

All the project files are conveniently located in the CD's Examples directory. To access the project files for Project 3, "Welding Sparks," for example, locate the following directory on the accompanying CD: Examples\Chap03.

We recommend that you copy the project files to your hard drive, but this is not absolutely necessary if you don't intend to save the project files.

COLOPHON

LightWave [6.5] Magic was laid out and produced with the help of Microsoft Word, Adobe Acrobat, Adobe Photoshop, Collage Complete, and QuarkXpress on a variety of systems, including a Macintosh G4. With the exception of pages that were printed out for proofreading, all files—text, images, and project files—were transferred via email or ftp and edited on-screen.

All body text was set in the Bergamo family. All headings, figure captions, and cover text were set in the Imago family. The Symbol and Sean's Symbol typefaces were used throughout for special symbols and bullets.

LightWave [6.5] Magic was printed on 60# Mead Web Dull at Graphic Arts Center (GAC) in Indianapolis, Indiana. Prepress consisted of PostScript computer-to-plate technology (filmless process). The cover was printed on 12-pt. Carolina, coated on one side at Moore Langen Printing Company, Inc. in Terre Haute, Indiana.